M000114942

AGAINST THE TERROR OF NEOLIBERALISM

Cultural Politics & the Promise of Democracy

A Series from Paradigm Publishers
Edited by Henry A. Giroux

Empire and Inequality: America and the World Since 9/11 (2004), Paul Street

Caught in the Crossfire: Kids, Politics, and America's Future (2005), Lawrence Grossberg

Reading and Writing for Civic Literacy: The Critical Citizen's Guide to Argumentative Rhetoric (2005), Donald Lazere

Why Are We Reading Ovid's Handbook on Rape? Teaching and Learning at a Women's College (2005), Madeleine Kahn

Schooling and the Struggle for Public Life, Updated Edition (2005), Henry A. Giroux

Listening Beyond the Echoes: Media, Ethics, and Agency in an Uncertain World (2006), Nick Couldry

Michel Foucault: Materialism and Education, Updated Edition (2006), Mark Olssen

Pedagogies of the Global: Knowledge in the Human Interest (2006), Arif Dirlik

Not Only the Master's Tools: African American Studies in Theory and Practice (2006), edited by Lewis R. Gordon and Jane Anna Gordon

The Giroux Reader (2006), Henry A. Giroux, edited and introduced by Christopher G. Robbins

Patriotic Correctness: Academic Freedom and Its Enemies (2008), John K. Wilson

Against the Terror of Neoliberalism (2008), Henry A. Giroux

Thinking Queerly: Posthumanist Essays on Ethics and Identity (2008), David Ross Fryer

AGAINST THE TERROR OF NEOLIBERALISM

Politics Beyond the Age of Greed

HENRY A. GIROUX

Paradigm Publishers
Boulder • London

Paradigm Publishers is committed to preserving ancient forests and natural resources. We elected to print *Against The Terror Of Neoliberalism* on 50% post consumer recycled paper, processed chlorine free. As a result, for this printing, we have saved:

7 Trees (40' tall and 6-8" diameter)
3,092 Gallons of Wastewater
1,243 Kilowatt Hours of Electricity
341 Pounds of Solid Waste
670 Pounds of Greenhouse Gases

Paradigm Publishers made this paper choice because our printer, Thomson-Shore, Inc., is a member of Green Press Initiative, a nonprofit program dedicated to supporting authors, publishers, and suppliers in their efforts to reduce their use of fiber obtained from endangered forests.

For more information, visit www.greenpressinitiative.org

All rights reserved. No part of this publication may be transmitted or reproduced in any media or form, including electronic, mechanical, photocopy, recording, or informational storage and retrieval systems, without the express written consent of the publisher.

Copyright © 2008 Paradigm Publishers

Published in the United States by Paradigm Publishers, 3360 Mitchell Lane Suite E, Boulder, CO 80301 USA.

Paradigm Publishers is the trade name of Birkenkamp & Company, LLC,
Dean Birkenkamp, President and Publisher.

Library of Congress Cataloging-in-Publication DataGiroux, Henry A.
Against the terror of neoliberalism : politics beyond the age of greed / Henry A. Giroux.
p. cm. — (Cultural politics and the promise of democracy)
Includes bibliographical references and index.
ISBN-13: 978-1-59451-520-0 (hardcover : alk. paper)
1. Neoliberalism—United States. 2. Authoritarianism—United States. 3. Youth—United States—Social conditions. 4. Racism—United States. 5. United States—Politics and government—1989- I. Title.
JC574.2.U6G57 2008
320.51—dc22

2007050082

Printed and bound in the United States of America on acid-free paper that meets the standards of the American National Standard for Permanence of Paper for Printed Library Materials.

Designed and typeset by Straight Creek Bookmakers.

12 11 10 09 08 1 2 3 4 5

For Susan,

for Brett, Chris, and Jack

Contents

Acknowledgments

This book was written at a very dire time in American history. Motivated by a sense a outrage and hope, it attempts to identify neoliberalism as a threat to democracy at home and abroad as well as to offer a productive series of analyses of how to stop its poisonous effects on all aspects of public and private life. As one of the most powerful ideologies of the twenty-first century, neoliberalism has become a breeding ground for militarism, rapacious profiteering, dissident profiling, and a new political and religious fundamentalism that undermines the presupposition that democracy is about sharing power and resources. In fact, democracy at the present time looks less like a reachable ideal than a forgotten ideology of the past. The Bush administration had done more to disable American democracy than any other American presidency. The rich receive huge tax breaks while millions of people live in dire poverty. Billions are added to the national debt, revealing a disdain for the security of future generations. Instead of promoting a surge in democracy, the United States promotes a surge in terrorism, fear at home, and death and destruction abroad. Total terror and permanent war reinforced by the ongoing militarization of society suggest an anti-politics in which thinking, debating, and critical human beings either are rendered superficial, punished, or, in more extreme cases, literally disappear. Democracy withers as civil liberties such as the rights to association, privacy, and due process are either viewed as useless or violated. As terror and certainty become all-encompassing and totalizing, the punishing state replaces the social state, making a mockery of those democratic values, ideals, and relations upon which American society was founded. Instead of furthering democratic ideals, the U.S. government has created a Gulag of secret prisons run by the CIA, imprisoned people in Guantanamo Bay while denying them any access to legal recourse, tortured people in prisons in Iraq, Afghanistan, and so-called black sites and, in more extreme cases, made so-called enemies of the state disappear. Similarly, the courts are now viewed as an extension of an imperial presidency, and cronyism and political corruption have cast a dark cloud over all aspects of governance. Under such circumstances, any claims to the United States being a democracy appear utterly hypocritical.

As war and fear become permanent fixtures in American society, the power of the United States is used to build empires abroad while constructing a security state at home. While lives are needlessly being lost in Iraq, collective protections are being dismantled and the hard currency of human suffering is becoming all the more evident as the gap between the rich and the poor expands and more and more children and adults descend into the black hole of poverty, joblessness, insecurity, and despair. Secrecy, surveillance, and lawlessness have become the hallmarks of a government that more closely resembles an authoritarian state than a robust democracy. Closer to home, a silent war is being waged against people of color who are being incarcerated at alarming rates. Academic freedom is increasingly under attack, a conservative Supreme Court appears intent on stripping women of their reproductive rights and legitimating the dictates of an imperial presidency, and the environment continues to be assaulted by neoliberal warriors and corporate moguls intent on reaping ever greater profits for themselves.

Fortunately, power is never completely on the side of domination, religious fanaticism, or political corruption. Nor is it entirely in the hands of those who view democracy as an excess or a burden. Increasingly, individuals and groups at home and around the globe including students, workers, feminists, educators, writers, environmentalists, senior citizens, and artists are organizing to challenge America's dangerous slide into the dredges of an authoritarianism that threatens democracy not only at home but also abroad. This book is composed in solidarity with them and with the next generation of young people who hopefully will never let this terrible assault on democracy happen again.

The second edition of this book could not have been written without the help of some close friends who offered invaluable criticisms and support. I would especially like to thank Sophia A. McClennen, Christopher Robbins, Jasmin Habib, David Clark, Stanley Aronowitz, Roger Simon, Ken Saltman, Donaldo Macedo, Grace Pollock, Brian McKenna, Tony Kashani, Doug Morris, Ira Shor, Brian McKenna, and Dean Birkenkamp. I am particularly grateful to my administrative assistant, Maya Sabados, whose efforts in helping me with this book far exceeded anything I could have imagined. As usual, most of the important ideas in the book were worked out as a result of various exchanges with my partner, Susan Searls Giroux. I am also grateful to my canine companion, Kaya, who has managed to keep me sane and calm in trying times. Needless to say, I bear the responsibility for the final outcome.

Some of the ideas in these chapters are drawn from work published in other places. A version of Chapter 1 was published as "The Emerging Authoritarianism in the United States: Political Culture Under the Bush/Cheney Administration," in *Symploke* 14: 1-2 (2007), pp. 98-151. Chapter 2, "Spectacles of Race and Pedagogies of Denial," appeared in *Communication Education* 52: 3/4 (July/October, 2003), pp. 191-211, available online at http://www.tandf.co.uk/journals/titles/03634523.asp; and sections of Chapter 6 were published in *JAC* 27:1 (2007), pp. 11-61.

Henry A. Giroux

Introduction
Slouching Toward Bethlehem

> In 1945 or 1950, if you had seriously proposed any of the ideas and policies in today's standard neo-liberal toolkit, you would have been laughed off the stage or sent off to the insane asylum.... The idea that the market should be allowed to make major social and political decisions; the idea that the State should voluntarily reduce its role in the economy, or that corporations should be given total freedom, that trade unions should be curbed and citizens given much less rather than more social protection—such ideas were utterly foreign to the spirit of the time. Even if someone actually agreed with these ideas, he or she would have hesitated to take such a position in public and would have had a hard time finding an audience.
>
> —Susan George[1]

What is often ignored by many theorists who alanyze the rise of neoliberalism in the United States is that it is not only a system of economic power relations, but also a political project of governing and persuasion intent on producing new forms of subjectivity and particular modes of conduct.[2] And while I want to develop this issue by analyzing the close link between the economic mechanisms of neoliberalism and its cultural politics of subjectification and self-regulation, I begin with a theoretical insight provided by the British media theorist, Nick Couldry, who insists that "every system of cruelty requires its own theatre," one that draws upon the rituals of everyday life in order to legitimate its norms, values, institutions, and social practices.[3] Neoliberalism represents one such system of cruelty, one that is reproduced daily through a regime of commonsense and a narrow notion of political rationality that "reaches from the soul of the citizen-subject to educational policy to practices of empire.[4] Wedded to the belief that the market should be the organizing principle for all political, social, and economic decisions, neoliberalism wages an incessant attack on democracy, public institutions, public goods, and noncommodified values. Under neoliberalism everything either is for sale or is plundered for profit. Public lands are looted by logging companies and corporate ranchers; politicians willingly hand the public's airwaves over to broadcasters and large corporate interests without a dime going into the public trust; corporations drive the nation's energy policies, and the war industries give war profiteering a new meaning as the government hands out contracts without any competitive bidding; the largesse of the government is then rewarded when the latter is bilked for millions by the same companies; the environment is polluted and despoiled in the name of profit-making just as the government passes legislation to make it easier for corporations to do so; public services are gutted in order to lower the taxes of major corporations; schools increasingly resemble malls or jails; and teachers, forced to raise revenue for classroom materials, increasingly function as circus barkers hawking everything from hamburgers to pizza parties—that is, when they are not reduced to prepping students to get higher test scores. The neoliberal economy with its relentless pursuit of market values now extends to the entirety of human relations. As markets are touted as the driving force of everyday life, big government is disparaged as either incompetent or a threat to individual freedom, suggesting that power should reside in markets and corporations rather than in governments and citizens. Citizenship has increasingly become a function of market values, and politics has been restructured as "corporations have been increasingly freed from social control through deregulation, privatization, and other neoliberal measures."[5]

Fortunately, the corporate capitalist fairy tale of neoliberalism has been challenged all over the globe by students, labor organizers, intellectuals, community activists, and a host of individuals and groups unwilling to allow democracy to be bought and sold by a combination of multinational corporations, corporate swindlers, international political institutions, and those government politicians who willingly align themselves with corporate interests and profits. From Seattle to Davos, people engaged in popular resistance are collectively taking up the challenge of neoliberalism and reviving both the meaning of resistance and the places where it comes about. Political culture is now global and resistance is amorphous, connecting students with workers, school teachers with parents, and intellectuals with artists. Groups protesting the attack on farmers in India whose land is being destroyed by the government in order to build dams now find themselves in alliance with young people resisting sweatshop labor in New York City. Environmental activists are joining up with key sections of organized labor as well as with groups protesting Third World debt. The collapse of the neoliberal showcase,

Argentina, along with numerous corporate bankruptcies and scandals starting with Enron, reveals the cracks in neoliberal hegemony and domination. In Latin America, a new wave of resistance to negative globalization and neoliberal structural adjustment policies has emerged among countries such as Chile, Peru, Argentina, and Venezuela.[6] In addition, the multiple forms of resistance against neoliberal capitalism are not limited by an identity politics focused on particularized rights and interests. On the contrary, a politics of identity has been expanded to address a broader crisis of political culture and democracy that connects the corporatization and militarization of public life with the collapse of the welfare state and the attack on civil liberties. Central to these new movements is the notion that neoliberalism has to be understood within a larger crisis of vision, meaning, education, and political agency. Democracy in this view is not limited to the struggle over economic resources and power; indeed, it also includes the creation of public spheres where individuals can be educated as political agents equipped with the skills, capacities, and knowledge they need to perform as autonomous political agents. I want to expand the reaches of this debate by arguing that any form of resistance against neoliberalism must address the discourses of political agency, civic education, and cultural politics as part of a broader struggle over the relationship between democratization (the ongoing struggle for a substantive and inclusive democracy) and the global public sphere.

We live at a time when the conflation of private interests, empire-building, and evangelical fundamentalism puts into question the very nature, if not existence, of the democratic process. Under the reign of neoliberalism, capital and wealth have been largely distributed upward while civic virtue has been undermined by a slavish celebration of the free market as the model for organizing all facets of everyday life. Political culture has been increasingly emptied of democratic values as collective life is organized around the modalities of privatization, risks, deregulation, and commercialization. When the alleged champions of neoliberalism invoke politics, they substitute "ideological certainty for reasonable doubt" and deplete "the national reserves of political intelligence" just as they endorse "the illusion that the future can be bought instead of earned."[7] Under attack is the social contract with its emphasis on enlarging the public good and expanding social provisions—such as access to adequate health care, housing, employment, public transportation, and education—that ensure a limited though important safety net and a set of conditions upon which democracy could be experienced and critical citizenship engaged. It has been replaced with a notion of national security based on fear, surveillance, and control rather than with a culture of shared responsibility. Self-reflection and collective empowerment are now reduced to self-promotion and self-interest and legitimated by a new and ruthless social Darwinism played out nightly on network television as a metaphor for the "naturalness" of downsizing, the celebration of hyper-masculinity, and the promotion of an unchecked competitive individualism over even the most limited notions of solidarity and collective struggle. Neoliberalism, with its celebration of markets, finance, and investors, "requires a new belief in the future ... the time of investment is now, the future must be lived in the present."[8] Gone is capitalism's promise of a better future for all. All that is left is the savagery of a war against all, and a future of hopelessness and cynicism.

Under neoliberal domestic restructuring and the foreign policy initiatives of the Washington Consensus, motivated by an evangelical belief in free-market democracy at home and free trade abroad, the United States in the last thirty years has witnessed the increasing obliteration of those discourses, social forms, public institutions, and noncommercial values that are central to the language of the common good, public commitment, and democratically charged politics. Civic engagement now appears impotent as corporations privatize public space and disconnect power from issues of equity, social justice, and civic responsibility. Proceeding outside democratic accountability, neoliberalism has allowed a handful of private interests to control as much of social life as possible in order to maximize their personal profit.

Abroad, neoliberal global policies have been used to pursue rapacious free-trade agreements and expand Western financial and commercial interests through the heavy-handed policies of the World Bank, the World Trade Organization, and the International Monetary Fund (IMF) in order to manage and transfer resources and wealth from the poor and less developed nations to the richest and most powerful nation-states and to the wealthy, corporate defenders of capitalism.[9] Third World and semi-peripheral states of Latin America, Africa, and Asia have become client states of the wealthy nations led by the United States. Loans made to the client states by banks and other financial institutions have produced severe dislocations and consequences for "social welfare programs such as health care, education, and laws establishing labor standards."[10] For example, the restrictions that the IMF and World Bank impose on countries as a condition for granting loans not only impose capitalist values, they also undermine the very possibility of an inclusive and substantive democracy. The results have been disastrous and can be seen both in the economic collapse of countries such as Nigeria and in the fact that "one third of the world's labor force—more than a billion people—are unemployed or underemployed."[11] Tracking twenty-six countries that received loans from the World Bank and the IMF, *The Multinational Monitor* spelled out the conditions that accompanied such loans:

> [c]ivil service downsizing; [p]rivatization of government-owned enterprises, with layoffs required in advance of privatization and frequently following privatization; [p]romotion of labor flexibility—regulatory changes to remove restrictions on the

> ability of government and private employers to fire or lay off workers; [m]andated wage reductions, minimum wage reductions or containment, and spreading the wage gap between government employees and managers; and [p]ension reforms, including privatization, that cut social security benefits for workers.[12]

At home, corporations increasingly not only design the economic sphere but also shape legislation and policy affecting all levels of government, and with limited opposition. As corporate power lays siege to the political process, the benefits flow to the rich and the powerful. Included in such benefits are reform policies that shift the burden of taxes from the rich to the middle class, the working poor, and state governments—as can be seen in the shift from taxes on wealth (capital gains, dividends, and estate taxes) to a tax on work, principally in the form of a regressive payroll tax. During the 2002–2004 fiscal period, tax cuts delivered $197.3 billion in tax breaks to the wealthiest 1 percent of Americans (i.e., households making more than $337,000 a year) while state governments increased taxes to fill a $200 billion budget deficit.[13] Equally alarming, a recent congressional study revealed that 63 percent of all corporations in 2000 paid no taxes while "[s]ix in ten corporations reported no tax liability for the five years from 1996 through 2000, even though corporate profits were growing at record-breaking levels during that period."[14] While the rich get huge tax cuts, the Pentagon is spending about "$6 billion a month on the war in Iraq or about $2 million a day."[15] Moreover, as part of an ongoing effort to destroy public entitlements, the Bush administration has reduced government-provided services, income, and health care; in addition, it has implemented cuts in Medicare and veterans' benefits as well as trimmed back or eliminated funds for programs for children and for public housing. Neoliberal policies justify privatizing social services through appeals to "personal responsibility as the proper functions of the state are narrowed, tax and wage costs in the economy are cut, and more social costs are absorbed by civil society and the family."[16] The hard currency of human suffering permeates the social order as health-care costs rise, one out of five children remain beneath the poverty line, and 47 million Americans bear the burden of lacking health insurance. In 2007, President Bush vetoed legislation that would have provided an additional and much-needed $35 billion to the highly successful and popular State Children's Health Insurance Program (S-chip). Bush's justification ranged from silly—as when he claimed the whole issue was a media myth—to the more transparent and ideologically driven argument that the program would expand "socialized-type medicine," interfere with private insurance, and cost too much. Actually, the costs for the bill would have come from levying a 61-cents-a-pack increase in the federal excise tax on cigarettes and other tobacco products, providing a further disincentive for smokers. Moreover, the program is run by insurers, doctors, and nurses who deliver the services. This bill would have provided health insurance for 3.8 million children from low-income families who are currently uninsured. Besides a veto, the Bush administration offers no alternative program to address the plight of the 9 million children uninsured and the millions underinsured. What becomes clear in this egregious act of presidential incompetence and moral indifference is that Bush the unflappable neoliberal warrior was willing to sacrifice the health of millions of poor children as part of his relentless attempts to destroy all vestiges of the welfare state and promote his pro-corporate, market-based fundamentalism.[17]

Draining the public treasury of funds and disparaging the social state does more than result in failed governance; it also puts people's lives at risk, as was obvious in the government's failure to provide decent care at Walter Reed Hospital for wounded soldiers returning from the wars in Iraq and Afghanistan. At the same time that it starves public programs and services, neoliberalism becomes complicitous with the transformation of the democratic state into a national security state that repeatedly uses its military and political power to develop a daunting police force and military-prison-education-industrial complex to punish workers, stifle dissent, and undermine the political power of labor unions and progressive social movements.

Within the discourse of neoliberalism, individual misfortune, like democracy itself, is now viewed either as an excess or as being in need of radical containment. The media, largely consolidated through corporate power, routinely provide a platform for high-profile right-wing pundits and politicians to remind us of how degenerate the poor have become, reinforcing the central neoliberal tenet that all problems are private rather than social in nature. Conservative columnist Ann Coulter captures the latter sentiment with a cruel vengeance with her comment that "[i]nstead of poor people with hope and possibility, we now have a permanent underclass of aspiring criminals knifing one another between having illegitimate children and collecting welfare checks."[18] Radio talk-show host Michael Savage also exemplifies the unabashed racism and fanaticism that emerge under a neoliberal regime in which ethics and justice appear beside the point. Buttressed by a right-wing media culture in which 91 percent of political talk radio is conservative,[19] Savage routinely refers to nonwhite countries as "turd world nations," homosexuality as a "perversion," and young children who are victims of gunfire as "ghetto slime."[20]

As Fredric Jameson argues in *The Seeds of Time,* it has now become easier to imagine the end of the world than the end of capitalism.[21] The breathless rhetoric of the global victory of free-market rationality, spewed forth by the mass media, right-wing intellectuals, and governments alike, has found its material expression both in an all-out attack on democratic values and in the growth of a range of social problems, including virulent and persistent poverty, joblessness, inadequate health care, racial apartheid in the inner cities, and increasing inequalities between the rich and the poor. Such issues appear to have been either removed from the inventory of public discourse and social policy or factored into talk-show spectacles in which the public becomes merely a staging area for venting private interests and emotions.

Within the discourse of neoliberalism that has taken hold of the public imagination, it becomes increasingly more difficult to talk about what is fundamental to civic life, critical citizenship, and a substantive democracy. In its dubious appeals to universal laws, neutrality, and selective scientific research, neoliberalism "eliminates the very possibility of critical thinking, without which democratic debate becomes impossible."[22] Hence, neoliberal policies that promote the cutthroat downsizing of the workforce, the bleeding of social services, the reduction of state governments to police precincts, the ongoing liquidation of job security, the increasing elimination of a decent social wage, the creation of a society of low-skilled workers, and the emergence of a culture of permanent insecurity and fear hide behind appeals to common sense and alleged immutable laws of nature.

When and where such nakedly ideological appeals strain both reason and imagination, religious faith is invoked to silence dissension. Society is now defended not as a space to nurture the most fundamental values and relations necessary to a democracy but, rather, as an ideological and political sphere "where religious fundamentalism comes together with market fundamentalism to form the ideology of American supremacy."[23] Similarly, American imperial ambitions have been legitimated by public relations intellectuals as part of the responsibilities of empire-building, now celebrated as a civilizing process for the rest of the globe. A culture of force buttressed by notions of "full spectrum dominance" and a permanent war on terror is now seen to function "in the service of spreading liberty and democracy."[24] Neoconservatives join hands with neoliberals and religious fundamentalists in broadcasting to the rest of the globe an American triumphalism in which the United States is arrogantly defined as "[t]he greatest of all great powers in world history."[25] Money, profits, and fear have become powerful ideological elements in arguing for opening up new markets and closing down the possibility of dissent at home. In such a scenario, a new kind of coercive state emerges as "authorized power is [sanctioned as the only type of] credible power ... [and] state appeals to fear [become] the only effective basis for obedience."[26] This becomes clear not only in the passage of repressive laws such as the USA PATRIOT Act and the Military Commissions Act of 2006 but also in the work of prominent neoconservatives such as David Frum and Richard Perle, who, without any irony intended, insist that "[a] free society is not an un-policed society. A free society is a self-policed society."[27] In what could only be defined as an Adam-Smith-joins-George-Orwell-in-a-religious-cult-in-California scenario, markets have become sacrosanct temples to be protected while citizens-turned-Army-of-God conscripts are urged to spy on one another and dissent is increasingly criminalized.[28] At the same time, democratic politics is increasingly derailed by the intersection of a free-market fundamentalism and an escalating militarism.[29] The consequences can be seen in the policy of anti-terrorism practiced by the Bush administration that mimics the very terrorism it wishes to eliminate. Not only does this policy of all-embracing anti-terrorism exhaust itself in a discourse of moral absolutes, militarism, revenge, and public acts of denunciation, it also strips community of democratic values by configuring politics in religious terms and defining every citizen and inhabitant of the United States as a potential terrorist. Politics becomes empty as citizens are reduced to obedient recipients of power, content to follow orders while shaming those who make power accountable. Under the dictates of a pseudo-patriotism, dissent is stifled in the face of a growing racism that condemns Arabs and people of color as less than civilized. The ongoing refusal of the American government to address with any degree of self-criticism or humanity the torture and violation of human rights exercised by American soldiers at Abu Ghraib prison in Iraq offers a case in point.[30] In light of the revelation of the most grotesque brutality, racism, and inhumanity exhibited by American soldiers against Arab prisoners captured on camera and video, powerful right-wing politicians and pundits such as Rush Limbaugh and Cal Thomas initially defended such actions as a way for young men to either "blow some steam off," engage in a form of harmless frat hazing, or give Muslim prisoners what they deserve. It gets worse. Commentators such as Newt Gingrich and Republican Senator James Inhofe went so far as to suggest that calling attention to such crimes not only undermined troop morale in Iraq but was also unpatriotic. That argument seems to have some credibility in the highest levels of government since, as of 2007, no high-ranking official has been legally charged with a crime. Defending torture and gross sexual humiliations by U.S. troops in Saddam's old jails is not merely insensitive political posturing; it is, more tellingly, indicative of how far the leadership of this country has strayed from any semblance of democracy. As a *New York Times* editorial pointed out in October 2007, the Bush administration has apparently turned the United States into a "nation that tortures human beings and then concocts legal sophistries to confuse the world and avoid accountability before American voters." The editorial goes on to state that "President Bush and his aides have not only condoned torture and abuse at secret prisons.... [whose techniques were] modeled on the dungeons of Egypt, Saudi Arabia and the Soviet Union.... but they have conducted a systematic campaign to mislead Congress, the American people and the world about those policies."[31]

Cleary, political culture, if not the nature of politics itself, has undergone revolutionary changes in the last two decades, reaching its most debased expression under the administration of the imperial presidency of President George W. Bush. Within this political culture, not only is democracy subordinated to the rule of a market, but corporate decisions are freed from territorial constraints and the demands of public obligations, just as economics is disconnected from its social consequences. Zygmunt Bauman captures what is new about the relationship among power, politics, and the shredding of social obligations in his comment that

> [t]he mobility acquired by "people who invest"—those with capital, with money which the investment requires—means the new, indeed unprecedented ... disconnection of power from obligations: duties towards employees, but also towards the younger and weaker, towards yet unborn generations and towards the self-reproduction of the living conditions of all; in short, the freedom from the duty to contribute to daily life and the perpetuation of the community.... Shedding the responsibility for the consequences is the most coveted and cherished gain which the new mobility brings to free-floating, locally unbound capital.[32]

As corporate power increasingly frees itself from any political limitations, it uses its power through the educational force of the dominant culture to put into place an utterly privatized notion of agency in which it becomes difficult for young people and adults to imagine democracy as a public good, let alone the transformative power of collective action. Democratic politics has become ineffective, if not banal, as civic language is increasingly impoverished and genuine spaces for democratic learning, debate, and dialogue such as schools, newspapers, popular culture, television networks, and other public spheres are either underfunded, eliminated, privatized, or subjected to corporate ownership. Under the politics and culture of neoliberalism, despite its tensions and contradictions, society is increasingly mobilized for the production of violence against the poor, immigrants, dissenters, and others marginalized because of their age, gender, race, ethnicity, and color. As I point out in Chapter 6, at the center of neoliberalism is a new form of politics in the United States, one in which radical exclusion is the order of the day—a politics in which the primary questions are no longer about equality, justice, or freedom but instead concern the survival of the slickest in a culture marked by fear, surveillance, and economic deprivation. As Susan George suggests, the question that now seems to define neoliberal "democracy" is "Who has a right to live or does not?"[33]

A key argument of this book is that neoliberalism is more than a neutral, economic discourse and logic that can be measured with the precision of a mathematical formula or defended through an appeal to the rules of a presumptively unassailable science that conveniently leaves its own history behind. On the contrary, rather than a paragon of economic rationality that offers the best "route to optimum efficiency, rapid economic growth and innovation, and rising prosperity for all who are willing to work hard and take advantage of available opportunities,"[34] it is an ideology that subordinates the art of democratic politics to the rapacious laws of a market economy.[35] More important, neoliberalism is a historical and socially constructed ideology that needs to be made visible, critically engaged, and shaken from the stranglehold of power it currently exercises over most of the commanding institutions of national and global life.[36] As a public pedagogy and political ideology, the neoliberalism of Friedrich Hayek and Milton Friedman[37] is far more ruthless than the classic liberal economic theory developed by Adam Smith and David Ricardo in the eighteenth and nineteenth centuries.[38] Neoliberalism has become the present conservative revolution because it harkens back to a period in American history—the Gilded Age—that supported the sovereignty of the market over the sovereignty of the democratic state and the common good.[39] Reproducing the future in the image of the distant past, it represents a struggle designed to roll back, if not dismantle, all of the policies put into place more than seventy years ago by the New Deal to curb corporate power and give substance to the liberal meaning of the social contract. The late Pierre Bourdieu captured what is new about neoliberalism when he said that neoliberalism is

> a new kind of conservative revolution [which] appeals to progress, reason and science (economics in this case) to justify the restoration and so tries to write off progressive thought and action as archaic. It sets up as the norm of all practices, and therefore as ideal rules, the real regularities of the economic world abandoned to its own logic, the so-called laws of the market. It reifies and glorifies the reign of what are called the financial markets, in other words the return to a kind of radical capitalism, with no other law than that of maximum profit, an unfettered capitalism without any disguise, but rationalized, pushed to the limit of its economic efficacy by the introduction of modern forms of domination, such as "business administration," and techniques of manipulation, such as market research and advertising.[40]

Neoliberalism has indeed become a broad-based political and cultural movement designed to obliterate public concerns and liquidate the welfare state, and make politics everywhere an exclusively market-driven project.[41] But neoliberalism does more than make the market "the informing principle of politics"[42] while allocating wealth and resources to those who are most privileged by virtue of their class, race, and power; its political culture and pedagogical practices also put into play a social universe and cultural landscape that support a particularly barbaric notion of authoritarianism, set in motion under the combined power of a religious and market fundamentalism and anti-terrorism laws that suspend civil liberties, incarcerate disposable populations, and provide the security forces necessary for capital to destroy those spaces where democracy can be nourished. All the while, the landscape and soundscape become increasingly militarized through a mass-mediated spectacle of violence whose underlying purpose is to conscript the public as soldiers in the "war on terrorism" while redefining democracy as a mix of war and American idealism. Neoliberalism does not merely produce militarized public spaces, economic inequality, iniquitous power relations, and a corrupt political system; it also promotes rigid exclusions from national citizenship and civic participation. As Lisa Duggan points out, "Neoliberalism cannot be abstracted from race and gender relations, or other cultural aspects of the body politic. Its legitimating discourse, social relations, and ideology are saturated with race, with gender, with sex, with religion, with ethnicity, and nationality."[43] Neoliberalism comfortably aligns itself with various strands of neoconservative and religious fundamentalisms waging imperial wars abroad as well as at home against those groups and movements that threaten its authoritarian misreading of the meaning of freedom, security, and productiveness.

One controversial example of how big corporations, particularly media conglomerates, use their power to simultaneously support neoliberal values, reactionary policies, and the politicians who produce them took place in 2004 when the Sinclair Broadcast Group, a Maryland-based media company whose holdings comprise sixty-two television stations, including several ABC affiliates, refused to air on its stations a special edition of *Nightline* with Ted Koppel. Sinclair was disturbed because Koppel had announced that he was going to read the names and show photographs of the faces of the then 721 U.S. soldiers killed in Iraq. Sinclair's refusal to air *Nightline* on its ABC stations was based on the argument that Koppel was making a political statement that allegedly undermined the war effort by drawing attention to its most troubling consequences. And its rationale for this act of censorship was that *Nightline* could have read the names of the thousands of citizens killed in terrorist attacks during the events of September 11, 2001. The problem with this accusation, as a statement from ABC made clear shortly after the charge, is that the network did broadcast a list of the 9/11 victims, one year after the gruesome event. What Sinclair did not mention was that it has been a generous contributor to the Republican Party and has lobbied successfully for policies that have allowed it to own even more stations. Sinclair shares the perspective of many of its corporate allies on the Right who believe that the costs of the war should be hushed up, in favor of news that portrays the Bush administration in a favorable light. After all, censoring the news is a small price to pay for the corporate windfalls that reward such acts. Free-market fundamentalism makes it easier for corporate power and political favoritism to mutually inform each other, reinforcing the ideological and political conditions for the perpetuation of a system of profits, money, market values, and power that, as Bill Moyers has pointed out, allows big corporations and big government to scratch each others' backs while canceling out the principles of justice and human dignity that inform a real democracy.[44]

The point I made earlier bears repeating: A key argument of this book is that neoliberalism has to be understood and challenged as both an economic theory and a powerful public pedagogy and cultural politics. That is, it has to be named and critically understood before it can be critiqued. The common-sense assumptions that legitimate neoliberalism's alleged historical inevitability have to be held up to the light so as to reveal the social damage they cause at all levels of human existence. Hence I not only attempt to identify and critically engage many of the most salient and powerful ideologies that inform and frame neoliberalism but also argue for making cultural politics and the notion of public pedagogy central to the struggle against neoliberalism—particularly since education and culture now play such prominent political and economic roles in both securing consent and producing capital. In fact, my position is similar to Susan Buck-Morss' argument that "[t]he recognition of cultural domination as just as important as, and perhaps even as the condition of possibility of, political and economic domination is a true 'advance' in our thinking."[45] Of course, this position is meant not to disavow economic and institutional struggles but, rather, to supplement them with a cultural politics that connects symbolic power and its pedagogical practices with material relations of power. In addition, I analyze how neoliberal policies work at the level of everyday life through the language of privatization and the lived cultural forms of class, race, gender, youth, and ethnicity. Finally, I attempt in every chapter to employ a language of both critique and possibility, engagement, and hope as part of a broader project of viewing democracy as a site of intense struggle over matters of representation, participation, and shared power.

Central to this book is the belief, as Alain Touraine argues, that neoliberal globalization has not "dissolved our capacity for political action."[46] Such action depends on the ability of various groups—the peace movement, the anti-corporate globalization movement, the human rights movement, the environmental justice movement—within and across national boundaries to form alliances in which matters of global justice, community, and solidarity provide a common symbolic space and multiple public spheres where norms are created, debated, and engaged as part of an attempt to develop a new political language, culture, and set of relations. Such efforts must be understood as part of a broader attempt not only to resist domination but also to defend all those social advances that strengthen democratic public spheres and services, demand new rights and modes of power sharing, and strive for social justice adequate to creating forms of collective struggle that can imagine and sustain democracy on a global level. The anti-corporate globalization struggle's slogan "Another World Is Possible!" demands, as

Alex Callinicos insightfully points out, a different kind of social logic, one that requires a powerful sense of unity and solidarity.

> Another *world*—that is, a world based on different social logic, run according to different priorities from those that prevail today. It is easy enough to specify what the desiderata of such an alternative social logic would be—social justice, economic efficiency, environmental sustainability, and democracy—but much harder to spell out how a reproducible social system embodying these requirements could be built. And then there is the question of how to achieve it. Both these questions—What is the alternative to capitalism? What strategy can get us there?—can be answered in different ways. One thing the anti-capitalist movement is going to have to learn is how to argue through the differences that exist and will probably develop around such issues without undermining the very powerful sense of unity that has been one of the movement's most attractive qualities.[47]

Callinicos' insight suggests that any viable struggle against neoliberal capitalism will have to rethink "the entire project of politics within the changed conditions of a global public sphere, and to do this democratically, as people who speak different political languages, but whose goals are nonetheless the same: global peace, economic justice, legal equality, democratic participation, individual freedom, mutual respect."[48] Indeed, one of the most central tasks facing intellectuals, activists, educators, and others who believe in an inclusive and substantive democracy is the utilization of theory to rethink the language and possibilities of politics as a way to imagine a future outside the powerful grip of neoliberalism. Critical reflection and social action in this discourse must acknowledge how the category of the global public sphere extends the space of politics beyond the boundaries of local resistance. Global problems need global institutions, global modes of dissent, global intellectual work, and global social movements.

In Chapter 1, I examine various debates about the growing authoritarianism in the United States (especially since the reelection of George W. Bush in 2004), with an emphasis on how neoliberal ideology becomes complicitous in reproducing the conditions for a new type of authoritarian domination. This chapter chronicles those forces that are not only suspicious of democracy but are aggressively at work to hollow out its substantive content and undercut its most basic values and principles. In Chapter 2, I illustrate how the discourse of neoliberalism privatizes the language of race while demonizing and punishing poor blacks and other youth of color as part of a larger attack on the welfare state. In this chapter, I focus on race as a category through which racial exclusions and violence are abstracted from public issues and considerations, whereby public considerations become privatized and reduced to matters of taste, character, and personal responsibility. In Chapter 3, I look at how a war is being waged against poor whites and kids of color, and how this war focuses on punishing students in public schools rather than on investing financially and intellectually in their education and future. This chapter explores how various aspects of everyday life, especially for young people, are being militarized and corporatized. In Chapter 4, I address what it means to understand neoliberalism as a form of public pedagogy and how the latter concept might become theoretically useful in rethinking strategies necessary to struggle individually and collectively against its most basic assumptions about the social order, work, education, and the larger global public sphere. In Chapter 5, I urge intellectuals to restore an enlightened notion of the future of democratic public life as well as forms of resistance to neoliberalism, grounded in the spirit of a militant hope and the creation of broader, democratic social movements. And, finally, in Chapter 6, I analyze the ideology of neoliberal common sense and consider how it functions as a form of cultural politics and public pedagogy to win various degrees of consent, especially as it bears down on and works through myriad aspects of everyday life. It is also here that I point to the emergence of the politics of disposability as a ruthless consequence of neoliberal governance, describe its connection to the demise of the social state, and conclude by addressing the democratic challenge of imagining a future beyond neoliberal ideology.

1
The Emerging Authoritarianism in the United States: Political Culture Under the Bush/Cheney Administration

> Hallmarks of totalitarian regimes have always included excessive reliance on secrecy, the deliberate stoking of fear in the general population, a preference for military rather than diplomatic solutions in foreign policy, the promotion of blind patriotism, the denial of human rights, the curtailment of the rule of law, hostility to a free press and the systematic invasion of the privacy of ordinary people.[1]

Introduction

How can we explain the reelection of George W. Bush in 2004 despite the flagrant lies about why the United States invaded Iraq, the passing of tax reform policies that reward the ultra-rich at the expense of the middle and lower classes, and the grandstanding over foreign policy decisions largely equated with bullying by the rest of the world? What is one to make of Bush's winning popular support for his reelection in light of his record of letting millions of young people slide into unemployment or underemployment, poverty, and hopelessness; his refusal to protect public health and the environment; and his promulgation of a culture of fear that is gutting the most cherished of American civil liberties? The reelection of George W. Bush makes clear what dominant intellectuals on the Left and Right have refused to acknowledge, though fiction writers such as Philip Roth seem to have a more prescient grasp of America's move toward authoritarianism.[2] The United States is not simply governed by a center-right party indifferent to the needs and will of the people; it is a country that is moving rapidly toward a form of authoritarianism that undermines any claim to being a liberal democracy. For those who cling to the illusion of democracy, even in its damaged forms, the issues that appear the most harmful to democracy are the war in Iraq, an imperial presidency, the record trade deficit, a soaring budget deficit, the ever-growing power of the military-industrial complex over American life, the attack on immigrants and people of color, the assault on civil liberties, and the horrifying concentration of wealth in the hands of the rich and elite corporations. Though seen as posing a threat to democracy, these issues are generally discounted as not being comparable to establishing the foundation for an emerging authoritarianism. This chapter sets out to show that a number of anti-democratic tendencies are now providing the conditions for a new form of authoritarianism, and to ignore this would be sheer folly.

Oppositional critics such as George Soros, respected philanthropist and multibillionaire, believe that the "Republican Party has been captured by a bunch of extremists."[3] Benjamin Ferencz, the chief prosecutor of Nazi war crimes at Nuremberg, has argued that George W. Bush should be tried for war crimes.[4] On the other hand, liberal apologists such as James Traub, a feature writer for the *New York Times,* put a different spin on the authoritarian direction in which the United States is moving. For Traub, any comparison between the Bush administration and fascism "constitutes a gross trivialization of the worst event in modern history."[5] According to Traub, *fascism* is a term that was abused by the Left in the 1960s and is being used recklessly once again by those criticizing the Bush regime. His argument holds that fascism is a historically specific movement whose ideology cannot be applied to contexts outside of the conditions in which it emerged. In short, Traub implies that any suggestion that the United States is becoming a fascist state is simply preposterous. Traub believes that whatever problems the United States faces have nothing to do with a growing authoritarianism. On the contrary, according to his view, we are simply witnessing the seizure of power by some extremists who not only represent a form of political exceptionalism and an annoying growth on the body politic but also have little to do with the real values that constitute the meaning of American democracy and national identity. Traub, in particular, like most of the dominant media in the United States, has no sense either of degrees and gradations of authoritarianism or of fascism as an ideology that can always reconstitute itself in different ideas, practices, and arguments. Instead, he clings to both a reductive understanding of fascism and a simplistic binary logic that strictly categorizes a country as authoritarian *or* democratic. He has no language for entertaining the possibility of a mixture of both systems, which would suggest a more updated if not different form of authoritarianism, or the malignant replication of many ideas characteristic of fascism within U.S. culture beyond the official sphere of state politics. What critics such as Traub ignore at their own peril is Hannah Arendt's prescient warning that elements of totalitarianism continue to be with us and that, rather than be relegated to the dustbin of history, the "still existing elements of totalitarianism would be more likely to crystallize into *new* forms."[6]

Elements of Authoritarianism in the United States

Revelations in the *New York Times* about the Bush administration's decision to allow the National Security Agency to spy on Americans without first obtaining warrants, the disclosure by the *Washington Post* of a network of covert prisons known as "black sites" established by the Central Intelligence Agency (CIA) in eight countries, the normalization of war, the rampant corruption involving the most powerful politicians in the Bush administration, the administration's political and moral laxity in the face of the Hurricane Katrina tragedy, and ongoing stories about widespread abuse and torture in Iraq and Afghanistan—these are just some of the elements reported in the popular press that corroborate a growing authoritarianism in American life. The Bush administration, as many notable and courageous critics ranging from Seymour M. Hersh to Gore Vidal and Robert Kennedy Jr. have pointed out, has tarnished the highest offices of government with unsavory corporate alliances, used political power unabashedly to pursue legislative policies that favor the rich and punish the poor, and disabled those public spheres not governed by the logic of the market. Sidney Blumenthal, former senior adviser to President Clinton and no radical, argues that the Bush administration has created a government that is tantamount to "a national security state of torture, ghost detainees, secret prisons, renditions and domestic eavesdropping."[7] Bob Herbert, an op-ed writer for the *New York Times,* insists that all of the surreptitious activities of the Bush regime offer Americans nothing less than a "road map to totalitarianism."[8]

Whereas the Clinton administration situated its key positions in the Treasury Department, the Bush administration relies on its defense experts—Cheney, Gates, and Rice—to develop its international policy. As war becomes the foundation for the administration's empire-driven foreign policy, real and symbolic violence combine with a number of anti-democratic tendencies to make the world more dangerous and the promise of global democracy difficult to imagine in the current historical moment.[9] Entire populations are now seen as disposable, and state sovereignty is no longer organized around the struggle for life but now entails an insatiable quest for the accumulation of capital, leading to what Achille Mbembe calls "necropolitics" or the destruction of human bodies.[10] The language of patriotic correctness and religious fanaticism is beginning to replace the language of social justice and equality, bespeaking the enduring attraction and "rehabilitation of fascist ideals and principles."[11]

In what follows, I argue that fascism and authoritarianism are important categories that need to be mined in order to explore the changing nature of power, control, and rule in the United States and the challenge that such changes pose to a democracy now under siege. I want to make clear from the outset that I am not suggesting the United States is engaged in a process of genocidal terror against racialized populations—though the increase in police brutality in the last decade against people of color coupled with the rise of a prison-industrial-military complex that primarily punishes black men cannot be overlooked.[12] Nor can the increased attack by the American government on the rights of many innocent Arabs, Muslims, and immigrants be understood as anything other than a kind of totalitarian time warp in which airport terminals now resemble state prisons as foreign nationals are fingerprinted, photographed, and interrogated.[13] Immigration detention is the fastest-growing form of incarceration in the United States and has pushed the number of people in prisons and jails in the United States over the 2.2 million mark. As the journalist Nina Bernstein points out, immigrants are not only being detained and imprisoned in record numbers but are dying for "lack of adequate healthcare" and insufficient "access to legal help, suicide prevention programs, and adequate oversight."[14] The Gulag that now spreads its tentacles and ensnares thousands of people in its network of secret detention centers, private prisons, and local jails was referred to in an editorial in the *New York Times* as "Gitmos Across America."[15] Given such circumstances, it is not difficult to argue that the United States is beset by a growing authoritarianism, the characteristics of which I will spell out below.

Fascism is not so much an ideological apparatus frozen in a particular historical period as it is a theoretical and political signpost for understanding how democracy can be subverted, if not destroyed. Bertram Gross in 1985 wrote a book titled *Friendly Fascism* in which he argued that if fascism came to the United States it would not embody the fascist characteristics that were associated with its legacies in the past. There would be no Nuremberg rallies, doctrines of racial superiority, government-sanctioned book burnings, death camps, or the abrogation of the constitution. In short, fascism would not take the form of an ideological grid from the past simply downloaded onto another country under different historical conditions. On the contrary, he believed that fascism would be an eternal danger and would have the ability to become relevant under new conditions, taking on familiar forms of thought that resonate with nativist traditions, experiences, and political relations.[16] Similarly, Umberto Eco, in his discussion of "Eternal Fascism," argues that any updated version of fascism will not openly assume the mantle of historical fascism; rather, new forms of authoritarianism will appropriate some of its elements. Like Gross, Eco maintains that fascism, if it comes to America, will have a different guise, although it will be no less destructive of democracy. He writes:

> Ur-Fascism [Eternal Fascism] is still around us, sometimes in plainclothes. It would be much easier for us if there appeared on the world scene somebody saying, "I want to reopen Auschwitz, I want the Blackshirts to parade again in the Italian squares." Life is not that simple. Ur-Fascism can come back under the most innocent of disguises. Our duty is to uncover it and to point our finger at any of its new instances—everyday, in every part of the world. Franklin Roosevelt's words of November 4, 1938, are worth recalling: "If American democracy ceases to move forward as a living force, seeking day and night by peaceful means to better the lot of our citizens, fascism will grow in strength in our land." Freedom and liberation are an unending task.[17]

In order to make a distinction between the old and new forms of fascism, I want to use the term *proto-fascism* for an emerging U.S. authoritarianism, not only because it suggests a different constellation of elements and forms pointing toward its reconstitution but also because it has "the beauty of familiarity, and rightly in many cases reveals a deliberate attempt to make fascism relevant in new conditions."[18] The point here is not to obscure the distinctiveness of the nature, force, or consequences of the old fascism but to highlight how some of its central elements are emerging in contemporary forms in the United States. Precise accounts of the meaning of fascism abound, and I have no desire, given its shifting nature, to impose a rigid definition with universal pretensions. But most scholars agree that fascism is a mass movement that emerges out of a failed democracy, and that its ideology is extremely anti-liberal, anti-democratic, and anti-socialistic. It is also marked by an "elaborate ideology which covers all aspects of man's existence and which contains a powerful chiliastic [messianic or religious] moment."[19] As a political philosophy, fascism exalts the nation and race—or some purified form of national identity—over the individual, supports centralized dictatorial power, demands blind obedience from the masses, and promotes a top-down revolution. As a social order, it is generally characterized by a system of terror directed against perceived enemies of the state; a monopolistic control of the mass media; an expanding prison system; a state monopoly of weapons; the existence of privileged groups and classes; control of the economy by a limited number of people; unbridled corporatism; "the appeal to emotion and myth rather than reason; the glorification of violence on behalf of a national cause; the mobilization and militarization of civil society; [and] an expansionist foreign policy intended to promote national greatness."[20]

Robert Paxton provides a working definition of fascism that points to both its anti-democratic moments and those elements that link it to the past and the present. Paxton's point is not to provide a precise definition of fascism but to understand the conditions that enable fascism to work and make possible its development in the future. Accordingly, fascism is

> [a] form of political behavior marked by obsessive preoccupation with community decline, humiliation or victimhood and by compensatory cults of unity, energy and purity, in which a mass-based party of committed nationalist militants, working in uneasy but effective collaboration with traditional elites, abandons democratic liberties and pursues with redemptive violence and without ethical or legal restraints goals of internal cleansing and external expansion.[21]

I argue in this chapter that the specter of fascism resides in the lived relations of a given social order and the ways in which such relations exacerbate the material conditions of inequality, undercut a sense of individual and social agency, hijack democratic values, and promote a deep sense of hopelessness and cynicism. In turn, this deep sense of despair on the part of the polity in the face of unaccountable corporate and political power, for instance, gives credence to Arendt's notion that at the heart of totalitarianism is the disappearance of thinking, debating, and speaking citizens who make politics possible. Fascism as both an ideology and a set of social practices emerges within the lived contradictions that mark such relations, scorning the present while calling for a revolution that rescues a deeply anti-modernist past as a way to revolutionize the future. Mark Neocleous touches on the anti-modernist nature of fascist ideology in his discussion of a "reactionary modernism" that is typical of the New Right:

> [The New Right] pitted itself against the existing order—the post-war "consensus" regarding welfarism and the quasi-corporate management of capitalism—in the light of an image of past national glory (a mythic and contradictory image, but no less powerful for that). The central elements of New Right politics—an aggressive leadership, uncompromising stance on law and order, illiberal attitude on moral questions generally and certain political questions such as race and immigration, an attack on the labor movement and a defense of private property, and a forthright nationalism—all combine in a politics of reaction: a reassertion of the principle of private property and capital accumulation as the *raison d'être* of modern society, alongside an authoritarian moralism requiring excessive state power as a means of policing civil society. If there is such a thing as the New Right distinct from "traditional" conservatism, then it lies in its being a reactionary modernism of our times.[22]

The emerging American proto-fascism that threatens the future of democracy can best be understood through an examination of several characteristics relating it both to an older form of fascism and to a set of contemporary conditions that give it a distinctive character. After documenting and analyzing these central, though far from exhaustive, features of proto-fascism under the current Bush administration, I want to conclude by examining how neoliberalism provides a unique set of conditions for both producing and legitimating the central tendencies of proto-fascism.

The cult of traditionalism, combined with a reactionary modernism, is a central feature of proto-fascism and is alive and well in Bush's America. The alliance of neoconservatives, extremist evangelical Christians, and free-market advocates on the political Right imagines a social order modeled on the presidency of William McKinley and the values of the robber barons. The McKinley presidency lasted from 1897 to 1901 and "had a consummate passion to serve corporate and imperial power."[23] This was an age when blacks, women, immigrants, and minorities of class "knew their place"; big government exclusively served the interests of the corporate monopolists; commanding institutions were under the sway of narrow political interests; welfare was a private enterprise; and labor unions were kept in place by the repressive forces of the state. All of these conditions are being reproduced under the leadership of the Republican Party, which until the 2006 elections held sway over all branches of government. William Greider, writing in *The Nation,* observes a cult of traditionalism and anti-modernism within the Bush administration and its return to a past largely defined through egregious inequality,[24] corporate greed, hyper-commercialism, political corruption, and an utter disdain for economic and political democracy.

A second feature connecting the old fascism to its updated version is the ongoing corporatization of civil society and the diminishment of public space. The latter refers to the fact that corporate space is destroying democratic public spheres, eliminating those public spaces where norm-establishing communication takes place. Viewed primarily as an economic investment rather than as a central democratic sphere for fostering the citizen-based processes of deliberation, debate, and dialogue, public space is consistently shrinking due to the relentless dynamic of privatization and commercialization.[25] The important notion that space can be used to cultivate citizenship is now transformed by a new "common sense" that links it almost entirely to the production of consumers.[26] The inevitable correlate to this logic is that providing space for democracy to grow is no longer a priority. As theorists such as Jürgen Habermas and David Harvey have argued, the idea of critical citizenship cannot flourish without the reality of public space.[27] Put differently, "the space of citizenship is as important as the idea of citizenship."[28] As a political category, space is crucial to any critical understanding of how power circulates, how disciplinary practices are constructed, and how social control is organized. Moreover, as Margaret Kohn points out in her landmark study on radical space, "spatial practices can ... contribute to transformative politics."[29] Space as a political category performs invaluable theoretical work in connecting ideas to material struggles, theories to concrete practices, and political operations to the concerns of everyday life. Without public space, it becomes more difficult for individuals to imagine themselves as political agents or to understand the necessity for developing a discourse capable of defending civic institutions. Public space confirms the idea of individuals and groups having a public voice, thus drawing a distinction between civic liberty and market liberty. The demands of citizenship affirm the social as a political concept in opposition to its conceptualization as a strictly economic category. The sanctity of the town hall or public square in American life is grounded in the crucial recognition that citizenship has to be cultivated in noncommercialized spaces. Indeed, democracy itself needs public spheres where education as a condition for democracy can germinate, where people can meet and democratic identities, values, and relations have the time "to grow and flourish."[30] Zygmunt Bauman captures the historical importance both of public spaces for nourishing civic discourses and engaging citizens and of the consequences of the current disappearance of noncommodified spheres as significant spaces in which powerful individuals can be held directly accountable for the ethical and material effects of their decisions:

> These meeting places ... public spaces—agoras and forums in their various manifestations, places where agendas are set, private affairs are made public ... were also the sites in which *norms were created*—so that justice could be done, and apportioned horizontally, thus re-forging the conversationalists into a *community,* set apart and integrated by the shared criteria of evaluation. Hence a territory stripped of public space provides little chance for norms being debated, for values to be confronted, to clash and to be negotiated. The verdicts of right and wrong, beauty and ugliness, proper and improper, useful and useless may only descend from on high, from regions never to be penetrated by any but a most inquisitive eye; the verdicts are unquestionable since no questions may be meaningfully addressed to the judges and since the judges left no address—not even an e-mail address—and no one can be sure where they reside. No room is left for the "local opinion leaders"; no room is left for the "local opinion" as such.[31]

The totalizing belief that commercial interests and commodification should be free of any regulation is equally matched by the belief that "every domain of human life should be open to the forces of the marketplace."[32] The values of the market and the ruthless workings of finance capital have become the template for organizing the rest of society.

A third feature of the emerging proto-fascism is the relationship between the construction of an ongoing culture of fear and a form of patriotic correctness designed to bolster a rampant nationalism and a selective popularism.[33] Fear is mobilized through both the war on terrorism and "the sovereign pronouncement of a 'state of emergency' [which] generates a wild zone of power, barbaric and violent, operating without democratic oversight in order to combat an 'enemy' that threatens the existence of not merely and not mainly its citizens, but its sovereignty."[34] As Stanley Aronowitz points out, the national security state is now organized through "a combination of internal terrorism and the threat of external terrorism," which works to reinforce "its most repressive functions."[35] The threat of outside terrorism redefines the rules of war since there is no traditional state or enemy to fight. One consequence is that all citizens and noncitizens are viewed as potential terrorists and must prove their innocence through either consent or complicity with the national security state. Under such circumstances, patriotic fervor marks the line between terrorists and nonterrorists.

Jingoistic patriotism is now mobilized in the highest reaches of government, in the media, and throughout society, put on perpetual display through the rhetoric of celebrities, journalists, and nightly television news anchors, and relentlessly buttressed by the never-ending waving of flags—on cars, trucks, clothes, houses, and the lapels of TV anchors—as well as through the use of mottoes, slogans, and songs. As a rhetorical ploy to silence dissent, patriotism is used to name as unpatriotic any attempt either to make governmental power and authority responsive to its consequences at home or to question how the appeal to nationalism is being used to legitimate the U.S. government's bad-faith aspirations to empire-building overseas. This type of anti-liberal thinking is deeply distrustful of critical inquiry, mistakes dissent for treason, constructs politics through the childish binary lens of good and evil and moral absolutes of "us and them," and views difference and democracy as threats to consensus and national identity. Such patriotic fervor fuels a system of militarized control that not only repudiates the authority of international law but also relies on a notion of preventive war in order to project the fantasies of unbridled American power all over the globe. Chalmers Johnson, Andrew Bacevich, and Richard Falk, among others, argue that it is precisely this style of imperial control—fed by the desire for incontestable military preeminence in the world—and the use of authoritarian modes of regulation by the state at home that have given rise to what Falk describes as the threat of global fascism posed by the current U.S. administration. He writes:

> But why fascist? ... First of all, the combination of unchallengeable military preeminence with a rejection by the US government of the restraining impact of international law and the United Nations.... Secondly, the US government in moving against terrorism has claimed sweeping power to deal with the concealed Al Qaeda network.... [T]he character of the powers claimed include secret detentions, the authority to designate American citizens as "enemy combatants" without any rights, the public consideration of torture as a permissible police practice in anti-terrorist work, the scrutiny applied to those of Muslim faith, the reliance on assassination directed at terrorist suspects wherever they are found, and numerous invasions of privacy directed at ordinary people.... The slide toward fascism at home is given tangible expression by these practices, but it is also furthered by an uncritical and chauvinistic patriotism, by the release of periodic alarmist

warnings of mega-terrorist imminent attacks that fail to materialize, and by an Attorney General, John Ashcroft [then Alberto Gonzales, until he resigned], who seems to exult in the authoritarian approach to law enforcement.[36]

A fourth feature of proto-fascism is the attempt to control the mass media through government regulation, consolidated corporate ownership, or sympathetic media moguls and spokespersons. The use of government regulation is evident in the Bush-appointed Federal Communications Commission's attempts to pass legislation favoring media monopolies, which would undermine opposition and organize consent through a "capillary network of associations with vast powers of social and cultural persuasion."[37] Indeed, media regulation has promoted rather than limited the consolidation of media ownership in the United States. As a powerful form of public pedagogy, the dominant media set the agenda for what information is included or excluded; they provide the narratives for understanding the past and present; they distinguish between high- and low-status knowledge; they offer modes of identity, legitimate particular values, and have the power to deeply influence how people define the future. The media do not merely manufacture consent, they go so far as to produce the news and dictate the knowledge, skills, and values through which citizenship is lived and democracy defined. In this process, the media have assumed a major role in providing the conditions necessary for creating citizens capable of participating fully in shaping and governing society by having access to a wide range of knowledge and information. At the risk of exaggerating this issue I must stress that, in the twenty-first century, media culture has become the most important educational force in creating citizens and social agents capable of putting existing institutions into question and making democracy work—or doing just the opposite.

Unfortunately, the power of the mass media along with the agenda it sets are now in the hands of a limited number of transnational corporations, and the number of owners is actually getting smaller. Robert McChesney and John Nichols argue that "the U.S. media system is dominated by about ten transnational conglomerates including Disney, AOL TimeWarner, News Corporation, Viacom, Vivendi Universal, Sony, Liberty, Bertelsmann, AT&T Comcast, and General Electric (NBC)."[38] Before the Telecommunications Act of 1996, a single firm could own no more than 28 radio stations nationally. With the passage of the law and the relaxation of restrictions, the radio industry has been in a state of upheaval as hundreds of stations have been sold. Three firms in the largest radio market now control access to more than half of the listening audience. One of the firms, Clear Channel Communications, owns 1,225 radio stations and 39 television stations in the United States and has equity interests in over 240 radio stations internationally. Not only does it reach more than 70 percent of the American public through its radio stations, it also operates approximately 776,000 outdoor advertising displays around the world, including billboards, street furniture, and transit panels. According to Source Watch, it "is a leading promoter, producer and marketer of live entertainment events and also owns leading athlete management and marketing companies."[39] Clear Channel is owned by a friend of the Bush family and it is a large contributor to right-wing political causes. The company makes no pretense about its conservative politics; in fact, it has gained a certain notoriety over the years for banning the Dixie Chicks and over 200 peace-related songs, including John Lennon's "Imagine," as well as allowing many of its stations to sponsor a number of pro-war rallies. *NOW with Bill Moyers* did a radio survey in February 2004 in which they discovered that "the top-rated talk radio stations across the country ran 310 hours of conservative talk each day and only five hours of views that were not right-wing."[40] Media concentration and the hijacking of media sources by right-wing interests severely restrict the range of views to which people have access and thereby undermine democracy by stripping citizens of the possibility for vigorous public debate, critical exchange, and civic engagement.

Under proto-fascism, the marketplace of ideas has almost nothing to do with what is crucial for citizens to know in order to be active participants in shaping and sustaining a vibrant democracy. On the contrary, the media largely serve to target audiences for advertising, to pander to the anti-democratic ideologies of the political elite, to reinforce the conventional wisdom of corporate interests, and to promote cynical withdrawal by a populace adrift in a sea of celebrity scandal and mindless infotainment. In a proto-fascist state, the media basically deteriorate into a combination of commercialism, propaganda, and entertainment. The Bush administration, in an attempt to preserve its power at all costs, has not only resorted to denouncing its critics as either irresponsible or un-American but also routinely pumps out propaganda by faking its own news, planting stories favorable to the Bush worldview at home and abroad, bribing conservative journalists such as Armstrong Williams and Karen Ryan, and simply relying on Fox News to divert attention from embarrassing revelations about government incompetence, failures, misdeeds, and lies. David Barstow and Robin Stein reported in the *New York Times* that "[i]n all, at least 20 federal agencies, including the Defense Department and the Census Bureau, have made and distributed hundreds of television news segments in the past four years, [as] records and interviews show.... Many were subsequently broadcast on local stations across the country without any acknowledgment of the government's role in their production. [Moreover, the Bush administration] spent $254 million in its first term on public relations contracts."[41] Under such circumstances, the media neither operate in the interests of the public good nor provide the pedagogical conditions necessary for producing critical citizens and defending a vibrant democracy. Instead, as McChesney and Nichols point out, concentrated mainstream media depoliticize the culture of politics, commercially carpet-bomb citizens, and denigrate public life.[42] Instead of performing an essential public service, the dominant media have become the primary pedagogical tool for promoting a culture of consent and conformity in which citizens are misinformed and public discourse is debased.

Even where critical thought does appear, whether in the university, the media, or other education sites, it is often attacked and disarmed through right-wing campaigns of intimidation, appeals to fear and security in order to refuse accountability, and pernicious suggestions that such criticism is un-American or even treasonous. Because of the critical nature of their work, reputable academic scholars such as Joseph Massad, Norman Finkelstein, Nadia Abu El-Haj, and others are either pilloried in the right-wing media, dismissed, or refused tenure, regardless of the quality of their scholarship.[43] Similarly, prominent critics of the government are routinely subjected to what has been called "Swift Boating," the relentless process of using ad hominem character assassination to viciously discredit the critics in highly personal terms. As Frank Rich points out, "The most prominent smear victims have been Bush political opponents with heroic Vietnam résumés: John McCain, Max Cleland, John Kerry. But the list of ... targets stretches from the former counterterrorism czar Richard Clarke to Specialist Thomas Wilson, the grunt who publicly challenged Donald Rumsfeld about inadequately armored vehicles last December."[44] An especially toxic assault was launched by the Bush administration against "the whistle-blower Joseph Wilson—the diplomat described by the first President Bush as 'courageous' and 'a true American hero' for confronting Saddam to save American hostages in 1991."[45] The Bush administration tried to punish former Ambassador Wilson (for having disclosed in a *New York Times* op-ed that a central argument of the administration's case for the Iraq war was false) by leaking the name of Wilson's wife, Valerie Plame, to conservative columnist Robert Novak, who revealed that she was a CIA operative. The attack on Wilson and the outing of his wife eventually led to the conviction in 2007 of I. Lewis Libby, the former chief of staff to Vice President Dick Cheney, on four felony counts for lying in a government investigation of the CIA leak.

Similarly, when the *New York Times* exposed the government's use of the National Security Agency to conduct warrant-free wiretapping on American citizens, Bush responded by discrediting the leak as "shameful" and called for a Justice Department investigation to locate the internal sources who had exposed yet another violation of individual rights. According to this logic, the real crime is the exposure of government wrongdoing, rather than the lawlessness and expression of absolute power revealed by such practices. Bush also implied that critics of his illegal wiretaps were guilty of giving aid and comfort to al Qaeda. As an editorial in *The Nation* pointed out, if this were true "the ranks of the treasonous now include leaders of the President's own party, and the *New York Times'* revelations of illegal wiretaps foretell an earthquake."[46] With such accusations, the Bush government, in its no-holds-barred war against terrorism, collapses the distinction "between enemies of the state and ordinary citizens" and in doing so emulates dictatorships of the latter part of the twentieth century in countries like Peru.[47] In Bush's Manichaean world of good and evil, the "appeal to absolutes blocks the road to open inquiry and genuine thinking."[48]

A fifth element of proto-fascism is the rise of an Orwellian version of Newspeak in the United States, or what Umberto Eco labels as the language of "eternal fascism," whose purpose is to produce "an impoverished vocabulary, and an elementary syntax [whose consequence is] to limit the instruments for complex and critical reasoning."[49] Under the Bush administration, especially since the tragic events of September 11, the tools of language, sound, and image are increasingly being appropriated in an effort to diminish the capacity of the American public to think critically. As the critical power of language is reduced in official discourse to a simulacrum of communication, it becomes more difficult for the American public to engage in critical debates, translate private considerations into public concerns, and recognize the distortions and lies that underlie much of the current government policies. What happens to critical language under the emergence of official Newspeak can be seen in the various ways in which the Bush administration and its official supporters both misrepresent by misnaming government policies and simply engage in lying to cover up their own regressive politics and policies.[50]

Many people have pointed to Bush himself as a mangler of the English language, but this charge simply repeats the obvious while privatizing a much more important issue connecting language to power. Bush's discursive ineptness may be fodder for late-night comics, but such analyses miss the crucial issue of how the Bush administration strategically manipulates discourse. For instance, Bush describes himself as a "reformer" while he promotes policies that expand corporate welfare, give tax benefits to the rich, and "erode the financial capacity of the state to undertake any but the most minimal welfare functions."[51] He defines himself as a "compassionate conservative," but he implements policies that result in "billions of dollars in cuts ... proposed for food stamp and child nutrition programs, and for health care for the poor."[52] Bush's public speeches, often mimicked in the media, are filled with what Renana Brooks has called "empty language"—that is, statements that are so abstract as to be relatively meaningless except to reinforce in simplistic terms an often reactionary ideological position. Brooks cites the example of Bush's comment on the complex relationship between malpractice suits and skyrocketing health care, which he reduces to "No one has ever been healed by a frivolous lawsuit." While Bush's own ideological position becomes clear in this comment, the complexity of the issue is completely trivialized and removed from public discussion. Bush uses language so as to suggest his decisions are largely benign, while covering up the grave constitutional implications of his actions. Referring to criticisms of his illegal wiretapping program, Bush responds with "When al-Qaeda or an al-Qaeda affiliate is making a phone call from outside the United States to inside the United States, we want to know why."[53] And in response to charges that his administration violates international law by using torture, he blithely states "In this new kind of war, we must be willing to question the enemy when we pick them up on the battlefield."[54] Of course, the "battlefield" is now considered any place on the planet, including the local bus stop, street, or mosque. On other occasions, when confronted with an obvious rhetorical misstep, Bush has quite simply denied that he made a particular claim. When the Downing Street Memo surfaced, making it clear that the Bush administration was intent on going to war and that such prewar claims as the weapons-of-mass-destruction argument and the alleged link between Iraq and al Qaeda were not true, Bush would often deflect questions regarding those claims by simply denying he made them. For instance, in a public forum in March 2006, Bush flatly lied by claiming in response to a hostile question that he had never said there "was a direct connection between September 11th and Saddam Hussein," but, of course, he did make such a statement on countless occasions.[55] Sometimes the distortions of official language are hard to miss, even among the media guards so quick to invoke patriotic correctness. One glaring example can be found in an interview between Terry Gross, host of National Public Radio's *Fresh Air,* and Grover Norquist, president of Americans for Tax Reform and also considered to be the chief architect of President Bush's tax plan. The topic for discussion was the estate tax, reviled as the "death tax" by conservative elites to gain popular support for its repeal even though the vast majority of Americans will not be affected by this tax. Gross suggested that since the estate tax affects only a small minority of people who get over $2 million in inheritance, the law eliminating it clearly privileges the rich, not the average American. Norquist responded by arguing that the morality behind her argument was comparable to the same type of morality that resulted in the death of millions of Jews under the Holocaust. When Gross challenged this specious analogy, Norquist argued illogically that "people" (read "liberals") who favored the estate tax could now be placed on the same moral plane as the Nazis who killed over 6 million Jews and untold others.[56] According to this logic, any critique of a minority group, but especially the rich, can be dismissed as being comparable to the kind of discrimination waged by the perpetrators of one of the worst mass murders in human history. Of course, there is the further implication that liberal critics should be punished for their views just as the Nazis were punished in Nuremberg for their crimes against humanity. This is a matter not just of using a desperate logic to dismiss counterarguments, or of silencing one's critics through distortion, but of actually demonizing those who hold the "wrong" views. Norquist's position is a contortion that fails to hide the fundamentalism that often drives this type of language.

Official Newspeak also trades in the rhetoric of fear in order to manipulate the public into a state of servile political dependency and unquestioning ideological support. Fear and its attendant use of moral panics create not only a rhetorical umbrella to promote other agendas but also a sense of helplessness and cynicism throughout the body politic. Hence the way Bush issued terror and security alerts during his first term—and, more generally, throughout his entire time in office, his reliance on panic-inducing references to 9/11, was almost always framed in the Manichean language of absolute good and evil. Bush's doublespeak also employs the discourse of evangelicalism, fully exploiting its attendant suggestion that whatever wisdom Bush has comes from his direct communion with God—a position not unlike that of Moses on Mount Sinai, and which, of course, cannot be challenged by mere mortals.[57]

While all governments sometimes resort to misrepresentations and lies, the Bush administration's doublespeak makes such action central to its maintenance of political power and its manipulation of the media and the public. Language is used in this context to say one thing but to actually mean its opposite.[58] This type of discourse mimics George Orwell's dystopian world of *1984*, where the Ministry of Truth actually produces lies and the Ministry of Love actually tortures people. Ruth Rosen points out that the Bush administration engages in a kind of doublespeak right out of Orwell's novel. For instance, Bush's Healthy Forest Initiative "allows increased logging of protected wilderness. The 'Clear Skies' initiative permits greater industrial air pollution."[59] With respect to the latter, the Bush administration produced Spanish-language public-service commercials hawking "Clear Skies" legislation, using these ads to claim that such legislation promoted "cleaner air" when in fact it has weakened restrictions on corporate polluters and eased regulations on some toxic emissions such as mercury. In other instances, legislation has been ignored altogether: J. P. Suarez, the Environmental Protection Agency's chief of enforcement, notified his staff that "the agency would stop pursuing Clean Air Act enforcement cases against coal burning power plants."[60] Eric Pianin reported in the *Washington Post* that "[t]he Bush administration has decided to allow thousands of the nation's dirtiest coal-fired power plants and refineries to upgrade their facilities without installing costly anti-pollution equipment as they now must do."[61] In addition, the Bush administration has weakened federal programs for cleaning up dirty waters and has removed scientific studies offering evidence of global warming from government reports.[62]

Even when it comes to children, Bush is undaunted in his use of deceptive language. In arguing for legislation that would shift financial responsibility to the states for the highly successful Head Start program, which provides over 1 million poor children with early educational, health, and nutrition services, Bush employed the phrase *opt in* to encourage Congress to pass new legislation reforming Head Start. While *opt in* sounds as if it refers to expanding the program, it actually undermines it because the states that are facing crushing deficits do not have the money to fund the program. Thus, the legislation would drastically weaken Head Start. Such language calls to mind the Orwellian logic that "war is peace, freedom is slavery, and ignorance is strength."

There is also abundant evidence by now that the Bush administration manipulated intelligence to legitimate its claim for a preemptive war with Iraq. The list of misrepresentations and rhetorical contortions includes the claims that Iraq was building nuclear weapons, that it was engaged in the production of biological and chemical agents, and that Saddam Hussein was working with Osama bin Laden and had direct ties to al Qaeda.[63] Even after the CIA reported on the fabrication of the administration's claim that Saddam Hussein had bought uranium from the African country of Niger in pursuit of developing a nuclear weapon, Bush included the assertion in his 2003 State of the Union Address.[64]

Charges of Newspeak come neither exclusively from the Left nor from cantankerous critics. *New York Times* op-ed writer and economist Paul Krugman, in his article "Standard Operating Procedure," asserts that "misrepresentation and deception are standard operating procedure for the [Bush] administration, which—to an extent never before seen in U.S. history—systematically and brazenly distorts the facts." And, in referring to Bush's selling of the Iraq war, Krugman argues that it is "arguably the worst scandal in American political history—worse than Watergate, worse than Iran-contra. Indeed, the idea that we were deceived into war makes many commentators so uncomfortable that they refuse to admit the possibility."[65]

In what has to rank as one of the most egregious distortions to have emerged from the Bush administration (or maybe just a delusional raving, as the *New York Daily News* suggests),[66] President Bush in an interview with *New Yorker* reporter Ken Auletta claimed that "[n]o president has ever done more for human rights than I have."[67] Such a statement is extraordinary given that Amnesty International condemned the United States in 2002 for being one of the world leaders in human rights violations. Similarly, a number of other organizations such as Human Rights Watch, U.S. Human Rights Network, the ACLU, and the Center for Constitutional Rights have accused the Bush administration itself of engaging in various human rights violations, including preventing foreign nationals held as prisoners at Guantanamo Bay from gaining access to U.S. courts; executing juvenile offenders; engaging in the racial profiling, detention, inhumane treatment, and deportation of Muslim immigrants after September 11, 2001; and refusing to ratify the American Convention on Human Rights, the Geneva Protocols, the International Covenant on Civil and Political Rights, the Convention on the Rights of the Child, and numerous other international agreements aimed at protecting human rights. As of 2007, the U.S. government has been condemned roundly at home and abroad for kidnapping people and sending them off to Syria and other authoritarian countries to be tortured, incarcerating prisoners in CIA-run super-secret prisons, and allowing the National Security Agency to secretly, if not illegally, store and monitor—with the assistance of AT&T, Bell South, and Verizon—the phone-call records of millions of Americans. Bob Herbert has argued that such practices are orchestrated through a campaign of fearmongering and power grabbing that keeps the American people too terrified to either notice or recognize that their basic constitutional rights are being trampled. He goes even further in writing:

> Well, I give you fair warning. This is a road map to totalitarianism. Hallmarks of totalitarian regimes have always included an excessive reliance on secrecy, the deliberate stoking of fear in the general population, a preference for military rather than diplomatic solutions in foreign policy, the promotion of blind patriotism, the denial of human rights, the curtailment of the rule of law, hostility to a free press and the systematic invasion of the privacy of ordinary people.[68]

A sixth element of proto-fascism is the growing collapse of the separation between church and state, on the one hand, and the increasing use of religious rhetoric as a marker of political identity and in the shaping of public policy, on the other. Religion has always played a powerful role in the daily lives of Americans. But it has never wielded such an influence in the highest levels of American government as it does in the current administration. Under the Bush presidency, the line between religion and secular politics is being erased as government officials, many now proxies for radical Christian evangelicals, embrace and impose on American society a rigid moralism and set of values that are largely bigoted, patriarchal, uncritical, and insensitive to real social problems such as poverty, racism, the crisis in health care, and the increasing impoverishment of America's children.[69] Instead of addressing these concrete problems, evangelicals with enormous political clout are waging a campaign to ban same-sex marriage, serve up creationism instead of science, privatize Social Security, eliminate embryonic stem-cell research, and overturn *Roe v. Wade* among other abortion rights cases. Rampant anti-intellectualism coupled with a rigid moralism boldly translate into everyday cultural practices and state policies as right-wing evangelicals such as Pat Robertson and James Dobson make public pronouncements on all manner of public and foreign policy issues while cultivating a close relationship with the White House. For example, Robertson, a Bush administration favorite, has called for the assassination of Hugo Chavez, the president of Venezuela, and suggested that the devastating stroke suffered by Prime Minister Ariel Sharon was "divine punishment for pulling Israel out of Gaza last summer."[70] Some of the more egregious anti-Islamic remarks made by the Christian Right have been compiled by Esther Kaplan, who writes:

> Franklin Graham, the son of traveling evangelist Billy Graham, whom President Bush credits with his religious awakening—the same Franklin Graham who had led Bush's inaugural prayer—denounced Islam on television as "a very evil and wicked religion." Reverend Jerry Vines, a past president of the 16-million-member Southern Baptist Convention, a religious organization with strong ties to the administration, called the Muslim prophet Muhammad a "demon-obsessed pedophile" ... while [Jerry] Falwell's characterization of Muhammad as "a terrorist" touched off a riot in Sholapur, India, that left nine people dead and one hundred injured.[71]

Not only have many Christian conservatives played a prominent role in shaping the Bush administration's policies toward the Middle East, providing further legitimation for the "war on terrorism," but public statements by the Christian Right such as those cited above have been widely reported in the Arab world, fueling hatred of the United States and providing a recruiting tool for Islamic terrorists.

The new place of religious fundamentalism in American politics attempts to "collapse the spiritual into the political (making politics into a religious mission) and the political into the spiritual (making religion into a political issue)."[72] Combining religious and political convictions with a rigid moralism impacts directly on people's lives. For instance, more and more conservative pharmacists are refusing to fill prescriptions for religious reasons. David Hager, who, before he was publicly outed for having an affair with a gay escort, was appointed by Bush to the FDA's Advisory Committee for Reproductive Health Drugs, "refuses to prescribe contraceptives to unmarried women (and believes the Bible is an antidote for premenstrual syndrome)."[73] Mixing medicine, politics, and religion means that some women are being denied birth control pills and that sex education inspired by faith-based institutions is promoting "abstinence-only education," despite a spate of research suggesting that such educational programs do not work. Most recently, Bush vetoed a bill calling for federal funding of stem-cell research. Clearly, this was done in order to satisfy his ultra-right-wing Christian supporters. The Bush administration has also succumbed to pressure from evangelicals by eliminating information from government websites about birth control, citing falsified scientific data such as assertions that using the birth control pill promotes higher rates of breast cancer, and producing school curricula that claim "half of all gay male teenagers in the U.S. are HIV positive."[74] Even popular culture is not immune from the Christian

Right's morality squad, given that it inspires a wave of criticism and censorship against all but the most sanitized facets of the entertainment industry, including children's shows that portray lesbian families positively or offer up alleged homoerotic representations, such as those attributed to the cartoon character SpongeBob SquarePants.[75]

The religious conservative movement not only has achieved an unprecedented political prominence with the election of George W. Bush but also seems to view him as its earthly leader. As *Washington Post* writer Dana Milbank puts it:

> For the first time since religious conservatism became a modern political movement, the president of the United States has become the movement's de facto leader—a status even Ronald Reagan, though admired by religious conservatives, never earned. Christian publications, radio and television shower Bush with praise, while preachers from the pulpit treat his leadership as an act of providence. A procession of religious leaders who have met with him testify to his faith, while Web sites encourage people to fast and pray for the president.[76]

Considered the leader of the Christian Right, Bush is regarded by many of his aides and followers as a leader with a higher purpose. Bush aide Tim Goeglein echoes this view: "I think President Bush is God's man at this hour, and I say this with a great sense of humility."[77] Ralph Reed, a long-time crusader against divorce, single-parent families, and abortion, and an influential voice of Georgia's Republican Party, assesses Bush's relationship with the Christian Right in more sobering political terms. He argues that the role of the religious conservative movement has changed in that it is no longer on the outskirts of power since it has helped to elect leaders who believe in its cause. Referring to the new-found role of the religious Right, he claims: "You're no longer throwing rocks at the building; you're in the building."[78] Bush has not disappointed his radical evangelical Christian following.

Apparently also believing himself on a direct mission from God, President Bush openly celebrates the virtues of evangelical Christian morality, prays daily, and expresses a fervent belief in Christianity in both his rhetoric and his policy choices. For example, while running as a presidential candidate in 2000, Bush proclaimed that his favorite philosopher was Jesus Christ. Furthermore, in a speech that outlined the dangers posed by Iraq, he stated: "We do not claim to know all the ways of Providence, yet we can trust in them, placing our confidence in the loving God behind all of life, and all of history. May He guide us now."[79] Stephen Mansfield, in his book *The Faith of George W. Bush,* claims that Bush told James Robinson, a Texas preacher: "I feel like God wants me to run for president. I can't explain it, but I sense my country is going to need me.... I know it won't be easy on me or my family, but God wants me to do it."[80] Surrounded by born-again missionaries, and with God rather than the most basic tenets of American democracy advising his leadership, Bush has relentlessly developed policies based less on social needs than on a highly personal and narrowly moral sense of divine purpose. Using the privilege of executive action, he has aggressively attempted to evangelize the realm of social services. For example, he has made available to a greater extent than any other president more federal funds to Christian religious groups that provide a range of social services. And he has eased the rules "for overtly religious institutions to access $20-billion in federal social service grants and another $8-billion in Housing and Urban Development money. Tax dollars can now be used to construct and renovate houses of worship as long as the funds are not used to build the principal room used for prayer, such as the sanctuary or chapel."[81] He has also provided more than $60 billion in federal funds for faith-based initiatives organized by religious charitable groups.[82] Not all religious groups, however, receive equal funding. The lion's share of federal monies goes to Christian organizations, thus undermining, via state sanction of some religions over others, the very idea of religious freedom. In addition, he has promised that such agencies can get government funds "without being forced to change their character or compromise their mission."[83] This means that such organizations and groups can now get federal money even though they discriminate on religious grounds in their hiring practices. The two programs that Bush showcased during his January 2003 State of the Union speech both "use religious conversion as treatment."[84] Bush has also created an office in the White House entirely dedicated to providing assistance to faith-based organizations applying for federal funding. Moreover, Bush is using school voucher programs to enable private schools to receive public money and refuses to fund schools that "interfere with or fail to accommodate prayer for bible study by teachers or students."[85] The former secretary of education, Rod Paige, made it clear how he felt about the separation of church and state when he told a Baptist publication that he believed that schools should teach Christian values. When asked to resign by a number of critics, Paige refused, and his office declined to clarify much less repudiate his suggestion that either public schools should teach Christian values or parents should take their kids out of such schools and send them to parochial schools. His office replied curtly: "The quotes are the quotes."[86]

Unfortunately, Bush's religious fervor appears more indebted to the God who believes in an eye-for-an-eye, a God of vengeance and retribution. As Jeremy Brecher points out, "the escalating rhetoric of the 'War against Terrorism' to the 'Axis of Evil' has provided a model for belligerence and potentially for nuclear conflict from India and Pakistan to Israel and Palestine."[87] Bush also appears indifferent to the seeming contradiction between his claim to religious piety and his willingness as the former governor of Texas to execute "more prisoners (152) than any governor in modern U.S. history."[88] Nor does he see the contradiction between upholding the word of God and imposing democracy on the largely Muslim population of Iraq through the rule of force and the barrel of a gun. Appealing to religion and fear, Bush has violated the constitutional rights of thousands of Muslims and Arabs who, since September 11, 2001, have been arrested, held in secret, and offered no legal recourse or access to their families. Such harsh treatment rooted in a notion of absolute good and evil represents more than an act of capricious justice; it also undermines "the presumption of innocence, as well as the constitutional rights to due process, to counsel, and to a speedy and public trial," and, in legitimating such treatment, "the Bush administration has weakened these protections for all, citizens and aliens alike. In the process, it has tarnished American democracy."[89] Indeed, whereas Bush and his religious cohorts claim they are working to exercise great acts of charity, it appears that the poor are being punished, and the only charity available is the handout being given to the rich. For instance, as funds were being distributed for faith-based initiatives, Congress not only passed legislation that eliminated a child tax credit that would have benefited about 2 million children but also agreed to a $350 billion tax cut for the rich while slashing domestic spending for programs that benefit the poor, elderly, and children. With the military budget and deficit raging out of control, the Bush administration in 2006 passed still another $70 billion tax cut for the super-rich.

The Bush administration has also refused to sign a United Nations Declaration on Children's Rights unless it eliminates sexual health services such as providing teenage sex education in which contraception or reproductive rights are discussed. On the domestic front, Bush has passed legislation halting "late-term" abortion, tried to pass legislation stopping the distribution of the morning-after pill, and eliminated financial support for international charities that provide advice on abortion. Such measures not only call into question the traditional separation between church and state but also undercut public services and provide a veneer of government legitimacy to religious-based organizations that prioritize religious conversion over modern scientific techniques. As Winnifred Sullivan, a senior lecturer at the University of Chicago Divinity School, puts it, the conservative evangelical proponents of the faith-based initiative "want government funds to go to the kinds of churches that regard conversion as part of your rehabilitation. It's a critique of secular professional social service standards."[90]

Behind the rhetoric of religious commitment is the reality of permanent war, the further immiseration of the poor, and the ongoing attacks on the notion of the secular state. There is also the force of intolerance and bigotry, the refusal to recognize the multiplicity of religious, political, linguistic, and cultural differences—those vast and diverse elements that constitute the democratic global sphere at its best. Hints of this bigotry are visible not only in the culture of fear and religious fundamentalism that shape Bush's world but also in those who serve them with unquestioning loyalty. This became clear when the national press revealed that a high-ranking Defense Department official called the war on terrorism a Christian battle against Satan. Lieutenant-General William Boykin, in his capacity as Deputy Under Secretary of Defense for Intelligence, while standing in front of pictures of Osama bin Laden, Saddam Hussein, and Kim Jong Il, asked the parishioners of the First Baptist Church of Broken Arrow, Oklahoma, the following question: "Why do they hate us? … The answer to that is because we are a Christian nation. We are hated because we are a nation of believers." He continued, "Our spiritual enemy will only be defeated if we come against them in the name of Jesus."[91] For Boykin, the war being fought in Iraq, Afghanistan, and, maybe eventually at home against other nonbelievers, is a holy war. And this language is not merely the ranting of a religious fanatic; it is symptomatic of a deeper strain of intolerance and authoritarianism that is emerging in this country. Such zeal can also be heard in the words of the late Reverend Jerry Falwell, who claimed on the airwaves that the terrorist attack of 9/11 was the result of God's judgment on the secularization of America. He stated: "I really believe that the pagans, and the abortionists, and the feminists, and the gays and lesbians, the ACLU, People for the American Way—all of them who have tried to secularize America—I point the finger in their face and say, 'You helped this happen.'"[92]

The emergence of a government-sanctioned religious fundamentalism has its counterpart in a political authoritarianism that undermines not only the most basic tenets of religious faith but also the democratic tenets of social justice and equality. Of course, this type of religious fundamentalism, supported largely by politicians and evangelical missionaries who run to the prayer groups and Bible-study cells sprouting up all over the Bush White House, has little to do with genuine religion or spirituality. Those who believe that biblical creationism rather than evolution should be taught in the schools, or that the United States "must extend God's will of liberty for other countries, by force if necessary," do not accurately represent the prophetic traditions in Islam, Christianity, or Judaism.[93] These traditions foster belief in a God who is giving and compassionate, not one who would endorse secular policies that bankrupt the government in order to benefit the rich or would produce laws that disadvantage the poor and impose more suffering on those already in need. Rather, a more representative Christian philosophy is espoused by the Reverend James Forbes Jr., head of the Riverside Church in New York City, who has asserted that "poverty is a weapon of mass destruction." Joseph Hough, the head of Union Theological Seminary, speaks for many religious leaders when he argues that what passes as Christianity in the Bush administration is simply a form of political machination masquerading as religion and making a grab for power:

> I'm getting tired of people claiming they're carrying the banner of my religious tradition when they're doing everything possible to undercut it. And that's what's happening in this country right now. The policies of this country are disadvantaging poor people every day of our lives and every single thing that passes the Congress these days is disadvantaging poor people more.... And anybody who claims in the name of God they're gonna run over people of other nations, and just willy-nilly, by your own free will, reshape the world in your own image, and claim that you're acting on behalf of God, that sounds a lot like Caesar to me.[94]

Kevin Phillips has argued that under the Bush administration, the Republican Party has emerged as "America's first religious party" and that "no leading world power in modern memory has [to a greater degree] become a captive of the sort of biblical inerrancy that dismisses modern knowledge and science."[95] Chris Hedges goes so far as to insist that the Republican Party is more than willing to turn the government over to the Christian Right, whose "ideology bears within it the tenets of a Christian fascism" and views democracy as the enemy of faith.[96] While the influence and control that right-wing evangelicals have over the government is debatable, what is clear is that they have a presence in the Bush administration that is unparalleled in American history. Moreover, the Bush administration's attempt to undo the separation between church and state is driven by a form of fundamentalism and animated by a biblical ideology that both discredits democratic values, public goods, and critical citizenship and spawns an irrationality evident in the innumerable contradictions among its rhetoric of piety, its celebration of militarism, its attack on minorities of sexual orientation, class, and race, its support for an imperial presidency, and its relentless grab for economic and political power—an irrationality that is the hallmark of both the old fascism and proto-fascism.

Along with religious fundamentalism and the other anti-democratic tendencies discussed above, forces that support the Bush administration's efforts to extend its power regardless of the consequences for democracy also include the increasing reality of a one-party system that exhibits a deep disdain for pluralism and resorts to corrupt attempts at redistricting; crass manipulation of voting rules; tactics designed to intimidate oppositional voter blocs, especially minorities; and the fraudulent use of voting machines. All such forces are intended to lock in a permanent Republican administration—not, of course, to be outdone by the setback in the 2006 congressional elections. Rampant cronyism and political corruption are exemplified in the scandal surrounding favorite-son lobbyist Jack Abramoff, the appointment of political hacks such as Michael Brown to head government agencies such as the Federal Emergency Management Agency (FEMA), the awarding of government contracts to donors who make big contributions to the Republican Party, and the placing of a number of right-wing evangelical supporters on government policymaking panels, despite their glaring incompetence to perform their appointed jobs. There is also the conservative language of hate, racism, and scapegoating that spews forth daily from infamous talking heads such as Ann Coulter, Rush Limbaugh, and Michael Savage, all of whom reflect a disdain for human rights and reveal something dreadful about the new narratives with which this government wants to define American culture. As Paul Gilroy points out, the war on terrorism has produced the "crudest expression of racial antipathy ... redolent of imperial and colonial domination."[97]

The alleged threat to domestic order has now also been extended to include others from the global South who are accused of endangering national security. From political theorist Samuel P. Huntington, who rails against the threat of "Hispanization," to CNN television host Lou Dobbs, who believes the United States is being overrun by illegal immigrants (who are spreading leprosy, no less!), to Pat Robertson, who publicly stated that Muslims were "worse than Nazis,"[98] there is a growing discourse of racist invective directed toward Mexican immigrants, Arabs, Muslims, and others who are perceived to imperil the "civilizational" distinctiveness of American culture, take away American jobs, or allegedly support acts of terrorism directed against the United States. There is also an increase in the surveillance of citizenry, euphemistically called the "special collection program," which is being conducted outside the jurisdiction of the courts; an increase in reports of U.S. human rights abuses such as torture, kidnapping, and making people "disappear"; the emergence of a hyper-nationalism fueled by racism; and a growing obsession with national security, crime, and law and order. Indeed, given that the Bush administration governs by "dividing the country along [the] fault lines of fear, intolerance, ignorance and religious rule,"[99] the future does not look bright for democracy. And I am not convinced that the anti-democratic forces that have been reinforced and solidified will evaporate once Bush leaves office. Such forces have certainly not lost their influence and power since the Democrats gained control of Congress in 2006.

While there are other elements central to proto-fascism, I want to explore in substantial detail the growing militarization of public space and culture in American society. Of course, the militarization of public space was a central feature of the old fascism. This feature is particularly important in the United States today because it poses the greatest risk to our civil liberties and to any semblance of democracy, and it has been a crucial force in the rise of the national security state.

The Politics of Militarization at Home and Abroad

In the contemporary context of globalization, militarism has become what David Theo Goldberg calls a "new regime of truth," a new epistemology defining what is fact and fiction, right and wrong, just and unjust.[100] The new ethos of militarization no longer occupies a marginal place in the American political landscape; indeed, it is reinforced daily by domestic and foreign policies that reveal a country obsessed with war and the military values, policies, and practices that drive it.[101] For instance, the military budget request for 2007 totals $462.7 billion, and as noted by Christopher Hellman, a respected military budget analyst from the Center for Arms Control and Nonproliferation, when "adjusted for inflation [the 2007 military budget] exceeds the average amount spent by the Pentagon during the Cold War, [and] for a military that is one-third smaller than it was just over a decade ago."[102] Moreover, the 2007 military budget request does not include supplemental funding for the wars in Iraq and Afghanistan, which for 2006 alone was $115 billion and from September 11, 2001, to the end of 2006 was more than $445 billion.[103] The U.S. military budget is "almost 7 times larger than the Chinese budget, the second largest spender ... almost 29 times as large as the combined spending of the six 'rogue states' (Cuba, Iran, Libya, North Korea, Sudan and Syria) who spent $14.65 billion [and is] more than the combined spending of the next 14 nations."[104] Such immense levels of defense spending by the federal government have grave implications for expanding a U.S. war machine that uses massive resources "devoted to the monopolistic militarization of space, the development of more usable nuclear weapons, and the strengthening of its world-girdling ring of military bases and its global navy, as the most tangible way to discourage any strategic challenges to its preeminence."[105] The projection of U.S. military force and power in the world can be seen in the fact that "the U.S. owns or rents 737 bases in about 130 countries—over and above the 6,000 bases" at home.[106] Chalmers Johnson claims that if there were an honest count "the actual size of the U.S. military empire would probably top 1,000 different bases overseas."[107] But America does more than simply produce massive amounts of death-dealing weapons; it is also the world's biggest arms dealer, with sales in 2006 amounting to "about $20.9 billion, nearly double the $10.6 billion the previous year."[108]

By regarding military power as the highest expression of social truth and national greatness, the Bush administration has opened a dangerous new chapter in American military history that now gives unfettered support to what C. Wright Mills has called a "'military metaphysics'—the cast of mind that defines international reality as basically military."[109] As Andrew Bacevich indicates, this mentality leads to a "tendency to see international problems as military problems and to discount the likelihood of finding a solution except through military means."[110] Similarly, Michael Hardt and Antonio Negri point out in *Multitude* that, in the current era, war has become the organizing principle of society and the foundation for politics and other social relations.[111] War in the current historical moment has assumed a measure of national greatness, at least as advocated by those in the highest reaches of government who invest it with mythic meaning, experience, and purpose. But there is more at work in the celebration of American militarism than a love affair with military knowledge, values, identities, and practices—and ultimately war. There is also the delusional jingoism, racism, and fundamentalism that more often than not justify violence, barbarism, human cruelty, and dehumanization. Chris Hedges gets it right in arguing that war is a form of "organized murder," and that when it is translated into a mythic reality it often has unforgivable and unimaginable painful consequences. Given the mix of lies, corruption, human suffering, needless deaths, mangled bodies, and sheer inhumanity that defines the Iraq war, his commentary written in 2003 seems especially prescient. He writes:

> [I]n mythic war we imbue events with meanings they do not have. We see defeats as signposts on the road to ultimate victory. We demonize the enemy so that our opponent is no longer human. We view ourselves, our people, as the embodiment of absolute goodness. Our enemies invert our view of the world to justify their own cruelty. In most mythic wars this is the case. Each side reduces the other to objects—eventually in the form of corpses.[112]

Broadly speaking, militarization refers to the related instances of the increasing centrality of the military in American society, the militarization of U.S. culture, and the growing propensity toward suppression of dissent. The process of militarization has a long history in the United States and is varied rather than static, changing under different historical conditions.[113] The militarizing of public space at home contributes to a narrowing of community as well as to an escalating concentration of unaccountable political power that threatens the very foundation of democracy in the United States. Militarization is no longer simply the driving force of foreign policy; it has become a defining principle for social changes throughout the country. Catherine Lutz captures the multiple registers and complex processes of militarization that have extensively shaped social life during the twentieth century:

> By militarization, I mean . . . an intensification of the labor and resources allocated to military purposes, including the shaping of other institutions in synchrony with military goals. Militarization is simultaneously a discursive process, involving a shift in general societal beliefs and values in ways necessary to legitimate the use of force, the organization of large standing armies and their leaders, and the higher taxes or tribute used to pay for them. Militarization is intimately connected not only to the obvious increase in the size of armies and resurgence of militant nationalisms and militant fundamentalisms but also to the less visible deformation of human potentials into the hierarchies of race, class, gender,

> and sexuality, and to the shaping of national histories in ways that glorify and legitimate military action.[114]

Lutz's definition of militarization is inclusive, attentive to the discursive, ideological, and material relations of power that serve war and violence. It also suggests the powerful cultural politics of militarization that works its way through everyday life, spawning particular notions of masculinity, sanctioning war as a spectacle and fear as a central formative component in mobilizing an affective investment in support of militarization. In other words, the forces of militarization, with their emphasis on the discursive production and material practice of violence, have produced a pervasive *culture* of militarization, which "inject[s] a constant military presence in our lives."[115] Unlike the old style of militarization in which all forms of civil authority were subordinate to military authority, the new ethos of militarization is organized to engulf the entire social order, legitimating its values as a central rather than peripheral aspect of American public life. Moreover, the values of militarism no longer reside in a single group nor are limited to a particular sphere of society. On the contrary, as Jorge Mariscal points out:

> In liberal democracies, in particular, the values of militarism do not reside in a single group but are diffused across a wide variety of cultural locations. In twenty-first century America, no one is exempt from militaristic values because the processes of militarization allow those values to permeate the fabric of everyday life.[116]

The growing influence of a military presence and ideology in American society is made visible, in part, by the fact that the United States now has more police, prisons, spies, weapons, and soldiers than at any other time in its history. The radical shift in the size, scope, and influence of the military can also be seen in the redistribution of domestic resources and government funding away from social programs into military-oriented security measures at home and abroad. According to journalist George Monbiot, the U.S. federal government "is now spending as much on war as it is on education, public health, housing, employment, pensions, food aid and welfare put together."[117] Meanwhile, the state is being radically transformed into a national security state, increasingly put under the sway of the military-corporate-industrial-educational complex. The military logic of fear, surveillance, and control is gradually permeating our public schools, universities, streets, media, popular culture, and criminal justice system.

Since the events of 9/11 and the wars in Afghanistan and Iraq, the military has assumed a privileged place in American society. President Bush not only celebrates the military presence in American culture, he cultivates it by going out of his way to give speeches at military facilities, talk to military personnel, and address veterans' groups. He often wears a military uniform when speaking to "captive audiences at military bases, defense plants, and on aircraft carriers."[118] He also takes advantage of the campaign value of military culture by using military symbolism as a political prop in order to attract the widest possible media attention. One now infamous and glaring instance occurred on May 1, 2003, when Bush landed in full aviator flight uniform on the USS *Abraham Lincoln* in the Pacific Ocean, where he officially proclaimed the end of the Iraq war. There was also his secret trip to Baghdad to spend Thanksgiving Day 2003 with the troops, an event that attracted worldwide coverage in all the media. But Bush has done more than take advantage of the military as a campaign prop to sell his domestic and foreign policies. His administration and the Republican Party, which until the 2006 election controlled all three branches of government, has worked toward establishing a "dangerous and unprecedented confluence of our democratic institutions and the military."[119]

Writing in *Harper's Magazine,* Kevin Baker claims that the military "has become the most revered institution in the country."[120] Soon after the Iraq war, a Gallup Poll reported that over 76 percent of Americans "expressed 'a great deal' or 'quite a lot' of confidence in their nation's military." And among a poll of 1,200 students conducted by Harvard University, 75 percent believed that the military most of the time would "do the right thing." In addition, the students "characterized themselves as hawks over doves by a ratio of two to one."[121] Given this pro-military attitude among university students, it should not surprise us that the Bruin Alumni Association at the University of California, Los Angeles, has targeted professors it describes as "radical" and posted their names on its website under the heading "The Dirty Thirty." The group is headed by former student and right-wing ideologue Andrew Jones, whose "Open Letter from the Bruin Alumni Association" describes its mission as combating "an exploding crisis of political radicalism on campus" and defines *radicalism* as holding any dissenting view of the war in Iraq, supporting affirmative action, or opposing "President Bush, the Republican Party, multi-national corporations, and even our fighting men and women." The Bruin Alumni Association does more than promote "McCarthy-like smears," intolerance, and anti-intellectualism through a vapid appeal for "balance"; it also initially offered $100 prizes to any students willing to provide information on their teachers' political views.[122] Of course, this has less to do with protesting genuine demagoguery than with attacking any professor who might raise critical questions about the status quo or hold the narratives of power accountable.

A narrowing view of politics and a growing support of the military have coincided with an attack on higher education by right-wing ideologues such as David Horowitz and Lynne Cheney (spouse of Vice President Dick Cheney), who view it as a "weak link" in the war against terror and a potential fifth column.[123] Horowitz also acts as the figurehead for various well-funded and -orchestrated conservative student groups such as the Young Americans and College Republicans; such groups perform the groundwork for his "Academic Bill of Rights" policy, which seeks out juicy but rare instances of "political bias"—whatever that is or however it might be defined—in college classrooms. One result of these efforts is that considerable sums of public money have been devoted to hearings in multiple state legislatures, most recently in Pennsylvania; another, as the *Chronicle of Higher Education* put it, has been the imposition of a "chilly climate" of self-policing of academic freedom and pedagogy.

Popular fears about domestic safety and internal threats accentuated by endless terror alerts have created a society that increasingly accepts the notion of a "war without limits" as a normal state of affairs. But fear and insecurity do more than produce a collective anxiety among Americans, exploited largely to get them to believe that they should vote Republican because it is the only political party that can protect them: In addition to producing manufactured political loyalty, such fears can be manipulated into a kind of "war fever." The mobilization of war fever, intensified through a politics of fear, carries with it a kind of paranoid edge, endlessly stoked by government alerts and repressive laws and used "to create the most extensive national security apparatus in our nation's history."[124] It is also reproduced in the Foxified media, which, in addition to constantly marketing the flag and interminably implying that critics of American foreign policy are traitors, offer up seemingly endless images of brave troops on the front line, heroic stories of released American prisoners, and utterly privatized commentaries on those wounded or killed in battle. *Time Magazine* embodied this representational indulgence in military culture by designating "The American Soldier" as the "Person of the Year" for 2003.[125] Not only have such ongoing and largely uncritical depictions of war injected a constant military presence in American life, they have also helped to create a civil society that has become more aggressive in its warlike enthusiasms. But there is more at work here than either the exploitation of troops for higher ratings or an attempt by right-wing political strategists to keep the American public in a state of permanent fear so as to remove pressing domestic issues from public debate. There is also the attempt by the Bush administration to convince as many Americans as possible that under the current "state of emergency" the use of the military internally in domestic affairs is perfectly acceptable, evident in the increasing propensity to use the military establishment "to incarcerate and interrogate suspected terrorists and 'enemy combatants' and keep them beyond the reach of the civilian judicial system, even if they are American citizens."[126] It is also evident in the federal government's attempt to try terrorists in military courts, and to detain prisoners "outside the provisions of the Geneva Convention as prisoners of war . . . at the U.S.

Marine Corps base at Guantanamo, Cuba[,] because that facility is outside of the reach of the American courts."[127]

As military values, ideology, and a hyper-masculine aesthetic begin to spread out into other aspects of American culture, citizens are recruited as foot soldiers in the war on terrorism, urged to spy on their neighbors' behaviors, watch for suspicious-looking people, and supply data to government sources in the war on terrorism. Major universities intensively court the military establishment for Defense Department grants and in doing so become less open to either academic subjects or programs that encourage rigorous debate, dialogue, and critical thinking. In fact, as higher education is pressured by both the Bush administration and its jingoistic supporters to serve the needs of the military-industrial complex, universities increasingly deepen their connections to the national security state in ways that are boldly celebrated. For instance, Pennsylvania State University (in addition to Carnegie Mellon University, the University of Pennsylvania, Johns Hopkins University, and a host of other public institutions) has entered into a formal agreement with the Federal Bureau of Investigation (FBI) in order to "create a link between [a] leading research university and government agencies." Graham Spanier, Penn State president and head of the new National Security Higher Education Advisory Board, stated that the collaboration "sends a positive message that leaders in higher education are willing to assist our nation during these challenging times."[128]

Public schools not only have more military recruiters roaming their corridors, providing a number of school services, and offering a range of gimmicks such as video game contests and concerts; they also have more military personnel teaching in the classrooms. Junior Reserve Officers Training Corps (JROTC) programs are increasingly becoming a conventional part of the school day. As a result of the No Child Left Behind Act, President Bush's educational law, "schools risk losing all federal aid if they fail to provide military recruiters full access to their students; the aid is contingent with complying with federal law."[129] Schools were once viewed as democratic public spheres that would teach students how to resist the militarization of democratic life, or at least learn the skills to peacefully engage domestic and international problems. Now they serve as recruiting stations for students.

Schools represent one of the most serious public spheres to come under the influence of military culture and values. Zero-tolerance policies turn public schools into prison-like institutions, as students' rights increasingly diminish under the onslaught of new disciplinary measures. Students in many schools, especially those in poor urban areas, are routinely searched, frisked, subjected to involuntary drug tests, maced, and carted off to jail. Elissa Gootman in a 2004 report on schools in New York City claims that "[i]n some places, schools are resorting to zero-tolerance policies that put students in handcuffs for dress code violations."[130] As educators turn over their responsibility for school safety to the police, the new security culture in public schools has turned them into "learning prisons," most evident in the ways in which schools are being "reformed" through the addition of armed guards, barbed-wired security fences, and lock-down drills.[131] A few years ago the police in Goose Creek, South Carolina, conducted an early-morning drug sweep at Stratford High School. When the officers arrived, they drew guns on students, handcuffed them, and made them kneel facing the wall.[132] No drugs were found in the raid. Though this incident was aired on the national news, there was barely any protest from the public. More recently, there have been reports of young children in kindergarten being handcuffed, taken out of school, and taken to the local police station where they were fingerprinted, had a mug shot taken, and were charged with a crime. The crime? In one highly publicized case, the child threw a tantrum in her kindergarten class.[133] It gets worse. Some schools are actually using sting operations in which undercover agents pretend to be students in order to catch young people suspected of selling drugs or committing any one of a number of school infractions. The consequences of such actions are far-reaching. As Randall Beger points out:

> Opponents of school-based sting operations say they not only create a climate of mistrust between students and police, but they also put innocent students at risk of wrongful arrest due to faulty tips and overzealous police work. When asked about his role in a recent undercover probe at a high school near Atlanta, a young-looking police officer who attended classes and went to parties with students replied: "I knew I had to fit in, make kids trust me and then turn around and take them to jail."[134]

The militarization of public high schools has become so commonplace that even in the face of the most flagrant disregard for children's rights, such acts are justified by both administrators and the public on the grounds that they keep kids safe. In schools across the country, surveillance cameras are being installed in classrooms. School administrators call this "school reform," but rarely do they examine the implications of what they are teaching kids who are put under constant surveillance.[135] The not-so-hidden curriculum here is that kids can't be trusted and that their rights are not worth protecting. At the same time, students are being educated to passively accept military sanctioned practices organized around maintenance of control, surveillance, and unquestioned authority—all conditions central to a police state and proto-fascism.

As the foregoing suggests, the rampant combination of fear and insecurity that is so much a part of the permanent war culture in the United States seems to bear down particularly hard on children, especially African-American youth. In many poor school districts, specialists are being laid off and crucial mental health services are being cut back. As Sara Rimer pointed out in the *New York Times,* much-needed student-based services and traditional, if not compassionate, ways of dealing with student problems are now being replaced by the juvenile justice system, which functions "as a dumping ground for poor minority kids with mental health and special-education problems.... The juvenile detention center has become an extension of the principal's office."[136] For example, in some cities, ordinances have been passed that "allow for the filing of misdemeanor charges against students for anything from disrupting a class to assaulting a teacher."[137] Children are no longer given a second chance for minor behavior infractions, nor are they simply sent to the guidance counselor, the principal, or detention. They now come under the jurisdiction of the courts and juvenile justice system.

Under the auspices of the national security state and the militarization of domestic life, containment policies have become the principal means to discipline working-class and minority youth and to restrict their ability to think critically and engage in oppositional practices. Marginalized students learn quickly that they are surplus populations and that the journey from home to school no longer means they will next move into a job; on the contrary, school is now a training ground for their "graduation" into containment centers such as prisons and jails that keep them out of sight, patrolled, and monitored so as to prevent them from becoming social cankers or political liabilities to white and middle-class populations concerned about their own safety. Schools increasingly function as zoning mechanisms to separate students marginalized by class and color. This follows the argument of David Garland, who points out that "[l]arge-scale incarceration functions as a mode of economic and social placement, a zoning mechanism that segregates those populations rejected by the depleted institutions of family, work, and welfare and places them behind the scenes of social life."[138] One indication of the disproportionate effects that black youth bear in paramilitarized schools can be found in the way in which they are disciplined relative to other groups, especially with regard to school suspensions and expulsion practices. For example, Howard Witt, a writer for the *Chicago Tribune,* writes:

> In every state but Idaho, a *Tribune* analysis of the data shows, black students are being suspended in numbers greater than would be expected from their proportion of the student population. In 21 states—Illinois among them—that disproportionality is so pronounced that the percentage of black suspensions is more than double their percentage of the student body. And on average across the nation, black students are suspended and expelled at nearly three times the rate of white students. No other ethnic group is disciplined at such a high rate, the federal data show.... Yet black students are no more likely to misbehave than other students from the same social and economic environments, research studies have found.[139]

Given these statistics, it is not surprising that only 42 percent of young, poor African Americans who enter the ninth grade actually graduate from high school. Nor is it surprising that such schools increasingly provide a direct pipeline for many black kids into joblessness, poverty, and the criminal justice system. The *New York Times* columnist, Bob Herbert, claims that parts of New York City are like a police state for young men, women, and children who happen to be black. He only has part of it right. What is missing in his comment is that the punishment and harassment that poor black kids experience extends far beyond the boundaries of New York City into almost every major urban city in America, especially in its schools.[140]

Instances of domestic militarization and the war at home can also be seen in the rise of the prison-industrial-educational complex and the militarization of the criminal justice system. The traditional "distinctions between military, police, and criminal justice are blurring."[141] The police now work in close collaboration with the military. This takes the form of receiving surplus weapons, arranging technology/information transfers, introducing SWAT teams modeled after the Navy Seals (indeed, such teams are experiencing a steep growth in police departments throughout the United States), and becoming more dependent on military models of crime control.[142] In short, the increasing use of military models in American life has played a crucial role in the paramilitarizing of the culture, providing both a narrative and a legitimation "for recent trends in corrections, including the normalization of special response teams, the increasingly popular Supermax prisons, and drug war boot camps."[143] From the paramilitaristic perspective, crime is no longer a social problem; it is now viewed as both an individual pathology and a matter of punishment rather than rehabilitation. Unsurprisingly, paramilitary culture increasingly embodies a racist and class-specific discourse and "reflects the discrediting of the social and its related narratives."[144] This is particularly evident in the singling out of America's inner cities as dangerous enclaves of crime and violence. The consequences for those communities have been catastrophic, especially in terms of the cataclysmic rise of the prison-industrial complex. As has been widely reported, the United States is now the biggest jailer in the world. Between 1985 and 2007 its prison population grew from 744,206 to 2.2 million (approaching the combined populations of Idaho, Wyoming, and Montana), and prison budgets jumped from $7 billion in 1980 to $40 billion in 2000.[145] As Sanho Tree points out:

> With more than 2 million people behind bars (there are only 8 million prisoners in the entire world), the United States—with one-twenty-second of the world's population—has one-quarter of the planet's prisoners. We operate the largest penal system in the world, and approximately one-quarter of all our prisoners (nearly half a million people) are there for nonviolent drug offenses.[146]

Yet, even as the crime rate plummets dramatically, more people, especially those of color, are being arrested, harassed, punished, and put in jail.[147] Of the 2.2 million people behind bars, 70 percent are people of color: 50 percent are African American and 17 percent are Latino.[148] A Justice Department report points out that on any given day in this country "more than a third of the young African American men aged 18–34 in some of our major cities are either in prison or under some form of criminal justice supervision."[149] The same department reported in April 2000 that "black youth are forty-eight times more likely than whites to be sentenced to juvenile prison for drug offenses."[150] When poor youth of color are not being warehoused in dilapidated schools or incarcerated, they are being aggressively recruited by the U.S. Army to fight the war in Iraq. For example, Carl Chery has reported that

> [w]ith help from *The Source* magazine, the U.S. military is targeting hip-hop fans with custom-made Hummers, throwback jerseys and trucker hats. The yellow Hummer, spray-painted with two black men in military uniform, is the vehicle of choice for the U.S. Army's "Take It to the Streets campaign"—a sponsored mission aimed at recruiting young African Americans into the military ranks.[151]

It seems that the Army has discovered hip-hop and urban culture, and that rather than listening to the searing indictment of poverty, joblessness, and despair that is one of their central messages, Army recruiters appeal to their most commodified elements by letting the "potential recruits hang out in the Hummer, where they can pep the sound system or watch recruitment videos."[152] Of course, the prospective recruits won't be shown any videos of Hummers being blown up in the war-torn streets of Baghdad.

Domestic militarization, also widespread in the realm of culture, functions as a mode of public pedagogy, instilling the values and the aesthetic of militarization through a wide variety of pedagogical sites and cultural venues. For instance, Humvee ads offer up the fantasy of military glamour and modes of masculinity that seem to guarantee virility for their owners by attempting to induce a mixture of fear and admiration from everyone else. One of the fastest-growing sports for middle-class suburban youth is the game of paintball "in which teenagers stalk and shoot each other on 'battlefields' (in San Diego, paintball participants pay an additional $50 to hone their skills at the Camp Pendleton Marine Base)."[153] And military recruitment ads flood all modes of entertainment, using sophisticated marketing tools and offering messages that resonate powerfully with particular forms of masculinity and directly serve as an enticement for recruitment. For example, the website *www.marines.com* opens with the sound of gunfire and then provides the following message: "We are the warriors, one and all. Born to defend, built to conquer. The steel we wear is the steel within ourselves, forged by the hot fires of discipline and training. We are fierce in a way no other can be. We are the marines."

From video games to Hollywood films to children's toys, popular culture is increasingly bombarded with militarized values, symbols, and images. Video games such as *Doom* have a long history of using violent graphics and shooting techniques that appeal to the most hyper-modes of masculinity. The Marine Corps was so taken with *Doom* in the mid-1990s that it produced its own version of the game, *Marine Doom,* and made it available to download for free. One of its developers, Lieutenant Scott Barnett, claimed at the time that it was a useful game to keep marines entertained. The military has found numerous ways to take advantage of the intersection between popular culture and the new electronic technologies. Such technologies are being employed not only to train military personnel but also to attract recruits, tapping into the realm of popular culture with its celebration of video games, computer technology, the Internet, and other elements of visual culture used by teenagers.[154] For instance, the army has developed online software that appeals to computer-literate recruits, and the most attractive feature of the software is a shooting game "that actually simulates battle and strategic-warfare situations."[155] When asked about the violence being portrayed, Brian Ball, the lead developer of the game, was crystal-clear about the purpose of the video: "We don't downplay the fact that the Army manages violence. We hope that this will help people understand the role of the military in American life."[156]

Capitalizing on its link with industry, the military now has a host of new war games in production. For instance, there is *America's Army,* one of the most popular and successful recruiting video games. This game teaches young people how "to kill enemy soldiers while wearing your pajamas [and also provides] plenty of suggestions about visiting your local recruiter and joining the real US Army."[157] Using the most updated versions of satellite technology, military-industry collaboration has also produced *Kuma: War.* This game, released in 2004, was developed by the Department of Defense and Kuma Reality Games. Updated weekly, it is a subscription-based product that "prepares gamers for actual missions based on real-world conflicts."[158] The game allows players to recreate actual news stories such as the raid that American forces conducted in Mosul, Iraq, in which Saddam Hussein's two sons, Uday and Qusay, were killed. Gamers can take advantage of real "true to life satellite imagery and authentic military intelligence to jump from the headlines right into the frontlines of international conflict."[159] Of course, the realities of carrying 80-pound knapsacks in 120-degree heat, dealing with panic-inducing anxiety and the fear of real people shooting real bullets or planting real bombs to kill or maim you and your fellow soldiers, and spending months, if not years, away from family are not among those experiences reproduced for instruction and entertainment.

The military uses the games to train recruits, and the video game makers offer products that have the imprimatur of a first-class fighting machine. And the popularity of militarized war games is on the rise. Nicholas Turse argues that as the line between entertainment and war disappears, a "'military-entertainment complex' [has] sprung up to feed the military's desire to bring out ever-more-realistic computer and video combat games. Through video games, the military and its partners in academia and the entertainment industry are creating an arm of media culture geared toward preparing young Americans for armed conflict."[160] Combat teaching games offer a perfect fit between the Pentagon, with its accelerating military budget, and the entertainment industry, with annual revenues of $479 billion, including $40 billion from the video game industry. The entertainment industry offers a stamp of approval for the Pentagon's war games, and the Defense Department provides an aura of authenticity for corporate America's war-based products. Collaboration between the Defense Department and the entertainment industry has been going on since 1997, but the permanent war culture that now grips the United States has given this partnership a new life and has greatly expanded its presence in popular culture.[161]

Young people no longer learn military values in training camp or in military-oriented schools. These values are now disseminated through the pedagogical force of popular culture itself, which has become a major tool used by the armed forces to educate young people about the ideology and social relations that inform military life—minus a few of the unpleasantries. The collaboration between the military and the entertainment industry offers forms of public pedagogy that "may help to produce great battlefield decision makers, but ... strike from debate the most crucial decisions young people can make in regard to the morality of a war—choosing whether or not to fight and for what cause."[162]

The popularity of militarized culture is apparent not only in the sales of video combat games but also in the sales of children's toys. Some of the best-selling items available at major retailers and major chain stores across the country are war-related toys. KB Toys stores in San Antonio, Texas, sold out in one day an entire shipment of fatigue-clad plush hamsters that dance to military music, and managers were instructed "to feature military toys in the front of their stores."[163] Sales of action figures have also soared. As Hasbro reported, "between 2001 and 2002, sales of *G.I. Joe* increased by 46 percent. And when toy retailer Small Blue Planet launched a series of figures called 'Special Forces: Showdown With Iraq,' two of the four models sold out immediately."[164] KB Toys took advantage of the infatuation with action toys related to the war in Iraq by marketing a doll that represented a pint-sized model of George W. Bush dressed in the U.S. pilot regalia he wore when he landed on the USS *Abraham Lincoln* on May 1, 2003. Japanese electronic giant SONY attempted to cash in on the war in Iraq by patenting the phrase "Shock and Awe" for use with video games. The phrase was coined by Pentagon strategists as part of a scare tactic associated with the massive air bombardment on Baghdad in the initial stages of the Iraq war. In addition, the *New York Times* reported that after September 11, 2001, "nearly two-dozen applications were filed for the phrase, 'Let's Roll'"—a phrase made famous by one of the passengers on the ill-fated hijacked plane that crashed in a field in Pennsylvania.

Even in the world of fashion, the ever-spreading chic of militarization and patriotism is making its mark. Army-Navy stores are doing a brisk business selling not only American flags, gas masks, aviator sunglasses, night-vision goggles, and other military equipment but also clothing with a camouflage look.[165] Even top designers are getting into the act. For instance, at a fashion show in Milan, Italy, many designers were "drawn to G.I. uniforms [and were] fascinated by the construction of military uniforms." One designer even "had beefy models in commando gear scramble over tabletops and explode balloons."[166]

As militarization spreads through the culture, it produces policies that rely more on force than on dialogue and compassion; it offers up modes of identification that undermine democratic values and tarnish civil liberties; and it makes the production of both symbolic and material violence a central feature of everyday life. As Chalmers Johnson, Andrew Bacevich, Carl Boggs, and Kevin Baker point out, militarization has become a central feature of American society as the United States has rapidly become a nation that "substitute[s] military solutions for almost everything, including international alliances, diplomacy, effective intelligence agencies, democratic institutions—even national security."[167] Within this ideology, masculinity is associated with violence, and action is often substituted for the democratic processes of deliberation and debate. Militarization is about the rule of force and the expansion of repressive state power. In fact, democracy appears as an excess in this logic and is often condemned by militarists as being a weak system of government. Echoes of this anti-democratic sentiment can be found in the USA PATRIOT Act with its violation of civil liberties, in the rancorous patriotism that equates dissent with treason, and in the discourse of public commentators who, in the fervor of a militarized culture, fan the flames of hatred and intolerance. One example that has become all too typical emerged after the September 11 attacks. Columnist Ann Coulter, in calling for a holy war on Muslims, wrote: "We should invade their countries, kill their leaders and convert them to Christianity. We weren't punctilious about locating and punishing only Hitler and his top officers. We carpet-bombed German cities; we killed civilians. That's war. And this is war."[168] While this statement does not reflect mainstream American opinion, the uncritical and chauvinistic patriotism and intolerance that inform it not only have become standard fare among many conservative radio hosts in the United States but are increasingly being legitimated in a wide variety of cultural venues. By blurring the lines between military and civilian functions, militarization deforms our language, debases democratic values, celebrates fascist modes of control, defines citizens as soldiers, and diminishes our ability as a nation to uphold international law and support a democratic global public sphere. Unless militarization is systematically exposed and resisted at every place where it appears in the culture, it will undermine the meaning of critical citizenship and do great harm to those institutions that are central to a democratic society.

Neoliberalism and the Death of Democracy

> I submit that neoliberalism has changed the fundamental nature of politics. Politics used to be primarily about who ruled whom and who got what share of the pie. Aspects of both these central questions remain, of course, but the great new central question of politics is, in my view, "Who has a right to live and who does not?" Radical exclusion is now the order of the day and I mean this deadly seriously.[169]

It is virtually impossible to understand the rise of such multifaceted authoritarianism in American society without analyzing the importance of neoliberalism as the defining ideology of the current historical moment.[170] While fascism does not need neoliberalism to develop, neoliberalism creates the ideological and economic conditions that can promote a uniquely American version of fascism.[171] Neoliberalism not only undermines vital economic and political institutions and public spaces central to a democracy but also has no vocabulary for recognizing anti-democratic forms of power. Even worse, it accentuates a structural relationship between the state and the economy that produces hierarchies, concentrates power in relatively few hands, unleashes the most brutal elements of a rabid individualism, destroys the welfare state, incarcerates a large proportion of its "disposable" population, economically disenfranchises large segments of the lower and middle classes, and reduces entire countries to pauperization.[172]

Under neoliberalism, the state makes a grim alignment with corporate capital and transnational corporations. Gone are the days when the state "assumed responsibility for a range of social needs"; instead, agencies of government now pursue a wide range of "'deregulations,' privatizations, and abdications of responsibility to the market and private philanthropy."[173] Deregulation promotes "widespread, systematic disinvestment in the nation's basic productive capacity."[174] Flexible production encourages wage slavery at home. And the search for ever greater profits leads to outsourcing, which accentuates the flight of capital and jobs abroad. Neoliberalism has become the prevailing logic in the United States, and according to Stanley Aronowitz, "the neoliberal economic doctrine proclaiming the superiority of free markets over public ownership, or even public regulation of private economic activities, has become the conventional wisdom, not only among conservatives but among social progressives."[175] The ideology and power of neoliberalism also cut across national boundaries. Throughout the globe, the forces of neoliberalism are on the march, dismantling the historically guaranteed social provisions provided by the welfare state, defining profit-making as the essence of democracy, and equating freedom with the unrestricted ability of markets to "govern economic relations free of government regulation."[176] Transnational in scope, neoliberalism now imposes its economic regime and market values on developing and weaker nations through structural adjustment policies enforced by powerful financial institutions such as the World Bank, the International Monetary Fund (IMF), and the World Trade Organization (WTO).[177] Secure in its dystopian vision that there are no alternatives, as Margaret Thatcher once put it, neoliberalism obviates issues of contingency, struggle, and social agency by celebrating the inevitability of economic laws in which the ethical ideal of intervening in the world gives way to the idea that we "have no choice but to adapt both our hopes and our abilities to the new global market."[178] Coupled with a new culture of fear, market freedoms seem securely grounded in a defense of national security, capital, and property rights.

In its capacity to dehistoricize and depoliticize society, as well as in its aggressive attempts to destroy all of the public spheres necessary for the defense of a genuine democracy, neoliberalism reproduces the conditions for unleashing the most brutalizing forces of capitalism and for accentuating the most central elements of proto-fascism. As the late Pierre Bourdieu argued, neoliberalism is a policy of depoliticization that attempts to liberate the economic sphere from all government controls:

> Drawing shamelessly on the lexicon of liberty, liberalism, and deregulation, it aims to grant economic determinisms a fatal stranglehold by liberating them from all controls, and to obtain the submission of citizens and governments to the economic and social forces thus liberated.... [T]his policy has imposed itself through the most varied means, especially juridical, on the liberal—or even social democratic—governments of a set of economically advanced countries, leading them gradually to divest themselves of the power to control economic forces.[179]

At the same time, neoliberalism uses the breathless rhetoric of the global victory of free-market rationality to cut public expenditures and undermine those noncommodified public spheres that serve as the repositories for critical education, language, and public intervention. Spewed forth by the mass media, right-wing intellectuals, and governments alike, neoliberal ideology, with its ongoing emphasis on deregulation and privatization, has found its material expression in an all-out attack on democratic values and on the very notion of the public sphere. Within the discourse of neoliberalism, the notion of the public good is devalued and, where possible, eliminated as part of a wider rationale for a handful of private interests to control as much of social life as possible in order to maximize personal profit. Public services such as health care, child care, public assistance, education, and transportation are now subject to the rules of the market. Construing the public good as a private good and the needs of the corporate and private sector as the only smart investments, neoliberal ideology produces, legitimates, and exacerbates the existence of persistent poverty, inadequate health care, racial apartheid in the inner cities, and growing inequalities between the rich and the poor.[180]

As Stanley Aronowitz points out, the Bush administration has made neoliberal ideology the cornerstone of its program and has been at the forefront in actively supporting and implementing the following policies:

> deregulation of business at all levels of enterprises and trade; tax reduction for wealthy individuals and corporations; the revival of the near-dormant nuclear energy industry; limitations and abrogation of labor's right to organize and bargain collectively; a land policy favoring commercial and industrial development at the expense of conservation and other proenvironment policies; elimination of income support to the chronically unemployed; reduced federal aid to education and health; privatization of the main federal pension program, Social Security; limitation on the right of aggrieved individuals to sue employers and corporations who provide services; in addition, as social programs are reduced, [Republicans] are joined by the Democrats in favoring increases in the repressive functions of the state, expressed in the dubious drug wars in the name of fighting crime, more funds for surveillance of ordinary citizens, and the expansion of the federal and local police forces.[181]

Central to both neoliberal ideology and its implementation by the Bush administration are the ongoing attempts by free-market fundamentalists and right-wing politicians to view government as the enemy of freedom (except when it aids big business) and to discount it as a guardian of the public interest. At the same time, there is a relentless attack on union membership and organized labor. Membership in unions, which "once constrained corporate economic and political power,"[182] now totals a mere 7.9 percent of the labor force in the private sector. The rabid neoliberalism of the Bush administration also fuels global policies that threaten the environment, especially in light of the Bush government's refusal to sign the Kyoto Protocol, designed to control greenhouse gas emissions and reduce global warming.

The call to eliminate big government is neoliberalism's great unifying idea and has broad popular appeal in the United States because it is a principle deeply embedded in the country's history and tangled up with its notion of political freedom. And yet, the right-wing appropriation of this tradition is racked with contradictions in terms of neoliberal policies. As William Greider points out:

> "Leave me alone" is an appealing slogan, but the right regularly violates its own guiding principle. The antiabortion folks intend to use government power to force their own moral values on the private lives of others. Free-market right-wingers fall silent when Bush and Congress intrude to bail out airlines, insurance companies, banks—whatever sector finds itself in desperate need. The hard-right conservatives are downright enthusiastic when the Supreme Court and Bush's Justice Department hack away at our civil liberties. The "school choice" movement seeks not smaller government but a vast expansion of taxpayer obligations.[183]

The advocates of neoliberalism have attacked what they call big government when it has provided essential services such as crucial safety nets for the less fortunate, but they had no qualms about using the government to bail out the airline industry after the economic nosedive that followed the 2000 election of George W. Bush and the events of 9/11. There have been no expressions of outrage from the cheerleaders of neoliberalism when the state has engaged in promoting various forms of corporate welfare by providing billions of dollars in direct and indirect subsidies to multinational corporations. In short, the government bears no obligation either to the poor and dispossessed or to the collective future of young people.

As the laws of the market take precedence over the laws of the state as guardians of the public good, the government offers less and less help in mediating the interface between the advance of capital and its rapacious commercial interests, and refuses to aid noncommodified interests and nonmarket spheres that create the political, economic, and social spaces and discursive conditions vital for critical citizenship and democratic public life. Within the discourse of neoliberalism, it becomes increasingly difficult for the average citizen to speak about political or social transformation, or even to challenge existing conditions, beyond a grudging nod toward rampant corruption, ruthless downsizing, the ongoing liquidation of job security, and the elimination of benefits for part-time and contract workers.

The liberal democratic vocabulary of rights, entitlements, social provisions, community, social responsibility, living wage, job security, equality, and justice seem oddly out of place in a country where the promise of democracy has been replaced by casino capitalism—a winner-take-all philosophy suited to lotto players and day traders alike. As corporate culture extends even deeper into the basic institutions of civil and political society, buttressed daily by a culture industry largely in the hands of concentrated capital, it is reinforced even further by the pervasive fear and public insecurity regarding the possibility that the future holds nothing beyond a watered-down version of the present. As the prevailing discourse of neoliberalism seizes the public imagination, there is no vocabulary for progressive social change, democratically inspired vision, or critical notions of social agency to expand the meaning and purpose of democratic public life. Against the reality of low-wage jobs, the erosion of social provisions for a growing number of people, the expanding war against young people of color at home, and empire-building wars abroad, the market-driven juggernaut of neoliberalism continues to mobilize desires in the interest of producing market identities and market relationships that ultimately sever the link between education and social change while reducing agency to the obligations of consumerism.

As neoliberal ideology and corporate culture extend even deeper into the basic institutions of civil and political society, there is a simultaneous diminishing of noncommodified public spheres—those institutions such as public schools, independent bookstores, churches, noncommercial public broadcasting stations, libraries, trade unions, and various voluntary institutions engaged in dialogue, education, and learning—that can address the relationship of the individual to public life, foster social responsibility, and provide a robust vehicle for public participation and democratic citizenship. As media theorists Edward Herman and Robert McChesney observe, noncommodified public spheres have historically played an invaluable role "as places and forums where issues of importance to a political community are discussed and debated, and where information is presented that is essential to citizen participation in community life."[184] Without these critical public spheres, corporate power often goes unchecked and politics becomes dull, cynical, and oppressive.[185] Moreover, the vacuum left by diminishing democracy is filled with religious zealotry, cultural chauvinism, xenophobia, and racism—the dominant tropes of neoconservatives and other extremist groups eager to take advantage of the growing insecurity, fear, and anxiety that result from increased joblessness, the war on terror, and the unraveling of communities. In this context, neoliberalism creates the economic, social, and political instability that helps feed both the neoconservative and the religious Right movements and their proto-fascist policy initiatives.

Especially troubling under the rule of neoliberalism is not simply that ideas associated with freedom and agency are defined almost exclusively through the prevailing ideology and principles of the market, but that neoliberal ideology also wraps itself in what appears to be an unassailable appeal to conventional wisdom. Defined as the paragon of modern social relations by Friedrich A. von Hayek, Milton Friedman, Robert Nozick, Francis Fukuyama, and other market fundamentalists, neoliberalism attempts to eliminate any engaged critique about its most basic principles and social consequences by embracing the "market as the arbiter of social destiny."[186] Neoliberalism empties the public treasury, privatizes formerly public services, limits the vocabulary and imagery available to recognize anti-democratic forms of power, and reinforces narrow models of individual agency. Equally important is its role in undermining the critical functions of a viable democracy by undercutting the ability of individuals to engage in the continuous translation between public considerations and private interests. It accomplishes this depoliticizing strategy, in part, by collapsing public issues into the realm of the private. As Bauman observes, "It is no longer true that the 'public' is set on colonizing the 'private.' The opposite is the case: it is the private that colonizes the public space, squeezing out and chasing away everything which cannot be fully, without residue, translated into the vocabulary of private interests and pursuits."[187] Divested of its political possibilities and social underpinnings, freedom offers few opportunities for people to translate private worries into public concerns and collective struggle.

The good life, in neoliberal discourse, "is construed in terms of our identities as consumers—we are what we buy."[188] For example, some neoliberal advocates argue that the health care and education crises faced by many states can be solved by selling off public assets to private interests. Blatantly demonstrating neoliberal ideology's contempt for noncommodified public spheres and democratic values, the Pentagon even considered, if only for a short time, turning the war on terror and security concerns over to futures markets, subject to online trading. In such exhibitions of market logic and casino capitalism, neoliberalism reveals its dream of a social order dominated by commercial spheres. At the same time, it aggressively attempts to empty the substance of critical democracy and replace it with a democracy of goods available to those with both purchasing power and the ability to expand the cultural and political power of corporations throughout the world. As a result of the consolidated corporate attack on public life, the maintenance of democratic public spheres from which to launch a moral vision or to engage in a viable struggle over politics loses all credibility—not to mention monetary support. As the alleged objectivity of neoliberal ideology remains largely unchallenged within dominant public spheres, individual critique and collective political struggle become more difficult.[189] As George Soros points out, this rigid ideology and inflexible sense of mission allow the Bush administration to believe that "because we are stronger than others, we must know better and we must have right on our side. This is where religious fundamentalism comes together with market fundamentalism to form the ideology of American supremacy."[190] The prevalence of neoliberalism means that the Bush administration, driven by an arrogance of power and an inflated sense of moral righteousness mediated largely by a false sense of certitude and a never-ending posture of triumphalism, can operate largely unchecked by public opposition.

As public space is increasingly commodified and the state becomes more closely aligned with capital, politics is defined largely by its policing functions rather than as an agency for peace and social reform. Besides the destruction of collective solidarities, neoliberalism refigures the relationship between the state and capital. As the state abandons its social investments in health, education, and the public welfare, it increasingly takes on the functions of an enhanced police or security state, the signs of which are most visible in the increasing use of the state apparatus to spy on and arrest its subjects, the incarceration of individuals considered disposable (primarily people of color), and the ongoing criminalization of social policies. Examples of the latter include anti-begging and anti-loitering ordinances that fine or punish homeless people for sitting or lying down too long in public places.[191] An even more despicable example of the barbaric nature of neoliberalism, with its emphasis on profits over people and its willingness to punish rather than serve the poor and disenfranchised, can be seen in the growing tendency of many hospitals across the country to have patients arrested and jailed if they cannot pay their medical bills. This policy, which is chillingly called "body attachment" and is "basically a warrant for ... the patient's arrest,"[192] represents a return to debtors' prison and is right out of the pages of George Orwell's *1984*. Its ideological counterpart is a public pedagogy that mobilizes power toward a social order marked by the progressive removal of autonomous spheres of cultural production such as journalism, publishing, and film; the destruction of collective structures capable of counteracting the widespread imposition of commercial values and effects of the market; the creation of a global reserve army of unemployed; and the subordination of nation-states to the real masters of the economy. Bourdieu emphasized the effects of neoliberalism on this dystopian world:

> First is the destruction of all the collective institutions capable of counteracting the effects of the infernal machine, primarily those of the state, repository of all of the universal values associated with the idea of the public realm. Second is the imposition everywhere, in the upper spheres of the economy and the state as at the heart of corporations, of that sort of moral Darwinism that, with the cult of the winner, schooled in higher mathematics and bungee jumping, institutes the struggle of all against all and cynicism as the norm of all action and behavior.[193]

Within this discourse, as Jean and John Comaroff have argued, "the personal is the only politics there is, the only politics with a tangible referent or emotional valence. It is in these privatized terms that action is organized, that the experience of inequity and antagonism takes meaningful shape."[194] Under such circumstances, neoliberalism portends the death of politics as we know it, strips the social of its democratic values, reconstructs agency in terms that are utterly privatized, and provides the conditions for an emerging form of proto-fascism that must be resisted at all costs. Neoliberalism not only enshrines unbridled individualism as a central feature of proto-fascism, it also destroys any vestige of democratic society by undercutting its "moral, material, and regulatory moorings," and in doing so it offers no language for understanding how the future might be grasped outside the narrow logic of the market.[195]

But there is even more at stake here than the obliteration of public concerns, the death of the social, the emergence of a market-based fundamentalism that undercuts the ability of people to understand how to translate privately experienced misery into collective action, and the elimination of the gains of the welfare state. There is also the growing threat of displacing "political sovereignty with the sovereignty of the market, as if the latter has a mind and morality of its own."[196] As democracy becomes a burden under the reign of neoliberalism, civic discourse disappears, and the reign of unfettered social Darwinism with its survival-of-the-slickest philosophy emerges as the template for a new form of proto-fascism. However, none of this will proceed further in the face of sufficient resistance. The increasing move toward proto-fascism is not inevitable. It is rather the case that the conditions have been put into place for democracy potentially to lose all semblance of meaning in the United States.

Against this encroaching form of fascism more is needed than moral outrage. What is needed is a new language for theorizing politics in the twenty-first century. Such a language must insist on the fundamental importance of what it means to live in a global information society marked not simply by the proliferation of new electronic technologies but also by new pedagogical sites in which the struggle over meaning is crucial to the struggle over the pedagogical conditions necessary for the emergence of democratic modes of agency and collective resistance.[197] Against the increasing alliance among global capitalism, political and religious fundamentalism, and an escalating militarism, there is a need for new social formations, collaborations, and movements in which it becomes possible to imagine a different world, one in which multitudinous networks are joined together not only by a language of critique but by a language of hope and concerted collective action. Within such a discourse, difference extends into solidarity, and opposition crosses borders and affirms both the collective possibilities of politics and the movement toward a more democratic future.

2
Spectacles of Race and Pedagogies of Denial

Race relations in the United States have changed considerably since W.E.B. Du Bois famously predicted in *The Souls of Black Folk* that "the problem of the 20th century is the problem of the color line."[1] This is not to suggest that race has declined in significance, or that the racial conditions, ideologies, and practices that provided the context for Du Bois' prophecy have been overcome; rather, the point is that they have been transformed, mutated, and recycled and have taken on new and in many instances more covert modes of expression.[2] Du Bois recognized that the color line was not fixed—its forms of expression changed over time, as a response to different contexts and struggles—and that one of the great challenges facing future generations would be not only to engage the complex structural legacy of race but also to take note of the plethora of forms in which it was expressed and experienced in everyday life. For Du Bois, race fused power and ideology and was deeply woven into both the public pedagogy of American culture and its geography, economics, politics, and institutions.

The great challenge Du Bois presents to this generation of students, educators, and citizens is to acknowledge that the future of democracy in the United States is inextricably linked "to the outcomes of racial politics and policies, as they develop both in various national societies and the world at large."[3] In part, this observation implies that how we experience democracy

---

This chapter is reprinted with permission from Henry A. Giroux, "Spectacles of Race and Pedagogies of Denial," *Communication Education* 52:3/4, pp. 19–21 (2003).

in the future will depend on how we name, think about, experience, and transform the interrelated modalities of race, racism, and social justice. It also suggests that the meaning of race and the challenges of racism change for each generation, and that the new challenges we face demand a new language for understanding how the symbolic power of race as a pedagogical force as well as a structural and materialist practice redefines the relationship between the self and the other, the private and the public. It is this latter challenge in particular that needs to be more fully addressed if racism is not to be reduced to an utterly privatized discourse that erases any trace of racial injustice by denying the very notion of the social and the operations of power through which racial politics are organized and legitimated.

When Du Bois wrote *The Souls of Black Folk,* racism was a visible and endemic part of the American political, cultural, and economic landscape. The racial divide was impossible to ignore, irrespective of one's politics. As we move into the new millennium, the politics of the color line and representations of race have become far more subtle and complicated than they were in the Jim Crow era when Du Bois made his famous pronouncement. And though far from invisible, the complicated nature of race relations in American society no longer appears to be marked by the specter of Jim Crow. A majority of Americans now believe that anti-black racism is a thing of the past, since it is assumed that formal institutions of segregation no longer exist. Yet, surveys done by the National Opinion Research Center at the University of Chicago have consistently found "that most Americans still believe blacks are less intelligent than whites, lazier than whites, and more likely than whites to prefer living on welfare over being self-supporting."[4] Contradictions aside, conservatives and liberals alike now view America's racial hierarchy as an unfortunate historical fact that has no bearing on contemporary society. Pointing to the destruction of the Southern caste system, the problematizing of whiteness as a racial category, the passing of civil rights laws, a number of successful lawsuits alleging racial discrimination against companies such as Texaco and Denny's, and the emergence of people of color into all aspects of public life, the color line now seems in disarray, a remnant of another era that Americans have fortunately moved beyond. Best-selling books such as Dinesh D'Souza's *The End of Racism,* Jim Sleeper's *Liberal Racism,* and Stephan and Abigail Thernstrom's *America in Black and White: One Nation, Indivisible* all proclaim racism as an obsolete ideology and practice.[5] And a large number of white Americans seem to agree. In fact, poll after poll reveals that a majority of white Americans believe that people of color no longer face racial discrimination in American life. For example, a recent Gallup Poll on "Black-White Relations" observes that "7 out of 10 whites believe that blacks are treated equally in their communities.... Eight in ten whites say blacks receive equal educational opportunities, and 83% say blacks receive equal housing opportunities in their communities. Only a third of whites believe blacks face racial bias from police in their areas."[6] For many conservative and liberal intellectuals, the only remaining remnant of racist categorization and policy in an otherwise color-blind society is affirmative action, which is ironically alleged to provide blacks with an unfair advantage in higher education, the labor force, "entitlement programs," and "even summer scholarship programs."[7]

The importance of race and the enduring fact of racism are relegated to the dustbin of history at a time in American life when the discourses of race and the spectacle of racial representations saturate the dominant media and public life. The color line is now mined for exotic commodities that can be sold to white youth in the form of rap music, hip-hop clothing, and sports gear. African American celebrities such as Michael Jordan, Etta James, and George Foreman are used to give market legitimacy to everything from gas grills to high-end luxury cars to clothes. Black public intellectuals such as Patricia Williams, Cornel West, Michael Dyson, and Henry Louis Gates command the attention of the *New York Times* and other eye-catching media. African Americans now occupy powerful positions on the Supreme Court and at the highest levels of political life. The alleged collapse, if not transformation, of the color line can also be seen in the emergence of the black elite, prominently on display in television sitcoms, fashion magazines, Hollywood movies, and music videos. On the political scene, however, the supposedly race-transcendent public policy is complicated by ongoing public debates over affirmative action, welfare, crime, and the prison-industrial complex. All of which suggests that whereas the color line has been modified and dismantled in places, race and racial hierarchies still exercise a profound influence on how most people in the United States experience their daily lives.[8] Popular sentiment aside, race—rather than disappearing—has retained its power as a key signifier in structuring all aspects of American life. As Michael Omi keenly observes: "Despite legal guarantees of formal equality and access, race continues to be a fundamental organizing principle of individual identity and collective action. I would argue that, far from declining in significance (as William Julius Wilson would have us believe), the racial dimensions of politics and culture have proliferated."[9]

Representations of race and difference are everywhere in American society, and yet racism as both a symbol and a condition of American life is either ignored or relegated to an utterly privatized discourse, typified in references to individual prejudices or to psychological dispositions such as expressions of "hate." As politics becomes more racialized, the discourse about race becomes more privatized. While the realities of race permeate public life, they are engaged less as discourses and sites where differences are produced within iniquitous relations of power than as either unobjectionable cultural signifiers or desirable commodities. The public morality of the marketplace works its magic in widening the gap between political control and economic power while simultaneously reducing political agency to the act of consuming. One result is a growing cynicism and powerlessness among the general population as the political impotence of public institutions is reinforced through the disparaging of any reference to ethics, equity, justice, or other normative principles that prioritize democratic values over market considerations. Similarly, as corporate power undermines all notions of the public good and increasingly privatizes public space, it obliterates those public spheres in which there might emerge criticism that acknowledges the tensions wrought by a pervasive racism that "functions as one of the deep, abiding currents in everyday life, in both the simplest and the most complex interactions of whites and blacks."[10] Indifference and cynicism breed contempt and resentment as racial hierarchies now collapse into power-evasive strategies such as blaming minorities of class and color for not working hard enough, refusing to exercise individual initiative, or practicing reverse-racism. In short, marketplace ideologies now work to erase the social from the language of public life so as to reduce all racial problems to private issues such as individual character and cultural depravity.

Black public intellectuals such as Shelby Steele and John McWhorter garner national attention by asserting that the subject and object of racism have been reversed. For Steele, racism has nothing to do with soaring black unemployment, failing and segregated schools for black children, a criminal justice system that resembles the old plantation system of the South, or police brutality that takes its toll largely on blacks in urban cities such as Cincinnati and New York. On the contrary, according to Steele, racism has produced white guilt, a burden that white people have to carry as part of the legacy of the civil rights movement. To remove this burden from white shoulders, blacks now have to free themselves from their victim status and act responsibly by proving to whites that *their* suffering is unnecessary.[11] They can do so through the spirit of principled entrepreneurialism—allowing themselves to be judged on the basis of hard work, individual effort, a secure family life, decent values, and property ownership.[12] It gets worse. John McWhorter, largely relying on anecdotes from his own limited experience in the academy at UCLA–Berkeley, argues that higher education is filled with African American students who are either mediocre or simply lazy, victims of affirmative action programs that coddle them because of their race while allowing them to "dumb down" rather than work as competitively as their white classmates. The lesson here is that the color line now benefits blacks rather than whites and that, in the end, for McWhorter, diversity rather than bigotry is the enemy of a quality education and functions largely to "condemn black students to mediocrity."[13]

Within this discourse, there is a glimmer of a new kind of racial reference, one that can imagine public issues only as private concerns. This is a racism that refuses to "translate private sufferings into public issues,"[14] a racism that works hard to remove issues of power and equity from broader social concerns. Ultimately, it imagines human agency as simply a matter of individualized choices, the only obstacle to effective citizenship and agency being the lack of principled self-help and moral responsibility. In what follows, I want to examine briefly the changing nature of the new racism by analyzing how some of its central assumptions evade notions of race, racial justice, equity, and democracy altogether. In the process, I analyze some elements of the new racism, particularly the discourse of color-blindness and neoliberal racism. I then address the ways in which the controversial Trent Lott affair demonstrated neoliberal racism as well as the racism of denial. I will conclude by offering some suggestions about how the new racism, particularly its neoliberal version, can be addressed as both a pedagogical and a political issue.

Neoliberalism and the Culture of Privatization

The public morality of American life and social policy regarding matters of racial justice are increasingly subject to a politics of denial. Denial in this case is not merely about the failure of public memory or the refusal to know, but an active ongoing attempt on the part of many conservatives, liberals, and politicians to rewrite the discourse of race so as to deny its valence as a force for discrimination and exclusion by either translating it as a threat to American culture or relegating it to the language of the private sphere. The idea of race and the conditions of racism have real political effects, and eliding them only makes those effects harder to recognize. And yet, the urgency to recognize how language is used to name, organize, order, and categorize matters of race not only has academic value, it also provides a location from which to engage difference and the relationship between the self and the other and between the public and private. In addition, the language of race is important because it strongly affects political and policy agendas as well. One only has to think about the effects of Charles Murray's book *Losing Ground* on American welfare policies in the 1980s.[15] But language is more than a mode of communication or a symbolic practice that produces real effects; it is also a site of contestation and struggle. Since the mid-1970s, race relations have undergone a significant shift and acquired a new character as the forces of neoliberalism have begun to shape how Americans understand notions of agency, identity, freedom, and politics itself.[16]

Part of this shift has to be understood within the emerging forces of transnational capitalism and a global restructuring in which the economy is separated from politics and corporate power is largely removed from the control of nation-states. Within the neoliberal register, globalization "represents the triumph of the economy over politics and culture ... and the hegemony of capital over all other domains of life."[17] Under neoliberal globalization, capital removes itself from any viable form of state regulation, power is uncoupled from matters of ethics and social responsibility, and market freedoms replace long-standing social contracts that once provided a safety net for the poor, the elderly, workers, and the middle class. The result is that public issues and social concerns increasingly give way to a growing culture of insecurity and fear regarding the most basic issues of individual livelihood, safety, and survival. Increasingly, a concern with either the past or the future is replaced by uncertainty, and traditional human bonds rooted in compassion, justice, and a respect for others are now replaced by a revitalized social Darwinism, played out nightly in the celebration of reality-based television, in which rabid self-interest becomes the organizing principle for a winner-take-all society. As insecurity and fear grip public consciousness, society is no longer identified through its allegiance to democratic values but through a troubling freedom rooted in a disturbing emphasis on individualism and competitiveness as the only normative measures to distinguish between what is a right or wrong, just or unjust, proper or improper action. Zygmunt Bauman captures this deracinated notion of freedom and the insecurity it promotes in his observation that

> [s]ociety no longer guarantees, or even promises, a collective remedy for individual misfortunes. Individuals have been offered (or, rather, have been cast into) freedom of unprecedented proportions—but at the price of similarly unprecedented insecurity. And when there is insecurity, little time is left for caring for values that hover above the level of daily concerns—or, for that matter, for whatever lasts longer than the fleeting moment.[18]

Within this emerging neoliberal ethic, success is attributed to thriftiness and entrepreneurial genius while those who do not succeed are viewed either as failures or as utterly expendable. Indeed, neoliberalism's attachment to individualism, markets, and anti-statism ranks human needs as less important than property rights and subordinates "the art of politics ... to the science of economics."[19] Racial justice in the age of market-based freedoms and financially driven values loses its ethical imperative to a neoliberalism that embraces commercial rather than civic values, private rather than pubic interests, and financial incentives rather than ethical concerns. Neoliberalism negates racism as an ethical issue and democratic values as a basis for citizen-based action. Of course, neoliberalism takes many forms as it moves across the globe. In the United States, it has achieved a surprising degree of success but is increasingly being resisted by labor unions, students, and environmentalists. Major protests against economic policies promoted by the World Bank, International Monetary Fund, and World Trade Organization have taken place in Seattle, Prague, New York, Montreal, Genoa, and other cities around the world. In the United States, a rising generation of students is protesting trade agreements like GATT and NAFTA as well as sweatshop labor practices at home and abroad and the corporatization of public and higher education. Unfortunately, anti-racist theorists have not said enough about either the link between the new racism and neoliberalism, on the one hand, or the rise of a race-based carceral state, on the other. Neither the rise of the new racism nor any viable politics of an anti-racist movement can be understood outside the power and grip of neoliberalism in the United States. Hence, at the risk of oversimplification and repetition within other chapters, I want to be a bit more specific about neoliberalism's central assumptions and how it frames some of the more prominent emerging racial discourses and practices.

Neoliberalism and the Politics of the New Racism

As mentioned in the preface, under the reign of neoliberalism in the United States, society is largely defined through the privileging of market relations, deregulation, privatization, and consumerism. Central to neoliberalism is the assumption that profit-making be construed as the essence of democracy and consuming as the most cherished act of citizenship. Strictly aligning freedom with a narrow notion of individual interest, neoliberalism works hard to privatize all aspects of the public good and simultaneously narrow the role of the state as both a gatekeeper for capital and a policing force for maintaining social order and racial control. Unrestricted by social legislation or government regulation, market relations as they define the economy are viewed as a paradigm for democracy itself. Central to neoliberal philosophy is the claim that the development of all aspects of society should be left to the wisdom of the market. Similarly, neoliberal warriors argue that democratic values be subordinated to economic considerations, social issues be translated as private dilemmas, part-time labor replace full-time work, trade unions be weakened, and everybody be treated as a customer. Within this market-driven perspective, the exchange of capital takes precedence over social justice, the making of socially responsible citizens, and the building of democratic communities. There is no language here for recognizing anti-democratic forms of power, developing nonmarket values, or fighting against substantive injustices in a society founded on deep inequalities, particularly those based on race and class. Hence, it is not surprising that under neoliberalism, language is often stripped of its critical and social possibilities as it becomes increasingly difficult to imagine a social order in which all problems are not personal, in which social issues provide the conditions for understanding private considerations, critical reflection becomes the essence of politics, and matters of equity and justice become crucial to developing a democratic society.

It is under the reign of neoliberalism that the changing vocabulary about race and racial justice has to be understood and engaged. As freedom is increasingly abstracted from the power of individuals and groups to actively participate in shaping society, it is reduced to the right of the individual to be free from social constraints. In this view, freedom is no longer linked to a collective effort on the part of individuals to create a democratic society. Instead, freedom becomes an exercise in self-development rather than social responsibility, reducing politics to either the celebration of consumerism or the privileging of a market-based notion of agency and choice that appears quite indifferent to how power, equity, and justice offer the enabling conditions for real individual and collective choices to be both made and acted upon. Under such circumstances, neoliberalism undermines those public spaces where noncommercial values and crucial social issues can be discussed, debated, and engaged. As public space is privatized, power is disconnected from social obligations and it becomes more difficult for isolated individuals living in consumption-oriented spaces to construct an ethically engaged and power-sensitive language capable of accommodating the principles of ethics and racial justice as a common good rather than as a private affair. According to Bauman, the elimination of public space and the subordination of democratic values to commercial interests narrows the discursive possibilities for supporting notions of the public good and creates the conditions for "the suspicion against others, the intolerance of difference, the resentment of strangers, and the demands to separate and banish them, as well as the hysterical, paranoiac concern with 'law and order.'"[20] Positioned within the emergence of neoliberalism as the dominant economic and political philosophy of our times, neoracism can be understood as part of a broader attack not only on difference but on the value of public memory, public goods, and democracy itself.

The new racism represents both a shift in how race is defined and a symptom of the breakdown of a political culture in which individual freedom and solidarity maintain an uneasy equilibrium in the service of racial, social, and economic justice. Individual freedom is now disconnected from any sense of civic responsibility or justice, focusing instead on investor profits, consumer confidence, the downsizing of governments to police precincts, and a deregulated social order in which the winner takes all. Freedom is no longer about either making the powerful responsible for their actions or providing the essential political, economic, and social conditions for everyday people to intervene in and shape their future. Under the reign of neoliberalism, freedom is less about the act of intervention than about the process of withdrawing from the social and enacting one's sense of agency as an almost exclusively private endeavor. Freedom now cancels out civic courage and social responsibility while it simultaneously translates public issues and collective problems into tales of failed character, bad luck, or simply indifference. As Amy Elizabeth Ansell points out:

> The disproportionate failure of people of color to achieve social mobility speaks nothing of the injustice of present social arrangements, according to the New Right worldview, but rather reflects the lack of merit or ability of people of color themselves. In this way, attention is deflected away from the reality of institutional racism and towards, for example, the "culture of poverty," the "drug culture," or the lack of black self-development.[21]

Appeals to freedom, operating under the sway of market forces, offer no signposts theoretically or politically for engaging racism as an ethical and political issue that undermines the very basis of a substantive democracy. Freedom in this discourse collapses into self-interest and as such is more inclined to organize any sense of community around shared fears, insecurities, and an intolerance of those "others" who are marginalized by class and color. But freedom reduced to the ethos of self-preservation and brutal self-interest makes it difficult for individuals to recognize the forms that racism often takes when draped in the language of either denial, freedom, or individual rights. In what follows, I want to explore two prominent forms of the new racism—color-blindness and neoliberal racism—and their connection to the New Right, corporate power, and neoliberal ideologies.

Unlike the old racism, which defined racial difference in terms of fixed biological categories organized hierarchically, the new racism operates in various guises proclaiming among other things race-neutrality, asserting culture as a marker of racial difference, or marking race as a private matter. Unlike the crude racism with its biological referents and pseudo-scientific legitimations, buttressing its appeal to white racial superiority, the new racism cynically recodes itself within the vocabulary of the civil rights movement, invoking the language of Martin Luther King, Jr., to argue that individuals should be judged by the "content of their character" and not by the color of their skin. Ansell, a keen commentator on the new racism, notes both the recent shifts in racialized discourse away from more rabid and overt forms of racism and its appropriation particularly by the New Right in the United States and Britain:

> The new racism actively disavows racist intent and is cleansed of extremist intolerance, thus reinforcing the New Right's attempt to distance itself from racist organizations such as the John Birch Society in the United States and the National Front in Britain. It is a form of racism that utilizes themes related to culture and nation as a replacement for the now discredited biological referents of the old racism. It is concerned less with notions of racial superiority in the narrow sense than with the alleged "threat" people of color pose—either because of their mere presence or because of their demand for "special privileges"—to economic, socio-political, and cultural vitality of the dominant (white) society. It is, in short, a new form of racism that operates with the category of "race." It is a new form of exclusionary politics that operates indirectly and in stealth via the rhetorical inclusion of people of color and the sanitized nature of its racist appeal.[22]

What is crucial about the new racism is that it demands an updated analysis of how racist practices work through the changing nature of language and other modes of representation. One of the most sanitized and yet most pervasive forms of the new racism is evident in the language of color-blindness. Within this approach, it is argued that racial conflict and discrimination are things of the past and that race has no bearing on an individual's or group's location or standing in contemporary American society. Color-blindness does not deny the existence of race but rejects the claim that race is responsible for massive inequalities between people of color and whites in all the major spheres of economic, political, social, and cultural life, especially in the areas of wealth, employment, housing, health care, and education. Put differently, inherent in the logic of color-blindness is the central assumption that race has no valence as a marker of identity or power when factored into the social vocabulary of everyday life and the capacity for exercising individual and social agency. As Charles Gallagher observes, "Within the color-blind perspective it is not race per se which determines upward mobility but how much an individual chooses to pay attention to race that determines one's fate. Within this perspective race is only as important as you allow it to be."[23] As Jeff, one of Gallagher's interviewees, puts it, race is simply another choice: "[Y]ou know, there's music, rap music is no longer, it's not a black thing anymore.... [W]hen it first came out it was black music, but now it's just music. It's another choice, just like country music can be considered like white hick music, you know it's just a choice."[24]

Hence, in an era "free" of racism, race becomes a matter of taste, lifestyle, or heritage but has nothing to do with politics, legal rights, educational access, or economic opportunities. Veiled by a denial of how racial histories accrue political, economic, and cultural weight to the social power of whiteness, color-blindness deletes the relationship between racial differences and power. In doing so it reinforces whiteness as the arbiter of value for judging difference against a normative notion of homogeneity.[25] For advocates of color-blindness, race as a political signifier is conveniently denied or seen as something to be overcome, allowing whites to ignore racism as a corrosive force for expanding the dynamics of ideological and structural inequality throughout society.[26] Color-blindness, then, is a convenient ideology for enabling whites to disregard the degree to which race is tangled up with asymmetrical relations of power, functioning as a potent force for patterns of exclusion and discrimination including but not limited to housing, mortgage loans, health care, schools, and the criminal justice system. If one effect of color-blindness is to deny racial hierarchies, another is that it offers whites the belief not only that America is now a level playing field but also that the success that whites enjoy relative to minorities of color is largely due to individual determination, a strong work ethic, high moral values, and a sound investment in education. In short, color-blindness offers up a highly racialized (though paraded as race-transcendent) notion of agency, while also providing an ideological space free of guilt, self-reflection, and political responsibility, despite the fact that blacks have a disadvantage in almost all areas of social life: housing, jobs, education, income levels, mortgage lending, and basic everyday services.[27] In a society marked by profound racial and class inequalities, it is difficult to believe that character and merit—as color-blindness advocates would have us believe—are the prime determinants for social and economic mobility and a decent standard of living. The relegation of racism and its effects in the larger society to the realm of private beliefs, values, and behavior does little to explain a range of overwhelming realities—such as soaring black unemployment, decaying cities, and segregated schools. Paul Street puts the issue forcibly in a series of questions that register the primacy of and interconnections among politics, social issues, and race:

> Why are African Americans twice as likely to be unemployed as whites? Why is the poverty rate for blacks more than twice the rate for whites? Why do nearly one out of every two blacks earn less than $25,000 while only one in three whites makes that little? Why is the median black household income ($27,000) less than two thirds of the median white household income ($42,000)? Why is the black family's median household net worth less than 10 percent that of whites? Why are blacks much less likely to own their own homes than whites? Why do African-Americans make up roughly half of the United States' massive population of prisoners (2 million) and why are one in three young, black male adults in prison or on parole or otherwise under the supervision of the American criminal justice system? Why do African Americans continue in severe geographic separation from mainstream society, still largely cordoned off into the nation's most disadvantaged communities thirty years after the passage of the civil rights fair housing legislation? Why do blacks suffer disproportionately from irregularities in the American electoral process, from problems with voter registration to the functioning of voting machinery? Why does black America effectively constitute a Third World enclave of sub-citizens within the world's richest and most powerful state?[28]

Add to this list the stepped-up resegregation of American schools and the growing militarization and lock-down status of public education through the widespread use of zero-tolerance policies.[29] Or the fact that African American males live on average six years less than their white counterparts. It is worth noting that nothing challenges the myth that America has become a color-blind post-racist nation more than the racialization of the criminal justice system since the late 1980s. As the sociologist Loic Wacquant has observed, the expansion of the prison-industrial complex represents a "de facto policy of 'carceral affirmative action' towards African Americans."[30] This is borne out by the fact that while American prisons house over 2 million inmates, "roughly half of them are black even though African Americans make up less than 13 percent of the nation's population.... According to the Justice Policy Institute there are now more black men behind bars than in college in the United States. One in ten of the world's prisoners is an African-American male."[31]

As one of the most powerful ideological and institutional factors for deciding how identities are categorized and power, material privileges, and resources distributed, race represents an essential political category for examining the relationship between justice and a democratic society. But color-blindness is about more than the denial of how power and politics operate to promote racial discrimination and exclusion; it is also an ideological and pedagogical weapon powerfully mobilized by conservatives and the Right for arguing that because of the success of the civil rights movement, racism has been eliminated as an institutional and ideological force, thus eradicating the need for government-based programs designed to dismantle the historical legacy and effects of racism in all dimensions of the social order.

Within the last twenty years, a more virulent form of the new racism has appeared that also affirms the basic principles of color-blindness; but instead of operating primarily as a discourse of denial regarding how power and politics promote racial discrimination and exclusion, neoliberal racism is about the privatization of racial discourse. It is also proactive, functioning aggressively in the public arena as an ideological and pedagogical weapon powerfully mobilized by various conservatives and right-wing groups. Neoliberal racism asserts the insignificance of race as a social force and aggressively roots out any vestige of race as a category at odds with an individualistic embrace of formal legal rights. Focusing on individuals rather than on groups, neoliberal racism either dismisses the concept of institutional racism or maintains that it has no merit. In this context, racism is primarily defined as a form of individual prejudice while appeals to equality are dismissed outright. For instance, racial ideologues Richard J. Herrnstein and Charles Murray write in *The Bell Curve:* "In everyday life, the ideology of equality censors and straitjackets everything from pedagogy to humor. The ideology of equality has stunted the range of moral dialogue to triviality.... It is time for America once again to try living with inequality, as life is lived."[32] Arguing that individual freedom is tarnished if not poisoned by the discourse of equality, right-wing legal advocacy groups such as the Center for Individual Rights (CIR) and the Foundation for Individual Rights in Education argue that identity politics and pluralism weaken rather than strengthen American democracy because they pose a threat to what it means for the United States "to remain recognizably American."[33] But such groups do more than define American culture in racist and retrograde terms; they also aggressively use their resources—generously provided by prominent right-wing conservative organizations such as the Lynde and Harry Bradley Foundation, the John M. Olin Foundation, the Adolph Coors Foundation, and the Scaife Family Foundation—to challenge racial preference policies that are not based on a "principle of state neutrality."[34] With ample resources at their disposal, advocates of neoliberal racism have successfully challenged a number of cases before the Supreme Court over the legality of affirmative action programs, campus speech codes, hiring practices, the Violence Against Women Act, and the elimination of men's sports teams in higher education.[35] Hence, neoliberal racism provides the ideological and legal framework for asserting that since American society is now a meritocracy, government should be race neutral, affirmative action programs dismantled, civil rights laws discarded, and the welfare state eliminated. As Nikhil Aziz observes, "The Right argues that, because racism has been dealt with as a result of the civil rights movement, race should not be a consideration for hiring in employment or for admission to educational institutions, and group identities other than 'American' are immaterial."[36]

Neoliberal racism is unwilling to accept any concept of the state as a guardian of the public interest. Motivated by a passion for free markets that is matched only by an anti-government fervor, neoliberal racism calls for a hollowing out of the social welfare functions of the state, except for its role in safeguarding the interests of the privileged and the strengthening of its policing functions. Rejecting a notion of the public good for private interest, advocates of neoliberal racism want to limit the state's role in public investments and social programs as a constraint on both individual rights and the expression of individual freedom. In this view, individual interests override any notion of the public good, and individual freedom operates outside any ethical responsibility for its social consequences. The results of this policy are evident in right-wing attacks on public education, health care, environmental regulations, public housing, race-based scholarships, and other public services that embrace notions of difference. Many of these programs benefit the general public, though they are relied on disproportionately by the poor and people of color. As Zsuza Ferge points out, what becomes clear about neoliberal racism is that "the attack on the big state has indeed become predominantly an attack on the welfare functions of the state.... The underlying motif is the conviction that the supreme value is economic growth to be attained by unfettered free trade equated with freedom *tout court*.... The extremely individualist approach that characterizes this ethic justifies the diagnosis of many that neoliberalism is about the 'individualization of the social.'"[37] By preventing the state from addressing or correcting the effects of racial discrimination, state agencies are silenced, thus displacing "the tensions of contemporary racially charged relations to the relative invisibility of private spheres, seemingly out of reach of public policy intervention."[38]

The relentless spirit of self-interest within neoliberal racism offers an apology for a narrow market-based notion of freedom in which individual rights and choices are removed from any viable notion of social responsibility, critical citizenship, and substantive democracy. By distancing itself from any notion of liberal egalitarianism, civic obligation, or a more positive notion of freedom, neoliberal racism does more than collapse the political into the personal—invoking character against institutional racism and individual rights against social wrongs. Indeed, it claims, as Jean and John Comaroff argue, that

> [t]he personal is the only politics there is, the only politics with a tangible referent or emotional valence. It is in these privatized terms that action is organized, that the experience of inequity and antagonism takes meaningful shape.... [Neoliberalism] is a culture that ... re-visions persons not as producers from a particular community, but as consumers in a planetary marketplace.[39]

Neoliberalism devitalizes democracy because it has no language for defending a politics in which citizenship becomes an investment in public life rather than an obligation to consume, relegated in this instance to an utterly privatized affair. The discourse of neoliberal racism has no way of talking about collective responsibility, social agency, or a defense of the public good. But the absences in its discourse are not innocent because they both ignore and perpetuate the stereotypes, structured violence, and massive inequalities produced by the racial state, the race-based attack on welfare, the destruction of social goods such as schools and health care, and the rise of the prison-industrial complex. And its attack on the principles of equality, liberty, economic democracy, and racial justice, in the final analysis, represents "a heartless indifference to the social contract, or any other civic-minded concern for the larger social good."[40] In fact, neoliberalism has played a defining role in transforming the social contract into the carceral contract, which substitutes punishment for social investment. Hence, it is not surprising how neoliberal arguments embracing the primacy of individual solutions to public issues such as poverty or the ongoing incarceration of black males are quick to defend public policies that are both punitive and overtly racist such as workfare for welfare recipients or the public shaming rituals of prison chain gangs, with an overabundance of black males always on display. Neoliberal racism's "heartless indifference" to the plight of the poor is often mirrored in an utter disdain for human suffering, as in Shelby Steele's nostalgic longing for a form of social Darwinism in which "failure and suffering are natural and necessary elements of success."[41]

It is interesting that whenever white racism is invoked by critics in response to the spectacle of racism, advocates of color-blindness and neoliberal racism often step outside the privatizing language of rights and have little trouble appropriating victim status for whites while blaming people of color for the harsh conditions under which so many have to live in this country. And in some cases, this is done in the name of a civility that is used to hide both the legacy and the reality of racism and a commitment to equality as a cornerstone of racial progress. A classic example of the latter can be found in *The End of Racism* by Dinesh D'Souza. He writes:

> Nothing strengthens racism in this country more than the behavior of the African-American underclass which flagrantly violates and scandalizes basic codes of responsibility and civility.... [I]f blacks as a group can show that they are capable of performing competitively in schools and the workforce, and exercising both the rights and responsibilities of American citizenship, then racism will be deprived of its foundation in experience.[42]

Spectacles of Race

Scripted denials of racism coupled with the spectacle of racial discourse and representations have become a common occurrence in American life. Power-evasive strategies wrapped up in the language of individual choice and the virtues of self-reliance provide the dominant modes of framing through which the larger public can witness in our media-saturated culture what Patricia Williams calls "the unsaid filled by stereotypes and self-identifying illusion, the hierarchies of race and gender circulating unchallenged," enticing audiences who prefer "familiar drama to the risk of serious democratization."[43] In what follows, I want to address the controversy surrounding the racist remarks made by Trent Lott at Strom Thurmond's centennial birthday celebration and how the Lott affair functions as an example of how controversial issues often assume the status of both a national melodrama and a scripted spectacle. I also want to analyze how this event functioned largely to privatize matters of white racism while rendering invisible the endorsement of systemic and state-fashioned racism. The Lott affair functions as a public transcript in providing a context for examining the public pedagogy of racial representations in media and print culture that are often framed within the ideology of the new racism in order to displace any serious discussion of racial exclusion in the United States. Finally, I offer some suggestions about how to respond politically to neoliberal racism and what the implications might be for a critical pedagogical practice aimed at challenging and dismantling it.

While attending Strom Thurmond's 100th birthday party on December 5, 2002, the then Senate majority leader, Trent Lott, offered the following salute to one of the most legendary segregationists alive: "I want to say this about my state: When Strom Thurmond ran for President, we voted for him. We're proud of it. And if the rest of the country had followed our lead, we wouldn't have had all these problems over all these years, either."[44]

Of course, for the historically aware, the meaning of the tribute was clear since Thurmond had run in 1948 on a racist Dixiecrat ticket whose official campaign slogan was "Segregation Forever!"

It took five days before the incident got any serious attention in the national media. But once the story broke, Lott offered an endless series of apologies that included everything from saying he was just "winging it" (until it was revealed that he made an almost identical remark as a congressman at a Reagan rally a few decades earlier), to having found "Jesus," to proclaiming he was now "an across the board" advocate of affirmative action.[45] The Lott story evoked a range of opinions in the media extending from a craven defense provided by conservative columnist Bob Novak (who argued that Lott's racist comments were just a slip of the tongue) to vociferous moral condemnation from all sides of the ideological spectrum. Once Lott's voting record on civil rights issues was made public, he became an embarrassment and liability to those politicians who denounced open racial bigotry but had little to say about structural, systemic, and institutional racism.[46] Under pressure from his Republican party colleagues, Lott eventually resigned as Senate majority leader, though he retained his Senate seat, and the story passed in the national media from revelation to spectacle to irrelevance. The shelf-life of the spectacle in the dominant culture is usually quite long—witness the Gary Condit affair—except when it offers the possibility for revealing how racist expressions privately license relations of power that reproduce a wide range of racial exclusions in the wider social order.

Lott's remarks cast him as a supporter of the old racism—bigoted, crude, and overtly racist. And, for the most part, the wrath his remarks engendered from the Republican Party and its media cheerleaders was mainly of the sort that allowed the critics to reposition themselves in keeping with the dictates of the logic of color-blindness and neoliberal racism. In doing so they distanced themselves from Lott's comments as a safe way to attest their disdain for the old racist bigotry and to provide a display of their moral superiority and civility while at the same time avoiding what Robert Kuttner has called some "inconvenient truths" when it came to talking about race. As Kuttner observes, "[Lott's] stated views made it more difficult for the Republican party to put on minstrel shows and offer speeches dripping with compassion, while appointing racist judges, battling affirmative action, resisting hate crimes legislation, and slashing social outlays that help minorities. Lott made it harder to hold down black voting in the name of 'ballot security' while courting black voters, and disguising attacks on public education as expanded 'choice' for black parents and stingy welfare reform as promoting self-sufficiency."[47] Of course, singling out Lott also suggested that he was, as an editorial in the *Wall Street Journal* claimed, a one-of-a-kind bad apple, an unfortunate holdover from the Jim Crow era that no longer exists in America. David Brooks, the editor of the conservative *National Review,* proclaimed with great indignation that Lott's views were not "normal Republican ideas" and, to prove the point, asserted that after hanging out with Republicans for two decades he had "never heard an overtly racist comment."[48]

Brooks, like many of his fellow commentators, seems to have allowed his ode to racial cleansing to cloud his sense of recent history. After all, it was only about a decade ago that Kirk Fordice, a right-wing Republican, ended his victorious campaign for governor—orchestrated largely as an attack on crime and welfare cheaters—with a "still photograph of a Black woman and her baby."[49] And of course this was just a few years after George H.W. Bush ran his famous Willie Horton ad and a short time before Dan Quayle in the 1992 presidential campaign used the racially coded category of welfare to attack a sitcom character, Murphy Brown. Maybe David Brooks was just unaware of the interview that John Ashcroft had given in 1999 to the neoconfederate magazine, *Southern Partisan,* "in which he 'vowed to do more' to defend the legacy of Jefferson Davis."[50] Or, as *New York Times* writer Frank Rich puts it in response to the apparent newfound historical amnesia about the overt racism displayed by the Republican Party in more recent times:

> Tell that to George W. Bush, who beat John McCain in the 2000 South Carolina primary after what *Newsweek* called "a smear campaign" of leaflets, e-mails and telephone calls calling attention to the McCains' "black child" (an adopted daughter from Bangladesh). Or to Sonny Perdue, the new Republican governor of Georgia, elected in part by demagoguing the sanctity of the confederate flag.[51]

One telling example of how the Trent Lott affair was removed from the historical record of racialized injustices, the realm of political contestation, and, indeed, any critical understanding of how racializing categories actually take hold in the culture can be found in the December 23, 2002, issue of *Newsweek,* which was devoted in entirety to the public uproar surrounding Lott's racist remarks.[52] *Newsweek* featured a 1962 picture of Lott on its cover with the caption "The Past That Made Him—and May Undo Him: Race and the Rise of Trent Lott." The stories that appeared in the magazine portrayed Lott either as an odd and totally out-of-touch symbol of the past ("A Man Out of Time," as one story headline read) or as an unrepentant symbol of racism that was no longer acceptable in American public life or in national politics. *Newsweek* ended its series on Lott with a short piece called "Lessons of the Trent Lott Mess."[53] The author of the article, Ellis Cose, condemned Lott's long history of racist affiliations, as did many other writers, but said nothing about why they were ignored by either the major political party or the dominant media over the last decade, especially given Lott's important standing in national politics. It is interesting to note that Lott's affiliation with the Council of Conservative Citizens (CCC)—a neoconfederate group that succeeded the notorious white Citizens Council, once referred to as the "uptown Klan"—was revealed in a 1998 story by Stanley Crouch, a writer for the *New York Daily News.* Surprisingly, the article was ignored at the time both by prominent politicians and by the dominant media. At issue here is the recognition that the history of racism in which Trent Lott participated is not merely his personal history but the country's history and, hence, should raise far more serious considerations about how the legacy of racism works through its cultural, economic, and social fabric. While Lott has to be held accountable for his remarks, his actions cannot be understood strictly within the language of American individualism—that is, as a bad reminder that the legacy of racism lives on in some old-fashioned politicians who cannot escape their past. In fact, Lott's remarks as well as the silence that allowed his racist discourse to be viewed in strictly personal and idiosyncratic terms must be addressed as symptomatic of a larger set of racist historical, social, economic, and ideological influences that still hold sway over American society. Collapsing the political into the personal, and serious reporting into talk-show clichés, Cose argues that the reason a person like Lott is serving and will continue to serve in the Senate, sharing power with America's ruling elite, is that "Americans are very forgiving folks."[54] This response is more than simply inane; it is symptomatic of a culture of racism that has no language for or interest in understanding systemic racism, its history, or how it is embodied in most ruling political and economic institutions in the United States. Or, for that matter, why it has such a powerful grip on American culture. The Trent Lott affair is important not because it charts an influential senator's fall from grace and power in the wake of an unfortunate racist remark made in public, but because it is symptomatic of a new racism that offers no resources for translating private troubles into public considerations.

The public pedagogy underlying the popular response to Trent Lott's racist remarks reveals how powerful the educational force of the culture is in shaping dominant conventions about race. Mirroring the logic of neoliberalism, the overall response to Lott both privatized the discourse of racism and attributed a racist expression to an unfortunate slip of the tongue, a psychological disposition, or the emotive residue of a man who is out of step with both his political party and the spirit of the country. But such an expression is not simply the assertion of a prejudiced individual; it is also a mode of exclusion, rooted in forms of authority largely used to name, classify, order, and devalue people of color. As David Theo Goldberg observes:

> As a mode of exclusion, racist expression assumes authority and is vested with power, literally and symbolically, in bodily terms. They are human bodies that are classified, ordered, valorized, and devalued.... When this authority assumes

> state power, racialized discourse and its modes of exclusion become embedded in state institutions and normalized in the common business of everyday institutional life.... As expressions of exclusion, racism appeals either to inherent superiority or to differences. These putative differences and gradations may be strictly physical, intellectual, linguistic, or cultural. Each serves in two ways: They purport to furnish the basis for justifying differential distributions or treatment, and they represent the very relations of power that prompted them.[55]

As part of the discourse of denial, the Trent Lott episode reveals how racism is trivialized through a politics of racial management in which racism is consigned to an outdated past, a narrow psychologism, the private realm of bad judgment or personal indiscretion. But racial discourse is not simply about private speech acts or individualized modes of communication; it is also about contested histories, institutional relations of power, ideology, and the social gravity of effects. Racist discourses and expressions should alert us to the workings of power and the conditions that make particular forms of language possible and others seemingly impossible, as well as to the modes of agency they produce and legitimate—an issue almost completely ignored in the mainstream coverage of the Lott affair. What was missing from such coverage is captured by Teun A. Van Dijk in his analysis of elite discourse and racism:

> Racism, defined as a system of racial and ethnic inequality, can survive only when it is daily reproduced through multiple acts of exclusion, inferiorization, or marginalization. Such acts need to be sustained by an ideological system and by a set of attitudes that legitimate difference and dominance. Discourse is the principal means for the construction and reproduction of this sociocognitive framework.[56]

Conclusion

Any attempt to address the politics of the new racism in the United States must begin by reclaiming the language of the social and affirming the project of an inclusive and just democracy. This suggests addressing how the politics of the new racism is made invisible under the mantle of neoliberal ideology—that is, raising questions about how neoliberalism works to hide the effects of power, politics, and racial injustice. What is both troubling and must increasingly be made problematic is that neoliberalism wraps itself in what appears to be an unassailable appeal to common sense. As Jean and John Comaroff observe:

> [T]here is a strong argument to be made that neoliberal capitalism, in its millennial moment, portends the death of politics by hiding its own ideological underpinnings in the dictates of economic efficiency: in the fetishism of the free

> market, in the inexorable, expanding "needs" of business, in the imperatives of science and technology. Or, if it does not conduce to the death of politics, it tends to reduce them to the pursuit of pure interest, individual or collective.[57]

Defined as the paragon of all social relations, neoliberalism attempts to eliminate an engaged critique about its most basic principles and social consequences by embracing the "market as the arbiter of social destiny."[58] More is lost here than neoliberalism's willingness to make its own assumptions problematic. Also lost is the very viability of politics itself. Not only does neoliberalism in this instance empty the public treasury, hollow out public services, and limit the vocabulary and imagery available to recognize anti-democratic forms of power and narrow models of individual agency, it also undermines the socially discursive translating functions of any viable democracy by undercutting the ability of individuals to engage in the continuous translation between public considerations and private interests and by collapsing the public into the realm of the private.[59] Divested of its political possibilities and social underpinnings, freedom finds few opportunities for rearticulating private worries into public concerns or individual discontent into collective struggle.[60] Hence, the first task in engaging neoliberalism is to reveal its claim to a bogus universalism and make clear how it functions as a historical and social construction. Neoliberalism hides the traces of its own ideology, politics, and history either by rhetorically asserting its triumphalism as part of the "end of history" or by proclaiming that capitalism and democracy are synonymous. What must be challenged is neoliberalism's "future-tense narrative of inevitability, demonstrating that the drama of world history remains wide open."[61]

But the history of the changing economic and ideological conditions that gave rise to neoliberalism must be understood in relation to the corresponding history of race relations in the United States and abroad. Most importantly, since the history of race is either left out or misrepresented by the official channels of power in the United States, it is crucial that the history of slavery, civil rights, racial politics, and ongoing modes of struggle at the level of everyday life be remembered and used pedagogically to challenge the historical amnesia that feeds neoliberalism's ahistorical claim to power and the continuity of its claims to common sense. The struggle against racial injustice cannot be separated from larger questions about what kind of culture and society is emerging under the imperatives of neoliberalism, what kind of history it ignores, and what alternatives might point to a substantive democratic future.

Neoliberalism requires all levels of government to be hollowed out and largely reduced either to their policing functions or to maintaining the privileges of the rich and the interests of corporate power holders—both largely white. In this discourse, the state is not only absolved of its traditional social contract of upholding the public good and providing crucial social provisions and minimal guarantees for those who are in need of such services; it also embraces a notion of color-blind racelessness. State racelessness is built on the right-wing logic of "rational racists" such as D'Souza, who argues that "[w]hat we need is a separation of race and state."[62] As Goldberg points out, this means that the state is now held

> to a standard of justice protective of individual rights and not group results.... [T]his in turn makes possible the devaluation of any individuals considered not white, or white-like, the trashing or trampling of their rights and possibilities, for the sake of preserving the right to *private* "rational discrimination" of whites.... [Thus] racist discrimination becomes privatized, and in terms of liberal legality state protected in its privacy.[63]

Defined through the ideology of racelessness, the state removes itself from either addressing or correcting the effects of racial discrimination, reducing matters of racism to individual concerns to be largely solved through private negotiations between individuals, and adopting an entirely uncritical role in the way in which the racial state shapes racial policies and their effects throughout the economic, social, and cultural landscape. Lost here is any critical engagement with state power and how it imposes immigration policies, decides who gets resources and access to a quality education, defines what constitutes a crime, how people are punished, how and whether social problems are criminalized, who is worthy of citizenship, and who is responsible for addressing racial injustices. As the late Pierre Bourdieu argued, there is a political and pedagogical need, not only to protect the social gains, embodied in state policies, that have been the outcome of important collective struggles, but also "to invent another kind of state."[64] This means challenging the political irresponsibility and moral indifference that are the organizing principles at the heart of the neoliberal vision. As Bourdieu suggests, it is necessary to restore the sense of utopian possibility rooted in the struggle for a democratic state. The racial state and its neoliberal ideology need to be challenged as part of a viable anti-racist pedagogy and politics.

Anti-racist pedagogy also needs to move beyond the conundrums of a limited identity politics and begin to include in its analysis what it would mean to imagine the state as a vehicle for democratic values and a strong proponent of social and racial justice. In part, reclaiming the democratic and public responsibility of the state would mean arguing for a state in which tax cuts for the rich, rather than social spending, are seen as the problem; using the state to protect the public good rather than waging a war on all things public; engaging and resisting the use of state power to both protect and define the public sphere as utterly white; redefining the power and role of the state so as to minimize its policing functions and strengthen its accountability to the public interests of all citizens rather than to the wealthy and corporations. Removing the state from its subordination to market values means reclaiming the importance of social needs over commercial interests and democratic politics over corporate power; it also means addressing a host of urgent social problems that include but are not limited to the escalating costs of health care, housing, the schooling crisis, the growing gap between rich and poor, the environmental crisis, the rebuilding of the nation's cities and impoverished rural areas, the economic crisis facing most of the states, and the increasing assault on people of color. The struggle over the state must be linked to a struggle for a racially just, inclusive democracy. Crucial to any viable politics of anti-racism is the role the state will play as a guardian of the public interest and as a force in creating a multiracial democracy.

Further, it is crucial for any anti-racist pedagogy and politics to recognize that power does not just inhabit the realm of economics or state power, but is also intellectual, residing in the educational force of the culture and its enormous powers of persuasion. This means that any viable anti-racist pedagogy must make the political more pedagogical by recognizing how public pedagogy works to determine and secure the ways that racial identity, issues, and relations are produced in a wide variety of sites including schools, cable and television networks, newspapers and magazines, the Internet, advertising, churches, trade unions, and a host of other public spheres in which ideas are produced and distributed. This, in turn, means becoming mindful of how racial meanings and practices are created, mediated, reproduced, and challenged through a wide variety of "discourses, institutions, audiences, markets, and constituencies which help determine the forms and meaning of publicness in American society."[65] The crucial role that pedagogy plays in shaping racial issues reaffirms the centrality of a cultural politics that recognizes the relationship between issues of representation and the operations of power, the important role that intellectuals might play as engaged, public intellectuals, and the importance of critical knowledge in challenging neoliberalism's illusion of unanimity. But an anti-racist cultural pedagogy also suggests the need to develop a language of both critique and possibility and to wage individual and collective struggles in a wide variety of dominant public spheres and alternative counter-publics. Public pedagogy as a tool of anti-racist struggles understands racial politics, not only as a signifying activity through which subject positions are produced, identities inhabited, and desires mobilized, but also as the mobilization of material relations of power as a way of securing, enforcing, and challenging racial injustices. While cultural politics offers an opportunity to understand how race matters and racist practices take hold in everyday life, such a pedagogical and cultural politics must avoid collapsing into a romanticization of the symbolic, popular, or discursive. Culture matters as a rhetorical tool and mode of persuasion, especially in the realm of visual culture, which has to be taken seriously as a pedagogical force, but changing consciousness is only a precondition to changing society and should not be confused with what it means to actually transform institutional relations of power. In part, this means contesting the control of the media by a handful of transnational corporations.[66] The social gravity of racism as it works through the modalities of everyday language, relations, and cultural expressions has to be taken seriously in any anti-racist politics, but such a concern and mode of theorizing must also be accompanied by an equally serious interest in the rise of corporate power and "the role of state institutions and agencies in shaping contemporary forms of racial subjugation and inequality."[67] Racist ideologies, practices, state formations, and institutional relations can be exposed pedagogically and linguistically, but they cannot be resolved merely in the realm of the discursive. Hence, any viable anti-racist pedagogy needs to draw attention to the distinction between critique and social transformation, to critical modes of analysis, on the one hand, and to the responsibility of acting individually and collectively on one's beliefs on the other.

Another important consideration that has to be included in any notion of anti-racist pedagogy and politics is the issue of connecting matters of racial justice to broader and more comprehensive political, cultural, and social agendas. Neoliberalism exerts a powerful force in American life because its influence and power are spread across a diverse range of political, economic, social, and cultural spheres. Its ubiquity is matched by its aggressive pedagogical attempts to reshape the totality of social life in the image of the market, reaching into and connecting a wide range of seemingly disparate factors that bear down on everyday life in the United States. Neoliberalism is persuasive because its language of commercialism, consumerism, privatization, freedom, and self-interest resonates with and saturates so many aspects of public life. Differences in this discourse are removed from matters of equity and power and reduced to market niches. Agency is privatized and social values are reduced to market-based interests. And, of course, a democracy of citizens is replaced by a democracy of consumers. Progressives, citizens, and other groups who are concerned about matters of race and difference need to maintain their concerns with particular forms of oppression and subordination; yet, at the same time, the limits of various approaches to identity politics must be recognized so as not to allow them to become either fixed or incapable of making alliances with other social movements as part of a broader struggle over not just particular freedoms but also the more generalized freedoms associated with an inclusive and radical democracy.

I have not attempted to be exhaustive in suggesting what it might mean to recognize and challenge the new racism that now reproduces more subtle forms of racial subordination, oppression, and exclusion, though I have tried to point to some pedagogical and political concerns that connect racism and neoliberal politics. The color line in America is neither fixed nor static. Racism as an expression of power and exclusion takes many meanings and forms under different historical conditions. The emphasis on its socially and historically constructed nature offers hope because it suggests that what can be produced by dominant relations of power can also be challenged and transformed by those who imagine a more utopian and just world. The challenge of the color line is still with us today and needs to be recognized not only as a shameful example of racial injustice but also as a reprehensible attack on the very nature of democracy itself.

3
Disabling the Future: Youth in the Age of Market Fundamentalism

The promise of democracy in the United States appears to be receding as the dark clouds of authoritarianism increasingly spread through every facet of the state and civil society. Under such circumstances, war and violence have become the most prominent organizing principles of American life, evident not only in the ongoing and ill-fated wars in Iraq and Afghanistan but also in the assault being waged at home on democratic values, social provisions, and, increasingly, on all of those populations considered either unpatriotic because they do not conform to the dictates of an imperial presidency or disposable because they have been relegated to the human waste of global neoliberalism. The war at home has given rise not only to a crushing attack on civil liberties—most evident in the passing of the Military Commissions Act of 2006, which conveniently allows the Bush administration to detain indefinitely anyone deemed an enemy combatant while denying him or her recourse to the traditional right to challenge that detention through legal means—but also to an assault on those populations now considered disposable and redundant under the logic of a ruthless market fundamentalism. Disposable populations are relegated to the frontier zones of relative invisibility, removed from public view. They are warehoused in schools that resemble boot camps, dispersed to dank and dangerous workplaces far from the enclaves of the tourist industries, incarcerated in prisons that privilege punishment over rehabilitation, and consigned to the increasing army of the permanently unemployed. Rendered redundant as a result of the collapse of the social state, pervasive racism, a growing disparity in income and wealth, and a take-no-prisoners neoliberalism, increasing numbers of individuals and groups are being demonized and criminalized either by virtue of their status as immigrants or because they are young, poor, unemployed, disabled, or confined to low-paying jobs.[1] This is particularly true for young people, who are increasingly portrayed as a generation of suspects.

Youth have come to be seen as a problem rather than as a resource for investing in the future. They are now treated as a disposable population, defined either as cannon fodder for a barbaric war in Iraq and Afghanistan or as the source of most of society's problems. The "war" on working-class youth and young people of color is evident not only in the disproportionate numbers of such individuals who enlist to fight in the wars abroad but also in the silent war at home, in the cuts being made to domestic funding for health care, children's education, and other public services in order to finance Bush's war against terrorism, and, more boldly, in the militarization of schools through the addition of armed guards, barbed-wire security fences, and "lock-down" drills. According to Bernadine Dohrn, educators now turn over their responsibility for school safety to the new security culture, and minor infractions once handled by teachers are now handled by the police.

> A major consequence of the tidal wave of fear, violence, and terror associated with children has been adult legislative and policy decisions to criminalize vast sectors of youth behavior.... Schools have become military fortresses. Hanging out becomes illegal. Fewer systems want to work with adolescents in need. Youngsters who have themselves been neglected or abused by adults pose too many challenges and have too many problems to be addressed. Health care and mental health services are rarely organized for adolescents. Schools want to get rid of the troublemakers and the kids who bring down the test scores. Minor offenses are no longer dealt with by retail stores, school disciplinarians, parents, or youth workers, but rather the police are called, arrests are made, petitions are filed.[2]

Young people are now treated like inmates or prisoners of war, stripped of their rights and subject to indignities that historically were reserved for war zones. Domestic militarization functions to contain "minority populations," to deprive them of their elector rights (13 percent of all black men in the United States have lost their right to vote),[3] and to provide new sources of revenue for a system that "evokes the convict leasing system of the Old South."[4] It also actively promotes and legitimates retrograde and repressive social policies. For example, an increasing number of states, including California and New York, are now spending more on prison construction than on higher education.[5] In addition, School Resource Officers—armed and unarmed enforcement officials who implement safety and security measures in schools—are one of the fastest-growing segments of law enforcement in the United States.[6]

Zero-tolerance policies have been especially cruel in expanding the criminalization of youth behavior.[7] Rather than attempting to work with youth, listen to them, and make an investment in their psychological, economic, and social well-being, a growing number of cities are passing sweep laws—curfews and bans against loitering and cruising—designed not only to keep youth off the streets but also to make it easier to criminalize their behavior. For example, within the last decade "45 states ... have passed or amended legislation making it easier to prosecute juveniles as adults," and in some states "prosecutors can bump a juvenile case into adult court at their own discretion."[8] In Kansas and Vermont, a 10-year-old child can be tried in adult court. A particularly harsh example of the draconian measures being used against young people can be seen in the passing of Proposition 21 in California. This law makes it easier for prosecutors to try teens 14 and older in adult court if they are accused of felonies. These youth would automatically be put in adult prison and be given lengthy mandated sentences. The overall goal of the law is to largely eliminate intervention programs, increase the number of youth in prisons, especially minority youth, and keep them there for longer periods of time. Moreover, the law is at odds with a number of studies indicating that putting youth in jail with adults both increases recidivism and poses a grave danger to young offenders who, as a Columbia University study suggests, are "five times as likely to be raped, twice as likely to be beaten and eight times as likely to commit suicide than adults in the adult prison system."[9]

Paradoxically, the moral panic against crime and now terrorism that increasingly feeds the calls for punishment and revenge rather than rehabilitation programs for young people exists in conjunction with the disturbing fact that the United States is one of only seven countries in the world that permits the death penalty for juveniles.[10] In many states, youth cannot join the military, get their ears pierced, or get a marriage license until they are 18, but youth as young as 10 years old can be jailed as adults and condemned to death in some states. The prize-winning novelist Ann Patchett suggested in the *New York Times* that perhaps the problem is that "as Americans, we no longer have any idea what constitutes a child."[11] This strikes me as dubious. The ongoing attacks on children's rights, the endless commercialization of youth, the downsizing of children's services, and the increasing incarceration of young people suggest more than confusion. In actuality, such policies suggest that, at best, adult society no longer cares about children and, at worst, views them as objects of scorn and fear.

It would be a tragic mistake for those of us concerned about democracy either to separate the war in Iraq from the many problems Americans (especially young people) face at home or to fail to recognize how war is being waged by a reactionary government on multiple fronts. Alongside the criminalization of youth, we see the criminal erosion of educational care for the young. Instead of providing a decent critical education to young people from poverty-stricken homes, President Bush and his cohorts serve them more standardized tests, enforce abstinence programs instead of scientifically informed sex education, and advocate creationism updated as Intelligent Design instead of scientific reason.[12] Youth who are poor and racially marginalized fare even worse, often finding themselves in classes that are overcrowded and lacking in basic resources; they are also subject to policies designed to warehouse young people rather than to educate them or provide even basic literacy skills. Instead of offering young people vibrant public spheres and the skills to make use of them, the Bush government gives them a commercialized culture in which consumerism is the only condition of citizenship.

Critical thought and social justice seem to be in retreat as everybody is now a customer or client, and every relationship is judged against the bottom line. Hence, the ever-proliferating consumer and entrepreneurial subject replaces the concept of the responsible citizen, as the former complies with the neoliberal mantra "privatize or perish." Amid a proliferating social Darwinism—emulated daily on Reality TV programs—tribulation is viewed as a weakness and self-reliance is the ultimate virtue, which is another way of saying that people must face on their own, and alone, the increasingly difficult challenges of the social order. In short, private interests trump social needs; profit-gauging has become more important than social justice; and the increasing militarization and commercialization of public space now define what counts as the public sphere. The consequences for politics and public life are devastatingly obvious in the growing gap between the rich and the poor, in the downward spiral of over 37 million Americans into poverty and despair,[13] and in the utter trivialization of democracy itself. One register of the growing racism, inequality, and poverty in America can be found in the haunting images of New Orleans following Hurricane Katrina—of dead bodies floating in flooded streets, and of thousands of African Americans marooned on highways, abandoned in the Louisiana Superdome, and waiting for days to be rescued from the rooftops of flooded houses. Another register is on display in the reported annual earnings of the top twenty-five hedge fund managers, whose combined income averaged $14 billion."[14] Less fortunate CEOs of big companies had to settle for annual salaries ranging from $118 million a year to the paltry $1.35 million that CEO Amin Khoury was paid by BE Aerospace.[15] The dominant media, largely in the hands of a few corporations, have become cheerleaders for those in power and now communicate through a language that requires no effort to understand, erasing, as a consequence, everything that matters in a substantive democracy. In the winner-take-all society, inequality and private power rather than justice and equality shape the larger social order.

All of these issues raise the fundamental question of what it might mean to take youth seriously as a political and moral referent in order not only to gauge the health of a democratic society but also to identify the obligations of adults to future generations of young people. For over a century, Americans have embraced as a defining feature of politics the idea that all levels of government would assume a large measure of responsibility for providing the resources, social provisions, and modes of education that enable young people to prepare in the present for a better future, while expanding the meaning and depth of an inclusive democracy. This was particularly true under the set of policies inaugurated in the 1960s by President Lyndon Johnson's Great Society programs, which were designed to eliminate both poverty and racial injustice. Taking the social contract seriously, American society exhibited at least a willingness to fight for the rights of children, enact reforms that invested in their future, and provide the educational conditions necessary for them to be critical citizens. Within such a modernist project, democracy was linked to the well-being of youth, while the status of how a society imagined democracy and its future was contingent on how it viewed its responsibility toward future generations. That project was reversed in the new American reality under the second Bush administration. Instead of a federal budget that addressed the needs of children, the United States enacted federal policies that weakened government social programs, provided tax cuts for millionaires, and undercut or eliminated basic social provisions for children at risk. As *New York Times* op-ed columnist Paul Krugman points out, compassion and responsibility under the Bush administration gave way to "a relentless mean-spiritedness" and revealed "President Bush as someone who takes food from the mouths of babes and gives the proceeds to his millionaire friends." For Krugman, Bush's budgets have come to resemble a form of "top-down class warfare."[16]

Wars are almost always legitimated in terms of making the world safe for "our children's future," but the rhetoric belies how their future is often denied by the acts of aggression put into place by a range of state agencies and institutions that operate on a war footing. This would include the horrible effects of the militarization of schools, the use of the criminal justice system to redefine social issues such as poverty and homelessness as criminal violations, and the subsequent rise of the prison-industrial complex as a way to contain disposable populations such as youth of color who are poor and marginalized. Under the rubric of war, security, and anti-terrorism, children are "disappeared" from the most basic social spheres that once provided the conditions for a sense of agency and possibility, just as they are rhetorically excised from any discourse about the future. On the larger global stage, children are being forced into adult roles, "whether as soldiers or prostitutes or prisoners or heads of families; worse, many of these children are stateless."[17] Not only are such children deprived of a decent and nurturing childhood, they are stripped of a future that would guarantee them their place as engaged citizens. What is so troubling about the current historical moment is that youth no longer symbolize the future. And yet, any discourse about the future has to begin with the issue of youth because, more than any other group, they embody the projected dreams, desires, and commitment of a society's obligations to the future. This echoes a classical principle of modern democracy in which youth both symbolized society's responsibility to the future and offered a measure of its progress. In many respects, youth not only registered symbolically the importance of modernity's claim to progress; they also affirmed the centrality of the liberal, democratic tradition of the social contract in which adult responsibility was manifest in providing the educational conditions necessary for youth to make use of the freedoms they possessed.

For previous generations, the category of youth did even more than affirm that modernity's social contract was rooted in a conception of the future in which adult commitment was articulated as a vital public service; it also affirmed those vocabularies, values, and social relations that were central to a politics capable of defending vital institutions as a public good and nurturing a flourishing democracy. At stake here was the recognition that children constitute a powerful referent for addressing war, poverty, education, and a host of other important social issues. Moreover, as a symbol of the future, children provided an important moral compass to assess what Jacques Derrida called the promises of a "democracy to come."[18] A vocabulary that focused on children's current and future social importance was particularly central to public and higher education, which often defined and addressed its highest ideals through the recognition that how it educated youth was connected to the democratic future it hoped for and its claim as an important public sphere.

But just as education has now been separated from a viable model of democratic politics, youth have been separated both from the discourse of the social contract and from any ethical commitment to provide young people, through the public sphere, with the prospect of a decent and democratic future. Punishment and fear have replaced compassion and social responsibility as the most important modalities mediating the relationship of youth to the larger social order. As Lawrence Grossberg points out, "It has become common to think of kids as a threat to the existing social order and for kids to be blamed for the problems they experience. We slide from kids in trouble, kids have problems, and kids are threatened, to kids as trouble, kids as problems, and kids as threatening."[19] This was exemplified recently when the columnist Bob Herbert reported in the *New York Times* that "parts of New York City are like a police state for young men, women and children who happen to be black or Hispanic. They are routinely stopped, searched, harassed, intimidated, humiliated and, in many cases, arrested for no good reason."[20] No longer "viewed as a privileged sign and embodiment of the future,"[21] youth are now increasingly demonized by the popular media and derided by politicians looking for quick-fix solutions to crime and other social ills. While youth, particularly those of color, are increasingly associated in the media and by dominant politicians with a rising crime wave, what is really at stake in this discourse is a punishment wave, one that reveals a society that does not know how to address those social problems that undercut any viable sense of agency, possibility, and future for many young people. For example, John J. Dilulio, Jr., a former Bush adviser, argued in an influential article published in the conservative *Weekly Standard* that society faced a dire threat from an emerging generation of youth between the ages of 15 and 24, whom he aptly called "super-predators."[22]

Hollywood movies such as *Thirteen, Kids, Brick, Hard Candy,* and *Alpha Dog* consistently represent youth as either dangerous, utterly brainless, or simply without merit. A 2006 episode about youth on *60 Minutes* was suggestive of this kind of demonization. Highlighting the ways in which young people alleviated their alleged boredom, the show focused on the sport of "bum hunting," in which young people search out, attack, and savagely beat homeless people while videotaping the event in homage to the triumph of Reality TV. As reprehensible as this act is, it is also reprehensible to vilify young people by suggesting that such behavior is in some way characteristic of youth in general. Then again, in a society where the marketplace's limited imagination sees youth only as consumers, objects, or billboards to sell sexuality, beauty products, music, athletic gear, clothes, and a host of other products, it is not surprising that young people can be so easily misrepresented.

At the dawn of the new millennium, it is not at all clear that we believe any longer in youth, the future, or the social contract, even in its minimalist version. Since the Reagan/Thatcher revolution of the 1980s, we have been told that there is no such thing as society—and, indeed, following that nefarious pronouncement, institutions committed to public welfare have been disappearing ever since. Rather than being cherished as a symbol of the future, youth are now seen as a threat to be feared and a problem to be contained. A seismic change has taken place in which youth are now being framed as a threat to public life. If youth once symbolized the moral necessity to address a range of social and economic ills, they are now largely portrayed as the source of most of society's problems. Hence, youth now constitute a crisis that has less to do with improving the future than with denying it. A concern for children is the defining absence in most dominant discourses about the future and the obligations this implies for adult society. To witness the abdication of adult responsibility to children we need look no further than the current state of public schools in America.

Schooling and the Politics of Punishment

> Ironically, children are unsafe in public schools today not because of exposure to drugs and violence, but because they have lost their constitutional protections under the Fourth Amendment.[23]
>
> [A] veritable Kindergulag has been erected around schoolchildren, making them subject to arbitrary curfews, physical searches, arbitrarily applied profiling schemes, and … random, suspicionless, warrantless drug testing.… If you're a kid in the U.S. today, martial law isn't a civics class lecture unit. It is a fact of life as the war on drugs, the war on violence and a nearly hysterical emphasis on safety [have] come to excuse the infliction of every kind of humiliation upon the young.[24]

The criminalization of adolescent behavior and the "dangerousation" of the young now justify responses to youth that were unthinkable twenty years ago, including prosecution and imprisonment, the prescription of psychotropic drugs, psychiatric confinement, and zero-tolerance policies that turn schools into "learning prisons."[25] School has become a model for a punishing society in which children who violate a rule as minor as a dress-code infraction or slightly act out in class can be handcuffed, booked, and put in a jail cell. As noted in Chapter 1, such was the case recently in Florida when the police handcuffed and arrested 6-year-old Desrée Watson, who was then taken from her kindergarten school to the Highlander County jail where she was fingerprinted, photographed for a mug shot, and charged with a felony and two misdemeanors. Her crime? The 6-year-old had thrown a tantrum in her kindergarten class.[26] Couple this type of domestic terrorism with the fact that the United States is one of only five countries that locks up child offenders for life. In fact, compared to only a handful of cases in the other countries, there are 2,225 child offenders in the United States who will spend the rest of their lives incarcerated.[27] Another instance of how youth are on the receiving end of the punishing society can be found in the Bush administration's No Child Left Behind policy, which provides financial incentives to schools that implement zero-tolerance policies, in spite of their proven racial and class biases. In addition, drug-sniffing dogs, metal detectors, and cameras have become common features in schools, and administrators willingly comply with federal laws that give military recruiters the right to access the names, addresses, and telephone numbers of students in both public schools and institutions of higher education—even though there have been numerous cases of rape and sexual abuse by recruiters who used their power to commit criminal acts against young people. Trust and respect now give way to fear, disdain, and suspicion, creating an environment in which critical pedagogical practices wither while pedagogies of surveillance and testing flourish.[28] Moreover, fear and disdain are increasingly being translated into social policies that signal the shrinking of the democratic public sphere, the hijacking of civic culture, the increasing militarization of public space, and the shredding of students' Fourth Amendment rights. In Toledo, Ohio, a 14-year-old student who refused to put a bowling shirt over her low-cut midriff top was handcuffed, put in a police car, and placed in the "detention center at the Lucas County juvenile courthouse. She was booked on a misdemeanor charge and placed in a holding cell for several hours, until her mother, a 34-year-old vending machine technician, got off work and picked her up."[29] And in another scenario that appears hard to believe, "an 8-year-old boy in a special-education class [in an elementary school in Pennsylvania] was charged with disorderly conduct this fall for his behavior in a time-out room: urinating on the floor, throwing his shoes at the ceiling and telling a teacher, 'Kids rule.'"[30] Schools increasingly are resorting to the juvenile justice system to handle behavior problems that in the past would have been handled by school officials.

What are we to make of a school policy that allows the arrest of "two middle-school boys whose crime was turning off the lights in the girls' bathroom" or puts zero-tolerance policies in place that allow an 11-year-old girl to be arrested, handcuffed, and put in the back of a police cruiser "for hiding out in the school and not going to class"?[31] Not only do children's services suffer under such a policy, but increasingly children's rights are being trampled and fewer institutions are willing to protect these rights. Consequently, their voices are almost completely absent from the debates, policies, and legislative practices that are developed in order to meet their needs.

Emulating state and federal laws passed in the 1990s that were based on mandatory sentencing policies (e.g., the federal Gun-Free Schools Act of 1994), many educators first invoked zero-tolerance rules against those kids who brought guns to schools. Under this law, any school receiving federal funds for education has to impose a one-year mandatory expulsion on any public school student who brings to school a firearm, such as a gun, bomb, grenade, missile, or rocket. Schools have broadened the policy, which now includes a gamut of student misbehavior ranging from using or circulating drugs, cigarette smoking, and sexual harassment to *threatening* other students—all broadly conceived. Under zero-tolerance policies, forms of punishment that were once applied to adults now apply to first-graders. Originally aimed at "students who misbehave intentionally, the law now applies to those who misbehave as a result of emotional problems or other disabilities" as well.[32] Across the nation, school districts are lining up to embrace zero-tolerance policies. The turning point came after the Columbine High School shootings in Littleton, Colorado, in 1999, when zero-tolerance policies increased rapidly in public schools across the United States. According to the U.S. Department of Education, about 90 percent of school systems nationwide have implemented such policies in order to deal with either violence or threats.[33] In the post-Columbine era, a manufactured culture of fear cultivates a view of educational reform in which students appear to be a threat to public safety and schools increasingly begin to resemble minimum-security prisons. As Tyson Lewis argues,

> Columbine has become a watershed event in the history of school security, further intensifying the connections between penitentiaries and schools. In the aftermath of the school shooting, districts across the country began to implement a plethora of new surveillance measures, including the use of cameras in halls and night-vision cameras in parking lots, bomb-sniffing dogs, random locker checks, armed police guards, crime analysts, metal detectors, transparent backpacks, and computerized student ID cards. Fifteen to thirty percent of post-Columbine high schools now have metal detectors, and there are security cameras in half of primary and secondary schools. It's an understatement to argue that schools now represent a subsector of the larger prison-industrial complex.[34]

Unfortunately, any sense of perspective or guarantee of rights seems lost, as school systems across the country clamor for metal detectors, armed guards, high-tech surveillance systems, see-through knapsacks, and, in some cases, armed teachers. Indeed, in the aftermath of the Virginia Tech murders in April 2007, many legislators are calling for laws that would allow teachers to carry guns. Not surprisingly, some school systems are also investing in new software in order to "profile" students who might exhibit criminal behavior.[35] Overzealous laws relieve educators of exercising deliberation and critical judgment as more and more young people are either suspended or expelled from school, often for ludicrous reasons. For example, in October 2003 in Lee County, Florida, as reported in *USA Today*, a "boy was kicked out of school for a doodle that showed one stick figure shooting another. And in September, a Montgomery County, Texas, teen was suspended and arrested for violating his school's drug policy by loaning his inhaler to a classmate who was having a severe asthmatic attack."[36] Virginia fifth-graders who allegedly put soap in their teacher's drinking water were charged with a felony.[37] A 12-year-old boy in Louisiana who was diagnosed with a hyperactive disorder was suspended for two days after telling his friends in a food line "I'm gonna get you" if they ate all the potatoes! The police then charged the boy with making "terroristic threats," and he was incarcerated for two weeks while awaiting trial. A 14-year-old disabled student in Palm Beach, Florida, was referred to the police by the school principal for allegedly stealing two dollars from another student. He was then charged with strong-armed robbery and held for six weeks in an adult jail, even though it was his first arrest.[38] There is the absurd case of five students in Mississippi being suspended and criminally charged for throwing peanuts at each other on a school bus.[39] There is also the equally revealing example of a student brought up on a drug charge because he gave another youth two lemon cough drops.

Zero tolerance does more than offer a simple solution to a complex problem; it has become a code word for a "quick and dirty way of kicking kids out" of school rather than creating safe environments for them.[40] Instead of creating a culture of caring and compassion mediated by deliberation and critical judgment, school officials who rely upon zero-tolerance laws are reduced to adjuncts of the local police department, responsible for largely apprehending, punishing, and turning students over to the police. As child advocate Steven Drizin asserts, zero-tolerance policies largely "rob school principals and educators of the discretion to take into account the individual circumstances of each case in deciding how to appropriately sanction school misconduct."[41] Rather than trying to figure out what causes student misbehavior, educators now simply punish students who violate the rules, and often with unjust consequences. For example, the *Denver Rocky Mountain News* reported in June 1999 that "partly as a result of such rigor in enforcing Colorado's zero-tolerance law, the number of kids kicked out of public schools has skyrocketed since 1993—from 437 before the law to nearly 2,000 in the 1996–1997 school year."[42] In Chicago, the widespread adoption of zero-tolerance policies in 1994 resulted in a 51 percent increase in student suspensions for the next four years, and a 3,000 percent increase in expulsions, jumping "from 21 in 1994–'95 to 668" the following year.[43] In Connecticut, students are being pushed out of schools like never before. For example, "[t]he number of suspensions jumped about 90 percent from 1998–1999 to 2000–2001. In the 2000–2001 school year, 90,559 children were suspended from schools around the state, up from 57,626 two years earlier."[44] Annette Fuentes claims that "every year, more than 3 million students ... are suspended and nearly 100,000 more are expelled, from kindergarten through twelfth."[45] At the same time, there is a growing body of evidence to suggest that zero-tolerance policies simply exacerbate the very problems they are attempting to address. For instance, Harvard University's Civil Rights Project has reported that states with "higher rates of suspension also have higher school-dropout and juvenile-crime rates."[46] Within such a climate of disdain and intolerance, expelling students does more than pose a threat to innocent kids; it also suggests that local school boards are refusing to do the hard work of exercising critical judgment, trying to understand what conditions undermine school safety, and providing reasonable support services for all students as well as viable alternatives for the troubled ones. Moreover, it is hard to understand how any school board can justify suspending or expelling kindergarten children. As Shelley Geballe, co-president of Connecticut Voices for Children, argues:

> It is inexcusable to expel a kindergarten child. The goal of a kindergarten program should be to provide the skills of not only academics but behavior. Zero tolerance that results in pushing out kids is wrongheaded, and I get concerned particularly now that we have a reduction in access to mental-health services, we have teachers who may not be well trained in understanding the emotional and developmental needs of young kids, and you have the No Child Left Behind pressures that provide further incentives to push kids out to get those standardized test scores up.[47]

As Geballe points out, as a consequence of the No Child Left Behind program implemented by the Bush administration, with its investment in high-stakes testing, schools now have an incentive either to push underachieving students out or to do nothing to prevent them from leaving school. Raising test scores is now the major goal of educational reformers, and it puts a huge amount of pressure on principals who are expected to reach district goals. Such pressure played an important role in the Houston School System, which, though held up as a model by President George W. Bush, not only did nothing to prevent students from leaving school but also falsified dropout data in order for principals to get financial bonuses and meet district demands. Tamar Lewin and Jennifer Medina reported in the *New York Times* that large numbers of students who are struggling academically are being pushed out of New York City schools in order not to "tarnish the schools' statistics by failing to graduate on time."[48] As the criminalization of young people has entered into the classroom, it becomes easier for school administrators to punish students rather than to listen to them or, for that matter, to work with parents, community programs, religious organizations, and social service agencies.[49] Even though zero-tolerance policies clog up the courts and put additional pressure on an already overburdened juvenile justice system, educators appear to have few qualms about implementing them. And the results are far from inconsequential for the students themselves.

Most insidiously, zero-tolerance laws, while a threat to all youth and any viable notion of equal opportunity through education, reinforce in the public imagination the image of students of color as a source of public fear and a threat to public-school safety. Zero-tolerance policies and laws appear to be well-tailored for mobilizing racialized codes and race-based moral panics that portray black and brown urban youth as a frightening and violent threat to the safety of "decent" Americans. Not only do most of the high-profile zero-tolerance cases involve African American students, but such policies also reinforce the racial inequities that plague school systems across the country. For example, the *New York Times* has reported on a number of studies illustrating that "black students in public schools across the country are far more likely than whites to be suspended or expelled, and far less likely to be in gifted or advanced placement classes."[50] Even in a city such as San

Francisco, considered a bastion of liberalism, African American students pay a far greater price for zero-tolerance policies. As Libero Della Piana points out, "According to data collected by Justice Matters, a San Francisco agency advocating equity in education, African Americans make up 52 percent of all suspended students in the district—far in excess of the 16 percent of [African American youth in] the general population."[51] Marilyn Elias reported in an issue of *USA Today* that "[i]n 1998, the first year national expulsion figures were gathered, 31 percent of kids expelled were black, but blacks made up only 17 percent of the students in public schools."[52] And a more recent study by the U.S. Department of Education covering the 2000–2001 school year showed that zero-tolerance laws bear down more drastically on black youth, with one in eight blacks being suspended compared to only one in fifteen white youth.[53]

Feeding on moral panic and popular fear, zero-tolerance policies not only turn schools into an adjunct of the criminal justice system, they also further rationalize misplaced legislative priorities and provide profits for the security industries. And that has profound social costs. Instead of investing in early-childhood programs, repairing deteriorating school buildings, or hiring more qualified teachers, schools now spend millions of dollars to upgrade security, even when such a fortress mentality defies the simplest test of common sense. In Tewksbury Memorial High School, Massachusetts, the new security camera system feeds into the local police station and can cost up to $300,000. It gets worse. In the Cleveland Municipal School District, the cost for the safety and security budget increased after Columbine from $12.5 million to $21.3 million.[54] The culture of fear and surveillance has produced big costs for public schools and equally big profits for corporations. More metal detectors are now produced for schools than for airports and prisons. And all sorts of electronic equipment and products, including security cameras, student ID cards, and see-through backpacks, mean big profits for the security industry.

Young people are quickly realizing that schools have more in common with military boot camps and prisons than with other institutions in American society. In addition, as schools abandon their role as democratic public spheres and are literally "fenced off" from the communities that surround them, they lose their ability to become anything other than spaces of containment and control. In this context, discipline and training replace education for all but the privileged as schools increasingly take on an uncanny resemblance to oversized police precincts, tragically disconnected both from the students who inhabit them and from the communities that give meaning to their historical experiences and daily lives. As schools become militarized, they also lose their ability to provide students with the skills to cope with human differences, uncertainty, and the various symbolic and institutional forces that undermine political agency and democratic public life itself.

I want to conclude this section by reasserting that the growth and popularity of zero-tolerance policies within the public schools have to be understood as part of a broader crisis of democracy in which the market is now seen as the master design for all pedagogical encounters and the state is increasingly geared toward measures of militarization, containment, and surveillance rather than toward expansion of democratic freedoms and social investments. In this sense, the corporatizing of public schooling and the war against youth cannot be disassociated from the assault on those public spheres and public goods that provide the conditions for greater democratic participation in shaping society. Questions of safety mobilized largely by a culture of fear and legitimated through the ongoing demonization of young people in the wider society have transformed schools into what sociologist Loic Wacquant has called an extension of "a single carceral continuum" that operates through the registers of surveillance, control, punishment, and exclusion.[55] In this context, zero-tolerance legislation within the schools simply extends to young people the elements of harsh control and administration implemented in other public spheres where inequalities breed dissent and resistance.

Zero tolerance has become a metaphor for hollowing out the state and expanding the forces of domestic militarization, reducing democracy to consumerism, and replacing the ethic of mutual aid with an appeal to excessive individualism and social indifference.[56] According to such logic, the notion of the political increasingly equates power with domination and citizenship with consumerism and passivity. Under this insufferable climate of manufactured indifference, increased repression, unabated exploitation, and a war on Iraq that Senator Robert Byrd believes is rooted in the arrogance of unbridled power, young people have become the new casualties in an ongoing battle against justice, freedom, social citizenship, and democracy. Yet, as despairing as these conditions appear at the present moment, they increasingly have become the basis for a surge of political resistance on the part of many youth, intellectuals, labor unions, educators, and social movements.[57] Educators, young people, parents, religious organizations, community activists, and other cultural workers need to rethink what it would mean to both interrogate and break away from the dangerous and destructive ideologies, values, and social relations of zero-tolerance policies as they work in a vast and related number of powerful institutional spheres to reinforce modes of authoritarian control that are increasingly spreading through American society.

Disposable Youth and the Crisis of the Social

The organization of schools around safety and punishment suggests a dangerous imbalance between democratic values and the culture of fear.

Instead of security, zero-tolerance policies in the schools contribute to a growing climate of bigotry, hypocrisy, and intolerance that turns a generation of youth into criminal suspects. This particularly loathsome turn in "school reform" to penalizing children rather than attempting to listen to them and help them with their problems resonates with a change in the larger culture toward the ongoing criminalization of social problems. When the "War on Poverty" ran out of steam with the social and economic crisis that emerged in the 1970s, there was a growing shift at all levels of government from an emphasis on social investments to an emphasis on public control and social containment. The criminalization of social issues—starting with President Ronald Reagan's war on drugs[58] and the privatization of the prison industry in the 1980s, escalating to the war on immigrants in the early 1990s and the rise of the prison-industrial complex by the close of the decade—has now become part of everyday culture and provides a common reference point that extends from governing prisons and regulating urban culture to running schools. This is most evident in the emergence of zero-tolerance laws that have swept the nation since the 1980s and gained full legislative strength with the passage of the Violent Crime Control and Law Enforcement Act of 1994. Following the mandatory sentencing legislation and "get tough" policies associated with the war on drugs, this bill called for a "three strikes and you're out" policy that put repeat offenders, including nonviolent offenders, in jail for life, regardless of the seriousness of the crime. As I mentioned in Chapter 1, the United States is now the biggest jailer in the world, with more than 2.2 million people behind bars.

In spite of what we are told by the current Bush administration, conservative educators, the religious Right, and the cheerleaders of corporate culture, the greatest threat to education in this country does not come from disruptive students or the absence of lock-down safety measures and get-tough school policies. Nor are young people threatened by the alleged decline of academic standards, the absence of privatized choice schemes, or the lack of rigid testing measures. On the contrary, the greatest threat to young people comes from a society that refuses to view them as a social investment and that consigns approximately 13 million children to live in poverty, while also reducing critical learning to massive testing programs, refusing to pay teachers an adequate salary, promoting policies that eliminate most crucial health and public services, and defining masculinity through the degrading celebration of a gun culture, extreme sports, and the spectacles of violence that permeate corporate-controlled media industries. It also comes from a society that values a hollow notion of security more than basic rights, wages an assault on all nonmarket values and public goods, and engages in a ruthless transfer of wealth from the poor and middle class to the rich and privileged.

Instead of providing a decent education to poor young people, American society offers them the growing potential of being incarcerated. According to Bernadine Dohrn:

> As youth service systems (schools, foster care, probation, mental health) are scaling back, shutting down, or transforming their purpose, one system has been expanding its outreach to youth at an accelerated rate: the adult criminal justice system. All across the nation, states have been expanding the jurisdiction of adult criminal court to include younger children by lowering the minimum age of criminal jurisdiction and expanding the types of offenses and mechanisms for transfer or waiver of juveniles into adult criminal court. Barriers between adult criminals and children are being removed in police stations, courthouses, holding cells, and correctional institutions. Simultaneously, juvenile jurisdiction has expanded to include both younger children and delinquency sentencing beyond the age of childhood, giving law enforcement multiple options for convicting and incarcerating youngsters.[59]

This new reality is buttressed by the fact that the United States is now the only country in the world that sentences minors to death and spends "three times more on each incarcerated citizen than on each public school pupil."[60]

The impoverishment of the American educational system reflects the literal poverty of American children. The hard currency of human suffering that impacts children is evident in some astounding statistics that suggest a profound moral and political contradiction at the heart of one of the richest democracies in the world: For example, the rate of child poverty rose in 2004 to 17.6 percent, boosting the number of poor children to 12.9 million. In fact, "[a]bout one in three severely poor people are under age 17."[61] Moreover, children make up a disproportionate share of the poor in the United States in that "they are 26 per cent of the total population, but constitute 39 per cent of the poor."[62] Just as alarmingly, 9.3 million children lack health insurance, and millions lack affordable child care and decent early-childhood education. One of the most damaging statistics revealing how low a priority children are in America can be seen in the fact that among the industrialized nations the United States ranks first in billionaires and defense expenditures and yet ranks an appalling twenty-fifth in infant mortality. *New York Times* op-ed columnist Bob Herbert reports that in Chicago "there are nearly 100,000 young people, ages 16 to 24, who are out of work, out of school and all but out of hope.... Nationwide ... the figure is a staggering 5.5 million and growing."[63] The magnitude of this crisis is evident in some cities, such as the District of Columbia, where the child poverty rate is as high as 45 percent.[64] When broken down along racial categories, the figures become even more despairing: "In 2000, the poverty rate for African Americans was 22 percent, basically double the rate for the entire nation.... In Chicago the poverty rate for blacks is 29.4 percent and only 8.2

for whites. The poverty rate for black children is 40 percent, compared to 8 percent for white kids."[65] As we might expect, behind these grave statistics lies a series of decisions to favor economically those already advantaged at the expense of youth. Savage cuts to education, nutritional assistance for impoverished mothers, veterans' medical care, and basic scientific research help fund tax cuts for the inordinately rich.

This inversion of the government's responsibility to protect public goods from private threats further reveals itself in the privatization of social problems and the vilification of those who fail to thrive in the military-industrial-academic complex. Too many youth within this degraded economic, political, and cultural geography occupy a "dead zone" in which the spectacle of commodification exists alongside the imposing threat of massive debt, bankruptcy, the prison-industrial complex, and the elimination of basic civil liberties. Indeed, we have an entire generation of unskilled and displaced youth who have been expelled from shrinking markets, blue-collar jobs, and the limited political power granted to the middle-class consumer. Rather than investing in the public good and solving social problems, the state now punishes those who are caught in the downward spiral of its economic policies. Punishment, incarceration, and surveillance represent the face of the new expanded state. Consequently, the implied contract between the state and its citizens is broken, and social guarantees for youth, as well as civic obligations to the future, vanish from the agenda of public concern. As market values supplant civic values, it becomes increasingly difficult "to translate private worries into public issues and, conversely, to discern public issues in private troubles."[66] Within this utterly privatizing market discourse, alcoholism, homelessness, poverty, joblessness, and illiteracy are viewed not as social issues but, rather, as individual problems—that is, such problems are attributed to a character flaw or a personal failing, and in too many cases such problems are criminalized. Those who fall prey to social ills are doubly offensive to America's ethos of rabid capitalism because in failing to "get ahead," they threaten to reveal the flawed execution of an individualism that masquerades as meritocracy, and their very presence reveals the bankruptcy of America's ultimate measure of agency: the ability to consume goods. Unfortunately, consumer skills do not include translating private issues into public concerns.

Black youth are especially disadvantaged since they are often jobless in an economy that does not need their labor and hence constitute a surplus and disposable population. Bob Herbert points out that "black American males inhabit a universe in which joblessness is frequently the norm [and that] over the past few years, the percentage of black male high school graduates in their 20s who were jobless has ranged from well over a third to roughly 50 percent.... For dropouts, the rates of joblessness are staggering. For black males who left high school without a diploma, the real jobless rate at various times over the past few years has ranged from 59 percent to a breathtaking 72 percent." He further argues that "[t]hese are the kinds of statistics you get during a depression."[67]

Within such a climate of harsh discipline and moral indifference, it is easier to put young people in jail than to provide the education, services, and care they need to face problems of a complex and demanding society.[68] Conservative critics such as Abigail Thernstrom actually reinforce the ongoing toughening of school policy, the expansion of police power in the schools, and the vanishing rights of children by arguing that zero-tolerance policies are especially useful for minority and poor children. Thernstrom's comments on educational reform not only expand zero-tolerance policies to include the most trivial forms of transgression but also suggest a barely concealed, racially coded standard for punishing students. She writes: "They need schools where there is zero tolerance for violence, erratic or tardy attendance, inappropriate dress, late or incomplete homework, incivility toward staff and other students, messy desks and halls, trash on the floor and other signs of disorder."[69] The notion that children should be viewed as a crucial social resource who present for any healthy society important ethical and political considerations about the quality of public life, the allocation of social provisions, and the role of the state as a guardian of public interests appears to be lost in a society that refuses to invest in its youth as part of a broader commitment to a fully realized democracy. As the social order becomes more privatized and militarized, we face the problem of losing a generation of young people to a system of increasing intolerance and moral indifference. In many suburban malls, working-class white youth and youth of color cannot even shop or walk around without carrying either appropriate identification cards or being accompanied by their parents. Excluded from public spaces outside of schools that once offered them the opportunity to hang out with relative security, work with mentors in youth centers, and develop their own talents and sense of self-worth, young people are forced to hang out in the streets. They are increasingly subject to police surveillance, anti-gang statutes, and curfew laws, especially in poor urban neighborhoods. Gone are the youth centers, city public parks, outdoor basketball courts, and empty lots where kids used to play stick ball. Play areas are now rented out to the highest bidder and then "caged in by steel fences, wrought iron gates, padlocks and razor ribbon wire."[70]

Young people have become the new casualties in an ongoing war against justice, freedom, citizenship, and democracy, and this can be seen in the images used to represent children in trouble. In a society that appears to have turned its back on the young, what we are increasingly witnessing in the media are scenes of children handcuffed, sitting in adult courts before stern judges, and facing murder charges. These images are matched by endless films, videos, ads, documentaries, television programs, and journalistic accounts in which urban youth are depicted largely as gang-bangers, drug dealers, and rapists—thus violent, dangerous, and pathological. Or, when working-class youth are not directly demonized, television offers images of ruling-class youth in programs such as *Born Rich, Rich Girls,* and *The Simple Life,* suggesting that they are the group with the real problems, such as coping with envy management and figuring out ways to "dispel the voodoo of inherited wealth."[71] Such representations invoke ruling-class youth as an unapologetic paean to class power. In a society where 59 percent of college students say they will eventually be millionaires, the dominant press provides enormous coverage to celebrities such as Paris Hilton, the now-famous New York debutante and former prison inmate who, as reported in the media, "has stood for the proposition that wealth comes with no obligations of tact, taste or civic responsibility. For people who dream of someday putting unearned wealth to poor use, Ms. Hilton has been a beacon."[72] In today's media, class is less a metaphor for marking the unjust inequities of privilege than a way of celebrating wealth and power and rubbing it in the face of the poor. This is the popular-culture version of the neoliberal view of the world now so trendy among neoconservatives and the ultra-Right, whose policies reproduce and legitimize a growing appeal to "tough love"—an appeal that, in reality, is marked by a contempt for those who are impoverished, disenfranchised, or powerless. This is class politics waged vengefully in the realm of popular culture.

The growing attack on working-class youth, youth of color, and public education in American society may say less about the reputed apathy of the populace than about the bankruptcy of conventional political languages and the need for a new language and vision for expanding and deepening the meaning of democracy and making the education of youth central to such a project. Made over in the image of corporate culture, schools are no longer valued as a public good; hence, the legitimation of such schools no longer rests on their capacity to educate students according to the demands of critical citizenship but, rather, makes an appeal to private interests by enabling students to master the requirements of a market-driven economy. This is substituting education with training. Under these circumstances, many students increasingly find themselves in schools that lack any language for relating the self to public life, social responsibility, or the imperatives of democracy. In this instance, democratic education with its emphasis on social justice, respect for others, critical inquiry, equality, freedom, civic courage, and concern for the collective good is suppressed and replaced by an excessive emphasis on the language of privatization, individualism, self-interest, and brutal competitiveness. Lost in this commercial and privatizing discourse of schooling is any notion of democratic community or model of leadership capable of raising questions about what public schools should accomplish in a democracy and why under certain circumstances they might fail, or, for that matter, why public schools have increasingly adopted policies that bear a close resemblance to how prisons are run.

How does a society justify housing poor students in schools that are unsafe, decaying, and with little or no extracurricular activities while at the same time spending five times more annually—as high as $20,000 in many suburban schools—on each middle-class student, housing them in schools with Olympic-size swimming pools, the latest computer technology, and well-groomed buildings and grounds? What message is being sent to young people when in a state such as New York "more Blacks entered prison just for drug offenses than graduated from the state's massive university system with undergraduate, master's, and doctoral degrees combined in the 1990s"?[73] What message is being sent when, as federal deficits are soaring, the Bush administration provides tax cuts for the rich—in one instance, $114 billion in corporate tax concessions—while at the same time children face drastic cuts in education and health aid, as well as other massive cuts in domestic programs such as job training and summer employment opportunities? In this instance, the culture of domestic militarization, with its policies of containment, brutalization, and punishment, becomes more valued by the dominant social order than any consideration of what it means for a society to expand and strengthen the mechanisms and freedoms of a fully realized democracy.[74]

As the state is downsized and stripped of its financial resources, and as basic social services dry up, containment policies become the principal means to discipline youth and restrict their ability to think critically and engage in oppositional practices. At the academic level this translates into imposing accountability schemes on schools that are really about enforcing high-stakes testing policies. Such approaches de-skill teachers, reduce learning to the lowest common denominator, undermine the possibility of critical thinking, and prepare young people to be docile. Schools increasingly resemble other weakened public spheres as they cut back on trained psychologists, school nurses, and programs such as music, art, athletics, and valuable after-school activities. Jesse Jackson argues that, under such circumstances, schools not only fail to provide students with a well-rounded education, they often "bring in the police, [and] the school gets turned into a feeder system for the penal system."[75] Marginalized students learn quickly that they are surplus populations and that the journey from home to school no longer means they will next move into a job; on the contrary, school now becomes a training ground for their "graduation" into containment centers such as prisons and jails that keep them out of sight, patrolled, and monitored so as to prevent them from becoming a social canker or political liability to those white and middle-class populations concerned about their own safety.

At the current time, solutions involving social problems are difficult to imagine, let alone address. For many young people and adults today, the private sphere has become the only space in which to imagine any sense of hope, pleasure, or possibility. Culture as an activity in which young people actually produce the conditions of their own agency through dialogue, community participation, public stories, and political struggle is being eroded. In its place, we are increasingly surrounded by a "climate of cultural and linguistic privatization" in which culture has become something we consume rather than create, and the only kind of speech that is acceptable is that of the fast-paced shopper. Despite neoconservative and neoliberal claims that economic growth will cure social ills, the language of the market has no way of dealing with poverty, social inequality, or civil rights issues. It has no respect for noncommodified values and no vocabulary for recognizing and addressing respect, compassion, decency, ethics, or, for that matter, its own anti-democratic forms of power. It has no way of understanding that the revolutionary idea of democracy, as Bill Moyers points out, is about more than the freedom to shop, formal elections, or the two-party system; it is about "the means of dignifying people so they become fully free to claim their moral and political agency."[76] These are political and educational issues, not merely economic concerns.

In order to strengthen the public sphere, we must use its most widespread institutions, undo their metamorphoses into means of surveillance, commodification, and control, and reclaim them as democratic spaces. Schools, colleges, and universities come to mind—because of both their contradictions and their democratic potential, their reality and their promise. In what follows, I argue that youth as a political and moral referent is a central category for engaging the purpose and meaning of higher education and its relationship to a future whose democratic possibilities can be seized only if young people are provided with the knowledge, capacities, and skills they need to function as social agents, citizens, empowered workers, and critical thinkers. But such a task must begin with analysis of the degree to which higher education's role as a democratic public sphere is being threatened by a number of anti-democratic tendencies.

The Attack on Higher Education

In keeping with the progressive impoverishment of politics and public life over the past two decades, the university is increasingly being transformed into a training ground for corporate interests and, hence, receding from its role as a public sphere in which youth can become the critical citizens and democratic agents necessary to nourish a socially responsible future. Strapped for money and increasingly defined in the language of corporate culture, many universities are now modeled after the wisdom of the business world and seem less interested in higher learning than in becoming licensed storefronts for brand-name corporations—selling off space, buildings, and research programs to rich corporate donors. College presidents are now often called CEOs and have come to be known less for their intellectual leadership than for their role as fund-raisers and their ability to bridge the worlds of academe and business. Venture capitalists scour colleges and universities in search of big profits to be made through licensing agreements, the control of intellectual property rights, and investments in university spin-off companies. In the age of money and profit, academic subjects gain status almost exclusively through their exchange value on the market—a phenomenon all the more pronounced as the Bush administration attempts to wield more control over higher education, cut student aid, plunder public services, and push states to the brink of financial disaster. As higher education increasingly becomes a privilege rather than a right, many working-class youth either find it financially impossible to enter college or, because of increased costs, have to drop out. Those students who have the resources to stay in school are feeling the pressure of the job market and rush to take courses and receive professional credentials in business and the biosciences as the humanities lose majors and downsize. Not surprisingly, students are now referred to as "customers," while some university presidents even argue that professors should be labeled "academic entrepreneurs."[77] As higher education is corporatized, young people find themselves on campuses that look more like malls, and they are increasingly taught by professors who are hired on a contractual basis, have obscene workloads, and barely make enough money to pay off their student loans. Tenured faculty are called upon to generate grants, establish close partnerships with corporations, and teach courses that have practical value in the marketplace. There is little in this vision of the university that imagines young people as anything other than fodder for the corporation or appendages of the national security state. What was once the hidden curriculum of many universities—the subordination of higher education to capital—has now become an open and much-celebrated policy of both public and private higher education.

An even more pervasive threat facing higher education comes from the ongoing militarization of public life. The influence of militaristic truths, values, social relations, and identities now permeates and defines American culture. Universities invest their resources, engage in research projects, and accept huge amounts of defense contract money in order to provide the personnel, expertise, and tools necessary to expand the security imperatives of the U.S. government. The CIA and other intelligence agencies are developing diverse connections to higher education and in the process are shaping academic programs and allocating vast sums of money for research projects.[78]

As I mentioned in Chapter 1, public universities such as Penn State, Carnegie Mellon, the University of Pennsylvania, Johns Hopkins, and a host of others are expanding the reach and influence of the national security state by entering into formal agreements with agencies such as the FBI.[79] In an effort to weed out left-oriented educators, right-wing ideologues and students now monitor classes, list the names of dissident professors on websites, and report such instances to the popular press. Of course, this type of classroom intervention has less to do with protesting genuine demagoguery than with attacking any professor who might raise critical questions about the status quo or hold the narratives of power accountable.[80] Illegal and unethical spying at the national level now seems to offer yet another strategy to harass professors, insult students by treating them as if they were mindless, and provide a model for student participation in the classroom that mimics tactics used by fascist and Nazi plants in the 1930s.

Educators and Public Life

If public and higher education are to be reclaimed as sites of critical thinking, collective work, and public service, educators and students will have to redefine the knowledge, skills, research, and intellectual practices currently favored in schools and universities. Central to such a challenge is the need to position intellectual practice "as part of an intricate web of morality, rigor and responsibility" that enables teachers to speak with conviction, use the public sphere to address important social problems, and demonstrate alternative models for bridging the gap between schools and the broader society. Connective practices are key: It is crucial to develop intellectual practices that are collegial rather than competitive and that refuse instrumentality and privileged isolation, link critical thought to a profound impatience with the status quo, and connect human agency to the idea of social responsibility and the politics of possibility.

Connection also means being openly and deliberately political in one's pedagogical and intellectual work. Increasingly, as schools and universities are shaped by a culture of fear in which dissent is equated with treason, the call to be objective and impartial, whatever one's intentions, can easily echo what George Orwell called the "official truth" or the establishment point of view. Lacking a self-consciously democratic political focus, teachers and students under the corporate model of leadership are often reduced to the role of technicians or functionaries engaged in formalistic rituals, unconcerned with the disturbing and urgent problems that confront the larger society. In opposition to this model, with its claim to and conceit of political neutrality, I argue that public intellectuals should combine the mutually interdependent roles of critical educator and active citizen. This requires finding ways to connect the practice of classroom teaching with the operation of power in society at large. The educator as public intellectual becomes responsible for linking the diverse experiences that produce knowledge, identities, and social values in the university to the quality of moral and political life in wider society. Such an intellectual does not train students solely for jobs but, rather, educates them to question critically the institutions, policies, and values that shape their lives, their relationships to others, and their connection to the larger world.

Educators, then, must be responsible for preparing students to engage critically with the world; but they must also recognize the impact their students will have on the next generation of young people. The importance of such an educational challenge and project is evident in the findings of a survey conducted in 2005 by the John S. and James L. Knight Foundation. According to the survey, 36 percent of U.S. high school students believe that "newspapers should get government approval of stories before publishing."[81] This view, clearly much more at home with fascism than with critical democracy, is legitimated by the students' lack of education about student rights, First Amendment freedoms, and the meaning of a substantive democracy. Education cannot be decoupled from political democracy: A deliberately informed and purposeful—as opposed to doctrinaire—education should take place at all levels of schooling, but it gains a significant part of its momentum in colleges and universities among academics and students who will go back to schools, churches, synagogues, and workplaces in order to produce new ideas, concepts, and critical ways of understanding the world in which young people and adults live.

In order for pedagogy that encourages critical thought to have a real effect, it must include the message that all citizens, old and young, are equally entitled, if not equally empowered, to shape the society in which they live. If educators are to function as public intellectuals, they need to provide the opportunities for students to learn that the relationship between knowledge and power can be emancipatory, that their histories and experiences matter, and that what they say and do counts in their struggle to unlearn dominating privileges, productively reconstruct their relations with others, and transform, when necessary, the world around them. More specifically, educators need to argue for forms of pedagogy that close the gap between schooling and everyday life. Their curricula need to be organized around knowledges of communities, cultures, and traditions that give students a sense of history, identity, and place. These are dangerous times in the United States, especially for young people, and under such circumstances we need educators who combine rigor and clarity, on the one hand, and civic courage and political commitment, on the other. Collectively, teachers, students, activists, and others must willfully engage controversy, make connections that are otherwise hidden, deflate the claims of triumphalism, and bridge intellectual work and the operation of politics.

Chapter 3

Conclusion

The corporatization and militarization of public and higher education, the dumbing-down of rigorous scholarship, and the devaluing of the critical capacities of young people mark a sharp break from a once strong educational tradition in the United States, extending from Thomas Jefferson to John Dewey to Maxine Greene—a tradition that held that freedom flourishes in the worldly space of the public realm only through the work of educated critical citizens. Within this democratic tradition, education was not confused with training; rather, its critical function was propelled by the need to educate students as citizens capable of defining and implementing democratic goals such as freedom, equality, and justice. If we were to value schools and universities as social tools, we could continue this tradition and support their role in fostering the pedagogical practices that enable a notion of citizenship marked by a "politically interested and mobilized citizenry, one that has certain solidarities, is capable of acting on its own behalf, and anticipates a future of ever greater social equality across lines of race, gender, and class."[82]

In order for schools to become a meaningful site for educating youth for a democratic future, educators and others need to reclaim education as an ethical and political response to the demise of democratic public life. At stake here is the role of schools and colleges as public spheres committed to increasing the possibilities of democratic identities, values, and relations. This approach suggests new models of leadership, organization, power, and vision dedicated to opening up education to all groups, creating a critical citizenry, providing specialized work skills for jobs that really require them, democratizing relations of governance among administrators, faculty, and students, and taking seriously the imperative to disseminate an intellectual and artistic culture. Education may be one of the few sites left in which students learn the knowledge and skills that enable them not only to mediate critically between democratic values and the demands of corporate power and the national security state but also to distinguish between identities founded on democratic principles and identities steeped in forms of competitive, unbridled individualism that celebrate self-interest, profit-making, militarism, and greed.

Addressing education as a democratic endeavor begins with the recognition that higher education is more than an investment opportunity; citizenship is more than conspicuous consumption; learning is more than preparing students for the workplace, however important that task might be; and democracy is more than making choices at the local mall. Reclaiming schools as part of the public sphere begins with the crucial project of challenging, among other things, corporate ideology and its attendant notion of corporate time, which speeds up time and imagines time as units of labor, production, sales, and consumption, while focusing on short-term goals—largely defined by financial profit and the quick accumulation of capital.[83] Corporate time, with its accelerated and fragmented pace, is increasingly replacing public time. In public time, time slows down and, rather than being measured by the accumulation of money and goods, serves as a valuation of the opportunity for individuals and groups to share resources, debate, think otherwise, and consider the task of having a positive, long-term impact on the world. Public time fosters incremental and cumulative change, and enables pedagogical opportunities in which thinking, planning, and acting can be measured by their long-term political, ethical, and economic consequences. Moreover, as Zygmunt Bauman points out, public time privileges relating individual problems to social considerations and opens up the space for a discourse in which it can be recognized that justice is now a planetary issue and that "the injustices out of which models of justice are molded are no longer confined to immediate neighborhoods ... that what happens in one place has a bearing on how people in all other places live, hope or expect to live."[84] In contrast to corporate time, then, public time is a fundamental element in recognizing and providing the conditions for the enablement of democratic values, identities, relations, and institutions. Time in this instance is not a deficit but an essential condition, as Hannah Arendt argues, for thoughtfulness, critical agency, and social justice.

By taking back education as a site for public time, we could foster dialogue, critical thought, and critical exchange. This would, in turn, provide opportunities for knowledge that deepens democratic values, while encouraging pedagogical relations that question the future in terms that are political, ethical, and social. Public and higher education also need to be defended against those religious and secular ideologues who harbor a deep disdain for critical thought and healthy skepticism, and who look with displeasure upon any form of education that teaches students to read the world critically and to hold power and authority accountable. Education is not only about issues of work and economics but also about questions of justice, social freedom, and the capacity for democratic agency, action, and change, as well as the related issues of power, exclusion, and citizenship. These are educational and political issues, and they should be addressed as part of a broader effort to re-energize the global struggle for social justice and democracy.

Any viable notion of critical pedagogy should affirm and enrich the meaning, language, and knowledge forms that students actually use to negotiate and inform their lives. Indeed, educators can exercise their role as public intellectuals via such approaches by giving students the opportunity to understand how power is organized through the enormous number of "popular" cultural spheres that exist in American society, including libraries, movie theaters, schools, and high-tech media conglomerates that circulate signs and meanings through newspapers, magazines, advertisements, new information technologies, computers, films, and television programs. Needless to say, this position challenges neoconservative Roger Kimball's claim that "[p]opular culture is a tradition essential to uneducated Americans."[85] By laying claim to popular media, critical pedagogy not only asks important questions about how knowledge is produced and taken up but also provides the conditions for students to become competent and critically versed in a variety of literacies (not just the literacy of print), while at the same time expanding the conditions and options for the roles they might play as cultural producers (as opposed to simply teaching them to be critical readers).

A critically engaged pedagogy necessitates that we incorporate in our classrooms those electronically mediated knowledge forms that constitute the terrain of mass and popular culture. I am referring here to the world of media texts—videos, films, the Internet, Podcasts, and other elements of the new electronic technologies that operate through a combination of visual and print culture. Such an approach not only challenges the traditional definition of schooling as the only site of pedagogy by widening the application and sites of pedagogy to a variety of cultural locations but also alerts students to the educational force of the culture at large, what I discuss in the following chapter as the field of public pedagogy.

There is a lot of talk among social theorists about the death of politics brought on by a negative globalization characterized by markets without frontiers, deregulation, militarism, and armed violence, which not only feed one another but produce global unlawfulness and reduce politics to merely an extension of war.[86] I would hope that of all groups, educators, especially, would be mindful of the potential for a better future and would vocally and tirelessly challenge these nihilistic views by making it clear that critical education is a precondition for global justice and is at the very heart of expanding the public good and promoting democratic social change. Public and higher education may be among the few spheres left in which the promise of youth can be linked to the promise of democracy. Education in this instance becomes both an ethical and a political referent; it furnishes an opportunity for adults to provide the conditions for young people to become critically engaged social agents. Similarly, it points to a future in which democratic practices create the conditions for each generation of youth to struggle anew to sustain the promise of a democracy that has no end point and that must be continuously expanded into a world of new possibilities and opportunities for keeping justice and hope alive.

How we view, represent, and treat young people should be part of a larger public dialogue about how to imagine a future global democracy that is both strong and inclusive. In order to realize this future, we need to address what it means to make the political more pedagogical—that is, to make it into a discourse capable of articulating a new vocabulary as well as a new set of theoretical tools and social possibilities. These are the conditions that will allow us to re-vision civic engagement and social transformation while imagining a new understanding of politics in which the promise of democracy commands the most concrete urgency and action. We have entered a period in which the war against youth, especially poor youth of color, offers no apologies because it is too arrogant and ruthless to imagine any resistance. But the collective need and potential struggle for justice should never be underestimated even in the darkest of times. The great abolitionist Frederick Douglass rightly and bravely argued that freedom is an empty abstraction if people fail to act: "If there is no struggle, there is no progress." Teachers, parents, students, and others need to work diligently and tirelessly in order to, as Raymond Williams once put it, make despair unconvincing and hope practical for all members of society, but especially for young people, who deserve a future that does a great deal more than endlessly repeat the present.

4
Neoliberalism as Public Pedagogy

Neoliberalism as Public Pedagogy

> Our age is the time of "individual utopias," of utopias privatized, and so it comes naturally (as well as being a fashionable thing to do) to deride and ridicule such projects which imply a revision of the options which are collectively put at the disposal of individuals.[1]

The ascendancy of neoliberal corporate culture into every aspect of American life both consolidates economic power in the hands of the few and aggressively attempts to break the power of unions, decouple income from productivity, subordinate the needs of society to the market, and deem public services and goods an unconscionable luxury. But it does more. It thrives on a culture of cynicism, insecurity, and despair. Conscripts in a relentless campaign for personal responsibility, Americans are now convinced that they have little to hope for—and gain from—the government, nonprofit public spheres, democratic associations, public and higher education, and other nongovernmental social forces. With few exceptions, the project of democratizing public goods has fallen into disrepute in the popular imagination as the logic of the market undermines the most basic social solidarities. The consequences include not only a weakened social state but a growing sense of insecurity, cynicism, and political retreat on the part of the general public. The incessant calls for self-reliance that now dominate public discourse betray a hollowed-out and refigured state that neither provides adequate safety nets for its populace, especially those who are young, poor, or marginalized, nor gives any indication that it will serve the interests of its citizens in spite of constitutional guarantees. As Stanley Aronowitz and Peter Bratsis argue, "The nation-state lives chiefly as a repressive power [though it] also has some purchase on maintaining a degree of ideological hegemony over ... 'the multitude.'"[2] In short, private interests trump social needs, and economic growth becomes more important than social justice. The capitulation of labor unions and traditional working-class parties to neoliberal policies is matched by the ongoing dismantling of the welfare state. Within neoliberalism's market-driven discourse, corporate power marks the space of a new kind of public pedagogy, one in which the production, dissemination, and circulation of ideas emerges from the educational force of the larger culture. Public pedagogy in this sense refers to a powerful ensemble of ideological and institutional forces whose aim is to produce competitive, self-interested individuals vying for their own material and ideological gain. The culture of corporate public pedagogy largely cancels out or devalues gender, class-specific, and racial injustices of the existing social order by absorbing the democratic impulses and practices of civil society within narrow economic relations. Corporate public pedagogy has become an all-encompassing cultural horizon for producing market identities, values, and practices.

Under neoliberalism, dominant public pedagogy with its narrow and imposed schemes of classification and limited modes of identification uses the educational force of the culture to negate the basic conditions for critical agency. As Pierre Bourdieu has pointed out, political action is only "possible because agents, who are part of the social world, have knowledge of this world and because one can act on the social world by acting on their knowledge of this world."[3] Politics often begins when it becomes possible to make power visible, to challenge the ideological circuitry of hegemonic knowledge, and to recognize that "political subversion presupposes cognitive subversion, a conversion of the vision of the world."[4] But another element of politics focuses on where politics happens, how proliferating sites of pedagogy bring into being new forms of resistance, raise new questions, and necessitate alternative visions regarding autonomy and the possibility of democracy itself.

What is crucial to recognize in the work of theorists such as Raymond Williams, Stuart Hall, Pierre Bourdieu, Noam Chomsky, Robert McChesney, and others is that neoliberalism is more than an economic theory: It also constitutes the conditions for a radically refigured cultural politics. That is, it provides, to use Raymond Williams' term, a new mode of "permanent education" in which dominant sites of pedagogy engage in diverse forms of pedagogical address to put into play a limited range of identities, ideologies, and subject positions that both reinforce neoliberal social relations and undermine the possibility for democratic politics.[5] The economist William Greider goes so far as to argue that the diverse advocates of neoliberalism currently in control of the American government want to "roll back the twentieth century literally"[6] by establishing the priority of private institutions and market identities, values, and relationships as the organizing principles of public life. This is a discourse that wants to squeeze out ambiguity from public space, to dismantle the social provisions and guarantees provided by the welfare state, and to eliminate democratic politics by making the notion of the social impossible to imagine beyond the isolated consumer and the logic of the market.[7] The ideological essence of this new public pedagogy is well expressed by Grover Norquist, the president of the Americans for Tax Reform and arguably Washington's leading right-wing strategist, who has been quoted as saying: "My goal is to cut government in half in twenty-five years, to get it down to the size where we can drown it in the bathtub."[8]

These new sites of public pedagogy that have become the organizing force of neoliberal ideology are not restricted to schools, blackboards, and test taking. Nor do they incorporate the limited forms of address found in schools. Such sites operate within a wide variety of social institutions and formats including sports and entertainment media, cable television networks, churches, and channels of elite and popular culture such as advertising. Profound transformations have taken place in the public sphere, producing new sites of pedagogy marked by a distinctive confluence of new digital and media technologies, growing concentrations of corporate power, and unparalleled meaning-producing capacities. Unlike traditional forms of pedagogy, modes of pedagogical address are now mediated through unprecedented electronic technologies that include high-speed computers, new types of digitized film, and the Internet. The result is a public pedagogy that plays a decisive role in producing a diverse cultural sphere that gives new meaning to education as a political force. What is surprising about the cultural politics of neoliberalism is that cultural studies theorists have either ignored or largely underestimated the symbolic and pedagogical dimensions of the struggle that neoliberal corporate power has put into place for the last thirty years, particularly under the ruthless administration of George W. Bush.

Making the Pedagogical More Political

> The need for permanent education, in our changing society, will be met in one way or another. It is now on the whole being met, though with many valuable exceptions and efforts against the tide, by an integration of this teaching with the priorities and interests of a capitalist society, and of a capitalist society, moreover, which necessarily retains as its central principle the idea of a few governing, communicating with and teaching the many.[9]

At this point in American history, neoliberal capitalism is not simply too overpowering; on the contrary, "democracy is too weak."[10] Hence the increasing influence of money over politics, the increasing domination of public concerns by corporate interests, and the growing tyranny of unchecked corporate power and avarice. Culture combines with politics to turn struggles over power into entertainment, as occurred in California when Governor Davis was recalled and Arnold Schwarzenegger emerged as the new occupant in the governor's office. But more importantly, under neoliberalism, pedagogy has become thoroughly politicized in reactionary terms as it constructs knowledge, values, and identities through a dominant media that has become a handmaiden of corporate power. For instance, soon after the invasion of Iraq, the *New York Times* released a survey indicating that 42 percent of the American public believed that Saddam Hussein was directly responsible for the September 11 attacks on the World Trade Center and the Pentagon. CBS, too, released a news poll indicating that 55 percent of the public believed that Saddam Hussein directly supported the terrorist organization al Qaeda. A majority of Americans also believed that Saddam Hussein had weapons of mass destruction, was about to build a nuclear bomb, and would unleash it eventually on an unsuspecting American public. None of these claims had any basis in fact, since no evidence existed even to remotely confirm their validity. Of course, the aforementioned opinions held by a substantial number of Americans did not simply fall from the sky; they were ardently legitimated by President Bush, Vice President Cheney, Colin Powell, and Condoleezza Rice, while daily reproduced uncritically in all of the dominant media. These misrepresentations and strategic distortions circulated in the dominant press either with uncritical, jingoistic enthusiasm, as in the case of the Fox News Channel, or through the dominant media's refusal to challenge such claims—both positions, of course, in opposition to foreign news sources, such as the BBC, that repeatedly challenged such assertions. Such deceptions are never innocent and in this case appear to have been shamelessly used by the Bush administration to muster support both for the Iraq invasion and for an ideologically driven agenda "that overwhelmingly favors the president's wealthy supporters and is driving the federal government toward a long-term fiscal catastrophe."[11]

While not downplaying the seriousness of government deception, I believe there is another issue underlying these events in which the most important casualty is not simply the integrity of the Bush administration but democracy itself. One of the central legacies of modern democracy—with its roots in the Enlightenment classical liberal tradition, and most evident in the twentieth century in works as diverse as those of W.E.B. Du Bois, Raymond Williams, Cornelius Castoriadis, John Dewey, and Paulo Freire, among others—is the important recognition that a substantive democracy cannot exist without educated citizens. For some more conservative thinkers, the fear of democracy itself translated into an attack on a truly public and accessible education for all citizens. For others such as the progressive Walter Lippman, who wrote extensively on democracy in the 1920s, it meant creating two modes of education: one for the elite who would rule the country and be the true participants in the democratic process, and the other for the masses whose education would train them to be spectators rather than participants in shaping democratic public life. Du Bois recognized that such a bifurcation of educational opportunity was increasingly becoming a matter of common sense, but he rejected it outright.[12] Similarly in opposition to the enemies of democracy and the elitists, radical social critics such as Cornelius Castoriadis, Paulo Freire, and Stuart Hall believed that education for a democratic citizenry was an essential condition of equality and social justice and had to be provided through public, higher, popular, and adult education.

While Castoriadis and others were right about linking education and democracy, they had no way, in their time, of recognizing that the larger culture would extend, if not supersede, institutionalized education as the most important educational force in the developed societies. In fact, education and pedagogy have been synonymous with schooling in the public mind. Challenging such a recognition does not invalidate the importance of formal education to democracy, but it does require a critical understanding of how the work of education takes place in a range of other spheres such as advertising, television, film, the Internet, video games, and the popular press. Rather than invalidate the importance of schooling, it extends the sites of pedagogy and in doing so broadens and deepens the meaning of cultural pedagogy. The concept of public pedagogy also underscores the central importance of formal spheres of learning that unlike their popular counterparts—driven largely by commercial interests that more often miseducate the public—must provide citizens with the critical capacities, modes of literacies, knowledge, and skills that enable them both to read the world critically and to participate in shaping and governing it. Pedagogy at the popular level must now be a central concern of formal schooling itself. My point is not that public and higher education are free from corporate influence and dominant ideologies but, rather, that such models of education, at best, provide the spaces and conditions for prioritizing civic values over commercial interests (i.e., they self-consciously educate future citizens capable of participating in and reproducing a democratic society). In spite of these models' present embattled status and contradictory roles, institutional schooling remains uniquely placed to prepare students to both understand and influence the larger educational forces that shape their lives. Such institutions, by virtue of their privileged position and dedication to freedom and democracy, also have an obligation to draw upon those traditions and resources capable of providing a critical and humanistic education to all students in order to prepare them for a world in which information and power have taken on new and influential dimensions. One entry into this challenge is to address the contributions to such issues that cultural studies and critical pedagogy have made in the last few decades, particularly with respect to how the relationship between culture and power constitute a new site of both politics and pedagogy.

Cultural Studies and the Question of Pedagogy

> City walls, books, spectacles, events educate—yet now they mostly *miseducate* their residents. Compare the lessons, taken by the citizens of Athens (women and slaves included), during the performances of Greek tragedies with the kind of knowledge which is today consumed by the spectator of *Dynasty* or *Perdue de vue*.[13]

My own interest in cultural studies emerges out of an ongoing project to theorize the regulatory and emancipatory relationship among culture, power, and politics as expressed through the dynamics of what can be called public pedagogy. This project concerns, in part, the diverse ways in which culture functions as a contested sphere in the production, distribution, and regulation of power and how and where it operates both symbolically and institutionally as an educational, political, and economic force. Drawing upon a long tradition in cultural studies work, culture is viewed as constitutive and political, not only reflecting larger forces, but also constructing them; in short, culture not only mediates history, it shapes it. In this formulation, power is a central element of culture just as culture is a crucial element of power.[14] As Bauman observes, "Culture is a permanent revolution of sorts. To say 'culture' is to make another attempt to account for the fact that the human world (the world moulded by the humans and the world which moulds humans) is perpetually, unavoidably—and unremediably *noch nicht geworden* (not-yet-accomplished), as Ernst Bloch beautifully put it."[15]

I am suggesting that culture is a crucial terrain for theorizing and realizing the political as an articulation and intervention into the social, a space in which politics is pluralized, recognized as contingent, and open to many formations.[16] But culture is also a crucial sphere for articulating the dialectical and mutually constitutive dynamics between the global political circuits that now frame material relations of power and a cultural politics in which matters of representation and meaning shape and offer concrete examples of how politics is expressed, lived, and experienced through the modalities of daily existence. Culture, in this instance, is the ground of both contestation and accommodation, and it is increasingly characterized by the rise of mega-corporations and new technologies that are transforming radically the traditional spheres of economy, industry, society, and everyday life. I am referring not only to the development of new information technologies but also to the enormous concentration of ownership and power among a limited number of corporations that now control diverse media technologies and markets.[17] Culture plays a central role in producing narratives, metaphors, images, and desiring maps that exercise a powerful pedagogical force over how people think about themselves and their relationship to others. From this perspective, culture is the primary sphere in which individuals, groups, and institutions engage in the art of translating the diverse and multiple relations that mediate between private life and public concerns. It is also the sphere in which the translating and pedagogical possibilities of culture are under assault, particularly as the forces of neoliberalism dissolve public issues into utterly privatized and individualistic concerns.[18]

Against the neoliberal attack on all things social, culture must be defended as the site where exchange and dialogue become crucial affirmations of a democratically configured space of the social in which the political is actually taken up and lived out through a variety of intimate relations and social formations. Far from being exclusively about matters of representation and texts, culture becomes a site, event, and performance in which identities and modes of agency are configured through the mutually determined forces of thought and action, body and mind, and time and space. Culture is the public space where common matters, shared solidarities, and public engagements provide the fundamental elements of democracy. Culture is also the pedagogical and political ground on which communities of struggle and a global public sphere can be imagined as a condition of democratic possibilities. Culture offers a common space in which to address the radical demands of a pedagogy that allows critical discourse to confront the inequities of power and promote the possibilities of shared dialogue and democratic transformation. Culture affirms the social as a fundamentally political space just as it attempts within the current historical moment to deny its relevance and its centrality as a political necessity. And culture's urgency, as Nick Couldry observes, resides in its possibilities for linking politics to matters of individual and social agency as they are lived out in particular democratic spheres, institutional forms, and communities in process. He writes:

> For what is urgent now is not defending the full range of cultural production and consumption from elitist judgement but defending the possibility of any shared site for an emergent democratic politics. The contemporary mission of cultural studies, if it has one, lies not with the study of "culture" (already a cliché of management and marketing manuals), but with the fate of a "*common* culture," and its contemporary deformations.[19]

Central to any feasible notion of cultural studies is the primacy of culture and power, organized through an understanding of how the political becomes pedagogical, particularly in terms of how private issues are connected to larger social conditions and collective forces—that is, how the very processes of learning constitute the political mechanisms through which identities are shaped, desires mobilized, and experiences take on form and meaning within those collective conditions and larger forces that constitute the realm of the social. In this context, pedagogy is no longer restricted to what goes on in schools, but becomes a defining principle of a wide-ranging set of cultural apparatuses engaged in what Raymond Williams has called "permanent education." Williams rightfully believed that education in the broadest sense plays a central role in any viable form of cultural politics. He writes:

> What [permanent education] valuably stresses is the educational force of our whole social and cultural experience. It is therefore concerned, not only with continuing education, of a formal or informal kind, but with what the whole environment, its institutions and relationships, actively and profoundly teaches. ... [Permanent education also refers to] the field in which our ideas of the world, of ourselves and of our possibilities, are most widely and often most powerfully formed and disseminated. To work for the recovery of control in this field is then, under any pressures, a priority.[20]

Williams argued that any workable notion of critical politics would have to pay closer "attention to the complex ways in which individuals are formed by the institutions to which they belong, and in which, by reaction, the institutions took on the color of individuals thus formed."[21] Williams also foregrounded the crucial political question of how agency unfolds within a variety of cultural spaces structured by unequal relations of power.[22] He was particularly concerned about the connections between pedagogy and political agency, especially in light of the emergence of a range of new technologies that greatly proliferated the amount of information available to people while at the same time constricting the substance and ways in which such meanings entered the public domain. The realm of culture for Williams took on a new role in the latter part of the twentieth century, inasmuch as the actuality of economic power and its attendant networks of pedagogical control now exercised more influence than ever before in shaping how identities were produced and desires mobilized, as well as how everyday life acquired the force of common sense.[23] Williams clearly understood that making the political more pedagogical meant recognizing that where and how the psyche locates itself in public discourse, visions, and passions provides the groundwork for agents to enunciate, act, and reflect on themselves and their relations to others and the wider social order.

Unfortunately, Williams' emphasis on making the pedagogical more political has not occupied a central place in the work of most cultural studies theorists. Pedagogy in most cultural studies accounts is either limited to the realm of schooling, dismissed as a discipline with very little academic cultural capital, or rendered reactionary through the claim that it simply accommodates the paralyzing grip of governmental institutions that normalize all pedagogical practices. Within this discourse, pedagogy largely functions to both normalize relations of power and overemphasize agency at the expense of institutional pressures, embracing what Tony Bennett calls "all agency and no structure."[24] Such criticism, however, does little to explore or highlight the complicated, contradictory, and determining ways in which the institutional pressures of schools and other pedagogical sites and the social capacities of educators are mediated within unequal relations of power. Instead, Bennett simply reverses the formula and buttresses his own notion of governmentality as a theory of structures without agents. Of course, this position also ignores the role of various sites of pedagogy and the operational work they perform in producing knowledge, values, identities, and subject positions. But more importantly, it reflects the more general refusal on the part of many cultural studies theorists to take up the relationship between pedagogy and agency, on the one hand, and the relationship among the crises of culture, education, and democracy, on the other. Given such a myopic vision, left-leaning intellectuals who are dismissive of formal education sites have no doubt made it easier for the more corporate and entrepreneurial interests to dominate colleges and universities.

Unfortunately, many cultural studies theorists have failed to take seriously Antonio Gramsci's insight that "[e]very relationship of 'hegemony' is necessarily an educational relationship"—with its implication that education as a cultural pedagogical practice takes place across multiple sites as it signals how, within diverse contexts, education makes us both subjects of and subject to relations of power.[25] I want to build on Gramsci's insight by exploring in greater detail the connection among democracy, political agency, and pedagogy described in the work of the late French philosopher Cornelius Castoriadis. Castoriadis has made seminal, and often overlooked, contributions to the role of pedagogy and its centrality to a substantive democracy. I focus on this radical tradition in order to reclaim a legacy of critical thinking that refuses to decouple education from democracy, politics from pedagogy, and understanding from public intervention. This tradition of critical thought signals for educators and cultural studies advocates the importance of investing in the political as part of a broader effort to revitalize notions of democratic citizenship, social justice, and the public good. But it also signals the importance of cultural politics as a pedagogical force for understanding how people buy into neoliberal ideology, how certain forms of agency are both suppressed and produced, how neoliberals work pedagogically to convince the public that consumer rights are more important than the rights people have as citizens and workers, and how pedagogy as a force for democratic change enables understanding, action, and resistance.

Education and Radical Democracy

> Let us suppose that a democracy, as complete, perfect, etc., as one might wish, might fall upon us from the heavens: this sort of democracy will not be able to endure for more than a few years if it does not engender individuals that correspond to it, ones that, first and foremost, are capable of making it function and reproducing it. There can be no democratic society without democratic *paideia*.[26]

Castoriadis was deeply concerned about what it meant to think about politics and agency in light of the new conditions of capitalism that threatened to undermine the promise of democracy at the end of the twentieth century. Moreover, he argued, like Raymond Williams, that education, in the broadest sense, is a principal feature of politics because it provides the capacities, knowledge, skills, and social relations through which individuals recognize themselves as social and political agents. Linking such a broad-based definition of education to issues of power and agency also raises a fundamental question that goes to the heart of any substantive notion of democracy: How do issues of history, language, culture, and identity work to articulate and legitimate particular exclusions? If culture in this sense becomes the constituting terrain for producing identities and constituting social subjects, education becomes the strategic and positional mechanism through which such subjects are addressed, positioned within social spaces, located within particular histories and experiences, and always arbitrarily displaced and decentered as part of a pedagogical process that is increasingly multiple, fractured, and never homogenous.

Over the last thirty years Castoriadis has provided an enormous theoretical service in analyzing the space of education as a constitutive site for democratic struggle. He pursues the primacy of education as a political force by focusing on democracy both as the realized power of the people and as a mode of autonomy. In the first instance, he insists that "democracy means power of the people ... a regime aspiring to social and personal" freedom.[27] Democracy in this view suggests more than a simply negative notion of freedom in which the individual is defended against power. On the contrary, Castoriadis argues that any viable notion of democracy must reject this passive attitude toward freedom with its view of power as a necessary evil. In its place, he calls for a productive notion of power, one that is central to embracing a notion of political agency and freedom that affirms the equal opportunity of all to exercise political power in order to participate in shaping the most important decisions affecting their lives.[28] He ardently rejects the increasing "abandonment of the public sphere to specialists, to professional politicians,"[29] just as he rejects any conception of democracy that does not create the means for "unlimited interrogation in all domains" that close off in "advance not only every political question as well as every philosophical one, but equally every ethical or aesthetic question."[30] Castoriadis refuses a notion of democracy restricted to the formalistic processes of voting while at the same time arguing that the notion of participatory democracy cannot remain narrowly confined to the political sphere.

Democracy, for Castoriadis, must also concern itself with the issue of cultural politics. He rightly argues that progressives are required to address the ways in which every society creates what he calls its "social imaginary significations," which provide the structures of representation that offer individuals selected modes of identification, provide the standards for both the ends of action and the criteria for what is considered acceptable or unacceptable behavior, and establish the affective measures for mobilizing desire and human action.[31] The fate of democracy for Castoriadis is inextricably linked to the profound crisis of contemporary knowledge, characterized by increasing commodification, fragmentation, privatization, and a turn toward racial and patriotic conceits. As knowledge becomes abstracted from the demands of civic culture and is reduced to questions of style, ritual, and image, it undermines the political, ethical, and governing conditions for individuals and social groups to either participate in politics or construct those viable public spheres necessary for debate, collective action, and solving urgent social problems. As Castoriadis suggests, the crisis of contemporary knowledge provides one of the central challenges to any viable notion of politics. He writes:

> Also in question is the relation of ... knowledge to the society that produces it, nourishes it, is nourished by it, and risks dying of it, as well as the issues concerning for whom and for what this knowledge exists. Already at present these problems demand a radical transformation of society, and of the human being, at the same time that they contain its premises. If this monstrous tree of knowledge that modern humanity is cultivating more and more feverishly every day is not to collapse under its own weight and crush its gardener as it falls, the necessary transformations of man and society must go infinitely further than the wildest utopias have ever dared to imagine.[32]

Castoriadis is particularly concerned about how progressives might address the crisis of democracy in light of how social and political agents are being produced through dominant public pedagogies in a society driven by the glut of specialized knowledge, consumerism, and a privatized notion of citizenship that no longer supports noncommercial values and increasingly dismisses as a constraint any view of society that emphasizes public goods and social responsibility. What is crucial to acknowledge in Castoriadis' view of democracy is that the crisis of democracy cannot be separated from the dual crisis of representation and political agency. In a social order in which the production of knowledge, meaning, and debate is highly restricted, not only are the conditions for producing critical social agents limited, but also lost is the democratic imperative of affirming the primacy of ethics as a way of recognizing a social order's obligation to future generations. Ethics in this sense recognizes that the extension of power assumes a comparable extension in the field of ethical responsibility, a willingness to acknowledge that ethics means being able to answer in the present for actions that will be borne by generations in the future.[33]

Central to Castoriadis' work is the crucial acknowledgment that society creates itself through a multiplicity of organized pedagogical forms that provide the "instituting social imaginary" or field of cultural and ideological representations through which social practices and institutional forms are endowed with meaning, generating certain ways of seeing the self and its possibilities in the world. Not only is the social individual constituted, in part, by internalizing such meanings, but he or she acts upon such meanings in order to also participate in and, where possible, to change society. According to Castoriadis, politics within this framework becomes "the collective activity whose object" is to put into question the explicit institutions of society while simultaneously creating the conditions for individual and social autonomy.[34] Castoriadis' unique contribution to democratic political theory lies in his keen understanding that autonomy is inextricably linked to forms of civic education that provide the conditions for bringing to light how explicit and implicit power can be used to open up or close down those public spaces that are essential for individuals to meet, address public interests, engage pressing social issues, and participate collectively in shaping public policy. In this view, civic education brings to light "society's instituting power by rendering it explicit. . . . [I]t reabsorbs the political into politics as the lucid and deliberate activity whose object is the explicit [production] of society."[35] According to Castoriadis, political agency involves learning how to deliberate, make judgments, and exercise choices, particularly as the latter are brought to bear as critical activities that offer the possibility of change. Civic education as it is experienced and produced throughout a vast array of institutions provides individuals with the opportunity to see themselves as more than they simply are within the existing configurations of power of any given society. Every society has an obligation to provide citizens with the capacities, knowledge, and skills necessary for them to be, as Aristotle claimed, "capable of governing and being governed."[36] A democracy cannot work if citizens are not autonomous, self-judging, and independent, qualities that are indispensable for making vital judgments and choices about participating in and shaping decisions that affect everyday life, institutional reform, and governmental policy. Hence, civic education becomes the cornerstone of democracy in that the very foundation of self-government is based on people not just having the "typical right to participate; they should also be educated [in the fullest possible way] in order to be *able* to participate."[37]

Chapter 4

From a Pedagogy of Understanding to a Pedagogy of Intervention

> It is not the knowledge of good and evil that we are missing; it is the skill and zeal to act on that knowledge which is conspicuously absent in this world of ours, in which dependencies, political responsibility and cultural values part ways and no longer hold each other in check.[38]

Williams and Castoriadis were clear that pedagogy and the active process of learning were central to any viable notion of citizenship and inclusive democracy. Pedagogy looms large for both of these theorists not as a technique or *a priori* set of methods but as a political and moral practice. As a political practice, pedagogy illuminates the relationships among power, knowledge, and ideology, while self-consciously, if not self-critically, recognizing the role it plays as a deliberate attempt to influence how and what knowledge and identities are produced within particular sets of social relations. As a moral practice, pedagogy recognizes that what cultural workers, artists, activists, media workers, and others teach cannot be abstracted from what it means to invest in public life, presuppose some notion of the future, or locate oneself in a public discourse.

The moral implications of pedagogy also suggest that our responsibility as public intellectuals cannot be separated from the consequences of the knowledge we produce, the social relations we legitimate, and the ideologies and identities we offer up to students. Refusing to decouple politics from pedagogy means, in part, that teaching in classrooms or in any other public sphere should not only simply honor the experiences students bring to such sites, including the classroom, but also connect their experiences to specific problems that emanate from the material contexts of their everyday life. Pedagogy in this sense becomes performative in that it is not merely about deconstructing texts but about situating politics itself within a broader set of relations that addresses what it might mean to create modes of individual and social agency that enable rather than shut down democratic values, practices, and social relations. Such a project not only recognizes the political nature of pedagogy but also situates it within a call for intellectuals to assume responsibility for their actions—to link their teaching to those moral principles that allow them to do something about human suffering, as Susan Sontag has recently suggested.[39] Part of this task necessitates that cultural studies theorists and educators anchor their own work, however diverse, in a radical project that seriously engages the promise of an unrealized democracy against its really existing and radically incomplete forms. Of crucial importance to such a project is rejecting the assumption that theory can understand social problems without contesting their appearance in public life. Yet, any viable cultural politics needs a socially committed notion of injustice if we are to take seriously what it means to fight for the idea of the good society. I think Zygmunt Bauman is right in arguing that "[i]f there is no room for the idea of *wrong* society, there is hardly much chance for the idea of good society to be born, let alone make waves."[40]

Cultural studies theorists need to be more forcefully committed to linking their overall politics to modes of critique and collective action that address the presupposition that democratic societies are never too just or just enough, and such a recognition means that a society must constantly nurture the possibilities for self-critique, collective agency, and forms of citizenship in which people play a fundamental role in critically discussing, administrating, and shaping the material relations of power and ideological forces that bear down on their everyday lives. At stake here is the task, as Jacques Derrida insisted, of viewing the project of democracy as a promise, a possibility rooted in an ongoing struggle for economic, cultural, and social justice.[41] Democracy in this instance is not a sutured or formalistic regime; it is the site of struggle itself. The struggle over creating an inclusive and just democracy can take many forms, offers no political guarantees, and provides an important normative dimension to politics as an ongoing process of democratization that never ends. Such a project is based on the realization that a democracy that is open to exchange, question, and self-criticism never reaches the limits of justice. As Bauman observes:

> Democracy is not an institution, but essentially an anti-institutional force, a "rupture" in the otherwise relentless trend of the powers-that-be to arrest change, to silence and to eliminate from the political process all those who have not been "born" into power. . . . Democracy expresses itself in a continuous and relentless critique of institutions; democracy is an anarchic, disruptive element inside the political system; essentially, a force for *dissent* and change. One can best recognize a democratic society by its constant complaints that it is *not* democratic enough.[42]

By linking education to the project of an unrealized democracy, cultural studies theorists who work in higher education can move beyond those approaches to pedagogy that reduce it to a methodology like "teaching of the conflicts" or relatedly opening up a culture of questioning. In the most immediate sense, these positions fail to make clear the larger political, normative, and ideological considerations that inform such views of education, teaching, and visions of the future, assuming that education is predicated upon a particular view of the future that students should inhabit. Furthermore, both positions collapse the purpose and meaning of higher education, the role of educators as engaged scholars, and the possibility of pedagogy itself into a rather short-sighted and sometimes insular notion of method, specifically one that emphasizes argumentation and dialogue. There is a disquieting refusal in such discourses to raise broader questions about the social, economic, and political forces shaping the very terrain of higher education—particularly unbridled market forces, or racist and sexist forces that unequally value diverse groups of students within relations of academic power—or about what it might mean to engage pedagogy as a basis not merely for understanding but also for participating in the larger world. There is also a general misunderstanding of how teacher authority can be used to create the conditions for an education in democracy without necessarily falling into the trap of simply indoctrinating students.[43] For instance, liberal educator Gerald Graff believes that any notion of critical pedagogy that is self-conscious about its politics and engages students in ways that offer them the possibility for becoming critical—or what Lani Guinier calls the need to educate students "to participate in civic life, and to encourage graduates to give back to the community, which, through taxes, made their education possible"[44]—either leaves students out of the conversation or presupposes too much and simply represents a form of pedagogical tyranny. While Graff is a strong advocate of creating educational practices that open up the possibility of questioning among students, he refuses to connect pedagogical conditions that challenge how they think at the moment to the next step of prompting them to think about changing the world around them so as to expand and deepen its democratic possibilities. George Lipsitz criticizes academics such as Graff who believe that connecting academic work to social change is at best a burden and at worst a collapse into a crude form of propagandizing, suggesting that they are subconsciously educated to accept cynicism about the ability of ordinary people to change the conditions under which they live.[45] Teaching students how to argue, draw on their own experiences, or engage in rigorous dialogue says nothing about why they should engage in these actions in the first place. The issue of how the culture of argumentation and questioning relates to giving students the tools they need to fight oppressive forms of power, make the world a more meaningful and just place, and develop a sense of social responsibility is missing in work like Graff's because this is part of the discourse of political education, which Graff simply equates to indoctrination or speaking to the converted.[46] Here propaganda and critical pedagogy collapse into each other. Propaganda is generally used to misrepresent knowledge, promote biased knowledge, or produce a view of politics that appears beyond question and critical engagement. While no pedagogical intervention should fall to the level of propaganda, a pedagogy that attempts to empower critical citizens can't and shouldn't avoid politics. Pedagogy must address the relationship between politics and agency, knowledge and power, subject positions and values, and learning and social change while always being open to debate, resistance, and a culture of questioning. Liberal educators committed to simply raising questions have no language for linking learning to forms of public scholarship that would enable students to consider the important relationship between democratic public life and education, politics and learning. Disabled by the depoliticizing, if not slavish, allegiance to a teaching methodology, they have little idea of how to encourage students pedagogically to enter the sphere of the political, enabling them to think about how they might participate in a democracy by taking what they learn "into new locations—a third-grade classroom, a public library, a legislator's office, a park"[47]—or, for that matter, taking on collaborative projects that address the myriad problems citizens face in a diminishing democracy.

In spite of the professional pretense to neutrality, academics need to do more pedagogically than simply teach students how to be adept at forms of argumentation. Students need to argue and question, but they need much more from their educational experience. The pedagogy of argumentation in and of itself guarantees nothing, but it is an essential step toward opening up the space of resistance against authority, teaching students to think critically about the world around them, and recognizing interpretation and dialogue as conditions for social intervention and transformation in the service of an unrealized democratic order. As Amy Gutmann brilliantly argues, education is always political because it is connected to the acquisition of agency, to the ability to struggle with ongoing relations of power, and is a precondition for creating informed and critical citizens. Educators, she believes, need to link education to democracy and recognize pedagogy as an ethical and political practice tied to modes of authority in which the "democratic state recognizes the value of political education in predisposing [students] to accept those ways of life that are consistent with sharing the rights and responsibilities of citizenship in a democratic society."[48] This notion of education is tied not to the alleged neutrality of teaching methods but to a vision of pedagogy that is directive and interventionist on the side of reproducing a democratic society. Democratic societies need educated citizens who are steeped in more than just the skills of argumentation. And it is precisely this democratic project that affirms the critical function of education and refuses to narrow its goals and aspirations to methodological considerations. This is what makes critical pedagogy different from training. Indeed, it is precisely the failure to connect learning to its democratic functions and goals that provides rationales for pedagogical approaches that strip the meaning of what it means to be educated from its critical and democratic possibilities.

Raymond Williams and Castoriadis recognize that the crisis of democracy is not only about the crisis of culture but also about the crisis of pedagogy and education. Cultural studies theorists would do well to take account of the profound transformations occurring in the public sphere and reclaim pedagogy as a central category of cultural politics. The time has come for such theorists to distinguish professional caution from political cowardice and recognize that their obligations extend beyond deconstructing texts or promoting a culture of questioning. These are important pedagogical interventions, but they do not go far enough. We need to link knowing with action, and learning with social engagement, and this requires addressing the responsibilities that come with teaching students and others to fight for an inclusive and radical democracy by recognizing that education in the broadest sense is not just about understanding, however critical, but also about providing the conditions for assuming the responsibilities we have as citizens to expose human misery and to eliminate the conditions that produce it. I think Bauman is quite right in suggesting that as engaged cultural workers, we need to take up our work as part of a broader democratic project in which the good society

> is a society which thinks it is not just enough, which questions the sufficiency of any achieved level of justice and considers justice always to be a step or more ahead. Above all, it is a society which reacts angrily to any case of injustice and promptly sets about correcting it.[49]

Matters of responsibility, social action, and political intervention develop not simply out of social critique but also out of forms of self-critique. The relationship between knowledge and power, on the one hand, and scholarship and politics, on the other, should always be self-reflexive about what its effects are, how it relates to the larger world, whether or not it is open to new understandings, and what it might mean pedagogically to take seriously matters of individual and social responsibility. In short, this project points to the need for educators to articulate cultural studies, not only as a resource for theoretical competency and critical understanding, but also as a pedagogical practice that addresses the possibility of interpretation as intervention in the world. Cultural studies practitioners have performed an important theoretical task in emphasizing how meaning and value are constituted in language, representations, and social relations. They have been purposely attentive to a careful and thorough reading of a diverse number of cultural texts. They have rightly addressed in great detail and complexity how power makes demands on knowledge within various cultures of circulation and transformation and how knowledge functions as a form of power. But such a critical understanding, reading, and engagement with meaning is not enough. Politics demands more than understanding; it demands that understanding be coupled with a responsibility to others. This is central to the most basic requirement of taking seriously our role as moral and political agents who can both read the world and transform it.

Neoliberalism not only places capital and market relations in a no-man's-land beyond the reach of compassion, ethics, and decency; it also undermines those basic elements of the social contract and the political and pedagogical relations it presupposes in which self-reliance, confidence in others, and a trust in the longevity of democratic institutions provide the basis for modes of individual autonomy, social agency, and critical citizenship. One of the most serious challenges faced by cultural studies, then, is the need to develop a new language and the necessary theoretical tools for contesting a variety of forms of domination put into play by neoliberalism in the twenty-first century. Part of this challenge demands recognizing that the struggles over cultural politics cannot be divorced from the contestations and conflicts put into play through the forces of dominant economic and cultural institutions and their respective modes of education. In short, cultural studies advocates must address the challenge of how to problematize and pluralize the political, engage new sites of pedagogy as crucial, strategic public spheres, and situate cultural studies within an ongoing project that recognizes that the crisis of democracy is about the interrelated crises of politics, culture, education, and public pedagogy.

5
The Politics of Hope in Dangerous Times

> There is a time and place in the ceaseless human endeavor to change the world, when alternative visions, no matter how fantastic, provide the grist for shaping powerful political forces for change. I believe we are precisely at such a moment. Utopian dreams in any case never entirely fade away. They are omnipresent as the hidden signifiers of our desires. Extracting them from the dark recesses of our minds and turning them into a political force for change may court the danger of the ultimate frustration of those desires. But better that, surely, than giving in to the degenerate utopianism of neoliberalism (and all those interests that give possibility such a bad press) and living in craven and supine fear of expressing and pursuing alternative desires at all.

Under the prevailing reign of neoliberalism in the United States, hope appears foreclosed and progressive social change a distant memory. Imagining a life beyond capitalism or the prevailing culture of fear appears impossible at a time when the distinction between capitalism and democracy seems to have been erased. As market relations now become synonymous with a market society, freedom is reduced to a market strategy and citizenship either is narrowed to the demands of the marketplace or becomes utterly privatized. The upshot is that it has become easier to imagine the end of the world than the end of capitalism.[1] Within this dystopian universe, the public realm is increasingly reduced to an instrumental space in which individuality limits self-development to the relentless pursuit of personal interests, and the realm of autonomy is reduced to a domain of activity "in which ...

private goals of diverse kinds may be pursued."[2] This is evident in ongoing attempts by many liberals and conservatives to turn commercial-free public education over to market forces, dismantle traditional social provisions of the welfare state, divest all vestiges of the health-care system to private interests, and mortgage social security to the whims of the stock market. There is a growing sense in the American popular imagination that citizen involvement, social planning, and civic engagement are becoming irrelevant in a society where the welfare state is being aggressively dismantled.[3] Those traditional, if not imagined, public spheres in which people could exchange ideas, debate, and shape the conditions that structure their everyday lives increasingly appear to have little relevance or political significance in spite of the expressions of public good that followed the tragedy that took place on September 11, 2001. In the midst of growing fears about domestic security, coupled with Iraq war jingoism, dissent is now labeled as unpatriotic and is accompanied by the ongoing destruction of basic constitutional liberties and freedoms. As I have pointed out in previous chapters, under the USA PATRIOT Act, individuals can be detained by the government indefinitely without being charged, having no recourse to a lawyer or the benefit of a trial. The military has been given the right to engage in domestic surveillance, and the FBI can now gain access to library records in order to peruse an individual's reading habits. In the face of such assaults upon civil liberties, leading political figures such as former secretary of education William Bennett have taken out ads in the *New York Times* claiming that internal dissent both aids terrorists and poses an equally serious threat to the security of the United States. Increasingly, the appeal to patriotic fervor feeds a commercial frenzy that turns collective grief into profits and political responsibility into demagoguery. If the tragedy of the events of 9/11 served to resurrect noble concepts like public service and civic courage, the all-encompassing power of the market quickly converted them into forms of civic vacuity that spawned an endless array of consumer products including everything from shoes to flag pins. But the hijacking of the grief resulting from such egregious terroristic acts did more than serve as grist for expanding markets; it also provided a pretext for using the discourse of anti-terrorism to dismantle basic civil liberties, imprison the American public within a culture of fear and repression, provide huge revenues to major corporations supporting the Bush administration, and spend billions on military weaponry designed to give legitimacy to a foreign policy based on the dangerous threat of preemptive strikes against alleged enemies of the United States.

While the role of big government and public services made a brief comeback on behalf of the common good, especially in providing crucial services related to public health and safety, President Bush and his supporters remain wedded to the "same reactionary agenda he pushed before the attack."[4] Instead of addressing the gaps in both public health needs and the safety net for workers, young people, and the poor, the Bush administration pushed through both houses of Congress a stimulus plan based primarily on tax breaks for the wealthy and major corporations, while at the same time "pressing for an energy plan that features subsidies and tax breaks for energy companies and drilling in the arctic wilderness."[5] Investing in children, the environment, crucial public services, and those most in need, once again, gives way to investing in the rich and repaying corporate contributors. Such practices suggest that little has changed with respect to economic policy, regardless of all the talk about the past being irrevocably repudiated in light of the events of September 11. Where is the public outrage over a tax "stimulus" package that gives the wealthiest 1 percent of the population 50 percent of the total tax cut while it simultaneously refuses to enact legislation lessening the financial burden for older Americans on Medicare? Where is the outrage over the Bush administration's willingness to give billions in tax breaks to the wealthy while at the same time "student loans, child-care, food stamps, school lunches, job training, veterans programs, and cash assistance for the elderly and disabled poor are all being cut"?[6] Where is the outrage over a government that will spend up to $900 billion dollars on the cost of waging a war and maintaining postwar control of Iraq at the same time that it cuts veterans' benefits and gives the rich an exorbitant tax cut? Where is the outrage over the passing of legislation such as the USA PATRIOT Act and the Homeland Security Act that gives the government unprecedented power to spy on its citizens, suspend due process, and jail people for thirty days or more without filing any criminal charges? Where is the outrage over the Bush administration's ongoing assault on the environment, scornfully evident in the government's refusal to ratify the Kyoto treaty to reduce global warming (an example now being followed by Russia)? Where is the collective anger over a government bent on ingratiating corporate interests while gutting environmental protection laws such as the Clean Air Act, evident in its attempt to eliminate federal regulations that force power plants to reduce mercury emissions, its refusal to regulate enforcement cases against coal-burning power plants, and its unwillingness to put any restraints on auto companies that continue polluting the air with high levels of auto emissions?[7] Even more serious is the government's shameful refusal to address the plight of the 30 million people in the United States who live below the poverty line, the 74 million adults and children who have no health insurance, and the 1.4 million children who are homeless.[8]

Emptied of any substantial content, "democracy" even in its current deracinated state appears imperiled as individuals are unable to translate their privately suffered misery into public concerns and collective action. Civic engagement and political agency now appear impotent, and public values are rendered invisible in light of the growing power of multinational corporations to commercialize public space and disconnect power from issues of equity, social justice, and civic responsibility.[9] As the vast majority of citizens become detached from public forums that nourish social critique, political agency not only becomes a mockery of itself but is upended by market-based choices in which private satisfactions replace social responsibilities or, as Ulrich Beck puts it, biographic solutions become a substitute for systemic change.[10] As Cornelius Castoriadis argues, under such conditions, it becomes impossible to imagine politics as the autonomy of the collective, "which can be achieved only through explicit self-institution and self-governance."[11] From this perspective, contemporary notions of freedom—legitimated as an absence of restraint and a narrow form of self-interest—have nothing to do with real autonomy and effective freedom in which individuals function as critical thinkers capable of "putting existing institutions into question … [so that] democracy again becomes society's movement of self-institution—that is to say, a new type of regime in the full sense of the term."[12] As the space of criticism is undercut by the absence of public spheres that encourage the exchange of information, opinion, and critique, the horizons of a substantive democracy that abides by the promise of autonomous individuals and an autonomous society disappear against the growing isolation and depoliticization that mark the loss of politically guaranteed public realms—realms where the realized power of people, political participation, and engaged citizenship would otherwise make their appearance. Also rapidly disappearing are those public spaces and unmarketed cultural spaces in which people neither confuse the language of brand names with the language of autonomy and social engagement nor communicate through a commodified discourse incapable of defending vital institutions as a public good. One consequence is that political exhaustion and impoverished intellectual visions are fed by the increasingly popular assumption that there are no alternatives to the present state of affairs. As I have said in Chapter 1, neoliberalism violates the first rule of democratic politics by denying its own historical and contemporary relationship to power and ideology, and shrouding itself in a discourse of objectivity and historical inevitability.

At the same time, as Manuel Castells observes, economic power is removed from politics to the degree that it has become global and extraterritorial; power now flows beyond national boundaries, largely escaping from and defying the reach of traditional centers of politics that are nation based and local.[13] The space of power appears increasingly beyond the reach of governments and, as a result, nations and citizens are increasingly removed as political agents with regard to the impact that multinational corporations have on their daily lives. This does not mean that the state has lost all of its power. On the contrary, it now works almost exclusively to deregulate business, eliminate corporate taxes, dismantle the welfare state, and incarcerate so-called disposable populations. Once again, the result is not only general indifference but the elimination of those public spaces that reveal the rough edges of social order, disrupt consensus, and point to the need for modes of education that link learning to the conditions necessary for developing democratic forms of political agency and civic struggle.

As the promise of what Takis Fotopoulos calls an "inclusive democracy"[14]—with its emphasis on the abolishment of iniquitous power relations in all economic, political, and social spheres—recedes from public memory, unfettered brutal self-interests combine with retrograde social policies to make security a top domestic priority. One consequence is that all levels of government are being hollowed out as their policing functions increasingly overpower and mediate their diminishing social functions. Reduced to dismantling the gains of the welfare state and constructing policies that criminalize social problems such as homelessness and that prioritize penal methods over social investments, government is now discounted as a means of addressing basic economic, educational, environmental, and social problems. As I mentioned earlier in the book, zero-tolerance policies link the public schools to the prison system as a substitute for education. One consequence is that the distinction between prison and school has become blurred. The police, courts, and other disciplinary agencies have increasingly become the main forces used to address social problems and implement public policies that are largely aimed at minorities of race and color. Moreover, the increasing concerns for national security fueled by a hyped-up jingoism, especially in a post–Iraq war climate, have amplified the forces of domestic militarization in the United States, and the American people appear increasingly drawn together "through shared fears rather than shared responsibilities."[15] Misfortune breeds contempt, and poverty is confused with personal neglect. Across the social sphere, neoliberalism's dismissal of public goods, coupled with an ecology of fear, rewrites the meaning of community through the logic of government threats, anti-terror campaigns waged against minorities, the squelching of dissent, and a highly coordinated government and media blitz in support of the occupation of Iraq.

Labeled by neoliberals and right-wing politicians as the enemy of freedom (except when it aids big business), government is discounted as a guardian of the public interest. As a result, government bears no responsibility either for the poor and dispossessed or for the collective future of young people. The disappearance of those noncommodified public spaces such as libraries, independent bookstores, union halls, adult clubs, and other sites necessary for reactivating our political sensibilities as critical citizens, engaged public intellectuals, and social agents is happening at a time when public goods are being disparaged in the name of privatization and critical public forums are ceasing to resonate as sites of utopian possibility. The lack of justice and equity in American society increases proportionately to the lack of political imagination and collective hope.

Politics devoid of a radical vision often either degenerates into cynicism or appropriates a view of power that appears to be equated only with domination. It is therefore crucial that progressives, educators, concerned citizens, and other activists respond with a renewed effort to merge politics, pedagogy, and ethics with a revitalized sense of the importance of providing the conditions for constructing critical forms of individual and social agency rather than believing the fraudulent, self-serving hegemonic assumption that democracy and capitalism are the same or, indeed, that politics as a site of contestation, critical exchange, and engagement is in a state of terminal arrest. In part, this would demand engaging the alleged argument for the death of politics as symptomatic not only of the crisis of democracy but also of the more specific crisis of vision, education, agency, and meaning that disconnects public values and ethics from the very sphere of politics.

Some social theorists such as Todd Gitlin make the plunge into forms of political cynicism easier by suggesting that any attempt to change society through a cultural politics that links the pedagogical and the political will simply augment the power of the dominant social order.[16] Lost from such accounts is the recognition that democracy has to be struggled over, even in the face of a most appalling crisis of political agency. Within this discourse, little attention is paid to the fact that struggles over politics, power, and democracy are inextricably linked to creating democratic public spheres where individuals can be educated as political agents equipped with the skills, capacities, and knowledge they need not only to actually perform as autonomous social agents but also to believe that such struggles *are worth taking up*. Neither homogeneous nor nostalgic, *the public sphere* points to a plurality of institutions, sites, and spaces; it is a sphere in which people not only talk, debate, and reassess the political, moral, and cultural dimensions of publicness but also develop processes of learning and persuasion as a way of enacting new social identities and altering "the very structure of participation and the ... horizon of discussion and debate."[17]

The struggle over politics, in this instance, is linked to pedagogical interventions aimed at subverting dominant forms of meaning in order to generate both a renewed sense of agency and a critical subversion of dominant power itself. Agency now becomes the site through which, as Judith Butler has pointed out in another context, power is not transcended but reworked, replayed, and restaged in productive ways.[18] Central to my argument is the assumption that politics is not simply about power but also, as Cornelius Castoriadis points out, "has to do with political judgments and value choices,"[19] indicating that questions of civic education and critical pedagogy (learning how to become a skilled activist) are central to the struggle over political agency and democracy. Civic education and critical pedagogy emphasize critical reflexivity, bridge the gap between learning and everyday life, make visible the connection between power and knowledge, and provide the conditions for extending democratic rights, values, and identities while drawing upon the resources of history. However, among many educators and social theorists, there is a widespread refusal to address education as a crucial means either for expanding and enabling political agency or for recognizing that such education takes place, not only within schools but across a wide variety of public spheres mediated through the very mechanisms of culture itself.

Democracy has now been reduced to a metaphor for the alleged "free" market and has nothing to do with a more substantive rendering of the term, such as what Noam Chomsky calls "involving opportunities for people to manage their own collective and individual affairs."[20] It is not that a genuine democratic public space once existed in some ideal form and has now been corrupted by the values of the market; rather, these democratic public spheres, even in limited forms, seem no longer to be animating concepts for making visible the contradiction and tension between the reality of existing democracy and the promise of a more fully realized democracy. While liberal democracy offers an important discourse around issues of "rights, freedoms, participation, self-rule, and citizenship," it has been mediated historically, as John Brenkman observes, through the "damaged and burdened tradition" of racial and gender exclusions, economic injustice, and a formalistic, ritualized democracy which substituted the swindle for the promise of democratic participation.[21] Part of the challenge of creating a substantive and inclusive democracy lies in constructing new locations of struggle, vocabularies, and subject positions that allow people in a wide variety of public spheres to become more than they are now, to question what it is they have become within existing institutional and social formations, and, as Chantal Mouffe points out, "to give some thought to their experiences so that they can transform their relations of subordination and oppression."[22]

Despite the urgency of the current historical moment, educators should avoid crude anti-theoretical calls to action. More than ever, they can appropriate scholarly and popular sources and use theory as a critical resource to name particular problems and make connections between the political and the cultural, to break what Homi Bhabha has called "the continuity and the consensus of common sense."[23] As a resource, theory becomes an important way of critically engaging and mapping the crucial relations among language, texts, everyday life, and structures of power as part of a broader effort to understand the conditions, contexts, and strategies of struggle that will lead to social transformation. I am suggesting that the tools of theory emerge out of the intersection of the past and present and respond to and are shaped by the conditions at hand. Theory, in this instance, addresses the challenge of connecting the world of the symbolic, discursive, and representational to the social gravity and force of everyday issues rooted in material relations of power.

The overriding political project at issue here calls for educators and others to produce new theoretical tools (a new vocabulary and set of conceptual resources) for linking theory, critique, education, and the discourse of possibility to the creation of the social conditions for the collective production of what Pierre Bourdieu calls realist utopias.[24] Such a project points to constructing a new vocabulary for connecting what we read to how we engage in movements for social change, while recognizing that simply invoking the relationship between theory and practice, critique and social action, is not enough. For as John Brenkman points out, "theory becomes [a] closed circuit when it supposes it can understand social problems without contesting their manifestation in public life."[25] Theory as such is also symptomatic of a kind of retreat from the uneven battles over values and beliefs characteristic of some versions of postmodern conceptions of the political. Any attempt to give new life to a substantive democratic politics must, in part, produce alternative narratives to those employed by the producers of official memory and address what it means to make the pedagogical more political. This means engaging the issue of what kind of educational work is necessary within different types of public spaces to enable people to use their full intellectual resources and skills both to provide a profound critique of existing institutions and to enter into the public sphere in order to interrupt the operations of dominant power and fully address what Zygmunt Bauman calls the "hard currency of human suffering."[26]

If emancipatory politics is to meet the challenge of neoliberal capitalism, politics needs to be theorized not as a science or set of objective conditions but as a point of departure in specific and concrete situations. This means rethinking the very meaning of the political so that it can provide a sense of direction but no longer be used to provide complete answers. In short, such a politics entails that we ask why and how particular social formations have a specific shape and come into being, and what it might mean to rethink such formations in terms of opening up new sites of struggles and movements. Politics in this sense offers a notion of the social that is open and provisional, providing a conception of democracy that is never complete but constantly amenable to different understandings of the contingency of its decisions, mechanisms of exclusions, and operations of power.[27] In this formulation, the struggle for justice and against injustice never ends. In the absence of such languages and the public spheres that make them operative, politics becomes narcissistic, reductionist, and it caters to the mood of widespread pessimism and the cathartic allure of spectacle or the seductions of consumerism. Emptied of its political content, public space increasingly becomes either a site of self-display—a favorite space for the public relations intellectual, speaking ever so softly on National Public Radio—or a site for the reclaiming of a form of social Darwinism represented most explicitly in reality-based television with its endless instinct for the weaknesses of others and its masochistic affirmation of ruthlessness and steroidal power. Or, it becomes a site where citizenship is stripped of its civic responsibilities and is reduced to the narrow obligations and needs of an unfettered individualism. Escape, avoidance, and narcissism are now coupled with the public display, if not celebration, of those individuals who define agency in terms of their survival skills rather than their commitment to dialogue, critical reflection, solidarity, and relations that open up the promise of public engagement with important social issues. Indeed, Reality TV now embraces the arrogance of neoliberal power as it smiles back at us, while simultaneously legitimating downsizing and the ubiquity of the political economy of fear.

Educated Hope[28]

Against an increasingly oppressive corporate-based globalism, educators and other cultural workers need to resurrect a language of resistance and possibility, a language that embraces a militant utopianism while constantly being attentive to those forces that seek to turn such hope into a new slogan or punish and dismiss those who dare look beyond the horizon of the given. Central to any viable notion of politics is the recognition that hope must be part of a broader movement creating the pedagogical conditions for producing individual and social agents who are willing to "make use of the freedom they have and to acquire the freedom they are told they have but have not."[29] Hope, in this instance, is one of the preconditions for individual and social struggle, for the ongoing practice of critical education in a wide variety of sites, and for courage on the part of intellectuals inside and outside the academy who use the resources of theory to address pressing social problems. But hope is also a referent for civic courage and its ability to mediate the memory of loss and the experience of injustice as part of a broader attempt to open up new locations of struggle, contest the workings of oppressive power, and undermine various forms of domination. For hope to be more than an empty abstraction, it must be firmly anchored in the realities and contradictions of everyday life and have some hold on the present. This suggests a notion of hope that, as Derrida described it, is willing to take up the "necessity to rethink the concepts of the possible and the impossible" in the face of the current attacks on public life and democracy worldwide.[30]

As I have argued elsewhere, the philosopher Ernst Bloch provides important theoretical insights on the importance of hope.[31] He argues that hope must be concrete, a spark that not only reaches out beyond the surrounding emptiness of privatization but anticipates a better world in the future, a world that speaks to us by presenting tasks based on the challenges of the present time. For Bloch, utopianism becomes concrete when it links the possibility of the "*not yet*" with forms of political agency animated by a determined effort to engage critically with the past and present in order to address pressing social problems and realizable tasks.[32] Bloch believes that utopianism cannot be removed from the world and is not "something like nonsense or absolute fancy; rather it is *not yet* in the sense of a possibility; that it could be there if we could only do something for it."[33] As a discourse of critique and social transformation, utopianism in Bloch's view is characterized by a "militant optimism," one that foregrounds the crucial relationship between critical education and political agency, on the one hand, and the concrete struggles needed, on the other hand, to give substance to the recognition that every present is incomplete. For theorists such as Bloch, utopian thinking is anticipatory rather than messianic, mobilizing rather than therapeutic. At best, such thinking, as Anson Rabinach argues, "points beyond the given while remaining within it."[34] The longing for a more human society in this instance does not collapse into a retreat from the world but emerges out of critical and practical engagements with present behaviors, institutional formations, and everyday practices. Hope in this context does not ignore the worst dimensions of human suffering, exploitation, and social relations; on the contrary, it acknowledges the need to sustain the "capacity to see the worst and offer more than that for our consideration."[35] The great challenge to militant utopianism, with its hope of keeping critical thought alive, rests in the emerging consensus among a wide range of political factions that neoliberal democracy is the best we can do. The impoverishment of intellectuals—with their growing refusal to speak of addressing, if not ending, human suffering and social injustices—is now matched by the poverty of a social order that cannot conceive of any alternative to itself.

Feeding into the increasingly dominant view that society cannot be fundamentally improved outside of market forces, neoliberalism strips utopianism of its possibilities for social critique and democratic engagement. By doing so it undermines the need to reclaim utopian thinking as both a discourse of human rights and a moral referent for dismantling and transforming dominant structures of wealth and power.[36] At the same time, neoliberalism undermines both the language of solidarity and those public spaces in which it is nourished, acted upon, and translated into a vibrant social movement and political force.

The loss of hope and the collapse into cynicism can be found all across the ideological spectrum extending from the Left to the Right. What is shared among these groups is the presupposition that utopian thinking is synonymous with state terrorism and that progressive visionaries are nothing more than unrealistic, if not dangerous, ideologues. The alternative offered here is what Russell Jacoby calls a "convenient cynicism,"[37] the belief that human suffering, hardship, and massive inequalities in all areas of life are simply inherent in human nature and an irreversible part of the social condition. Or, in its liberal version, the belief that "America's best defense against utopianism as terrorism is preserving democracy as it currently exist[s] in the world"[38]—a view largely shared by ultra-conservatives such as Lynne Cheney, John Ashcroft, and Norman Podhoretz. Within this discourse, hope is foreclosed, politics becomes militarized, and resistance is privatized, aestheticized, or reduced to some form of hyper-commercialized escapism. Against a militant and radically democratic utopianism, the equation of terrorism and utopianism appears deeply cynical. Neoliberalism not only appears flat, it also offers up an artificially conditioned optimism—operating at full capacity in the pages of *Fast Company, Wired Magazine,* the *Wall Street Journal,* and *Forbes* as well as in the relentless entrepreneurial hype of figures such as George Gilder and the Nike and Microsoft revolutionaries—in which it becomes increasingly difficult to imagine a life beyond the existing parameters of market pleasures, mail-order catalogues, shopping malls, and Disneyland.[39] The profound anti-utopianism that is spurred on by neoliberalism, its myths of the citizen as consumer and markets as sovereign entities, and its collapse of the distinction between both market liberties and civic liberties, on the one hand, and a market economy and a market society, on the other, not only commodifies a critical notion of political agency, it also undermines the importance of multiple democratic public spheres.

Against the dystopian hope of neoliberalism, I want to argue for the necessity of educated hope as a crucial component of a radically charged politics "grounded in broad-based civic participation and popular decision making."[40] Educated hope as a form of oppositional utopianism makes visible the necessity for progressives and other critical intellectuals to be attentive to the ways in which institutional and symbolic power are tangled up with everyday experience. Any politics of hope must tap into individual experiences while at the same time linking individual responsibility with a progressive sense of social agency. Politics and pedagogy alike spring "from real situations and from what we can say and do in these situations."[41] At its best, hope translates into civic courage as a political and pedagogical practice that begins when one's life can no longer be taken for granted. In doing so, it makes concrete the possibility for transforming politics into an ethical space and public act that confront the flow of everyday experience and the weight of social suffering with the force of individual and collective resistance and the unending project of democratic social transformation. Emphasizing politics as a pedagogical practice and performative act, educated hope accentuates the notion that politics is not only played out on the terrain of imagination and desire but is also grounded in relations of power mediated through the outcome of situated struggles dedicated to creating the conditions and capacities for people to become critically engaged political agents.

Combining the discourse of critique and hope is crucial to affirming that critical activity offers the possibility for social change and to viewing democracy as a project and a task, as an ideal type that is never finalized and has a powerful adversary in the social realities it is meant to change. Postcolonial theorist Samir Amin echoes this call by arguing that educators should consider addressing the project of a more realized democracy as part of an ongoing process of democratization. According to Amin, democratization "stresses the dynamic aspect of a still-unfinished process" while rejecting notions of democracy that are given a definitive formula.[42] An oppositional cultural politics can take many forms, but given the current assault on democratic public spheres, it seems imperative that progressives revitalize the struggles over social citizenship, particularly those aimed at expanding liberal freedoms, ensuring the downward distribution of resources, and creating forms of collective insurance that provide a safety net for individual incapacities and misfortunes. Simultaneously, any viable cultural politics must address the necessity to develop collective movements that can challenge the subordination of social needs to the dictates of commercialism and capital.

Central to such a politics would be a critical public pedagogy that attempts to make visible alternative models of radical democratic relations in a wide variety of sites. These spaces can make the pedagogical more political by raising fundamental questions such as: What is the relationship between social justice and the distribution of public resources and goods? What conditions, knowledge, and skills are prerequisites for political agency and social change? At the very least, such a project involves understanding and critically engaging dominant public transcripts and values within a broader set of historical and institutional contexts. It means moving beyond the often paralyzing language of critique or the refusal to relate the discourse of politics to the everyday relations through which people experience their lives. It also means refusing to offer scripted narratives that fix people in a particular notion of identity, agency, or future. As I have stressed before, many educators have failed to take seriously Antonio Gramsci's insight that "[e]very relationship of 'hegemony' is necessarily an educational relationship"—with its implication that education as a cultural pedagogical practice takes place across multiple sites as it signals how, within diverse contexts, education makes us both subjects of and subject to relations of power.[43] Education in this sense assigns critical meaning to action, connects understanding with engagement, and links engagement with the hope of democratic transformation. In other words, it is a precondition for producing subjects capable of making their own histories within diverse economies of power and politics. As Edward Said has insisted, education mediated through the politics of hope is not about "appropriating power and then using it to create new forms of orthodoxy and antidemocratic authority ... but [about] the employment of the simpler, and indeed more elegant, spur of trying right now to alleviate human suffering, reducing the wakefulness of corporate profligacy and redirecting resources back to communities and individuals."[44] In what follows, I comment on what it would mean to make the pedagogical more political as part of a broader effort to reclaim the radically democratic role of public and higher education, as well as what it would mean to address educators as critical public intellectuals.

Public Intellectuals and Higher Education

In opposition to the corporatizing of schooling, educators need to define public and higher education as a resource vital to the promise and realization of democratic life. Such a task points, in part, to the need for academics, students, parents, social activists, labor organizers, and artists to join together and oppose the transformation of higher education into commercial spheres, to resist what Bill Readings has called a consumer-oriented, corporate university more concerned about accounting than accountability.[45] As Zygmunt Bauman reminds us, schools are among the few public spaces left where students can learn the "skills for citizen participation and effective political action. And where there are no [such] institutions, there is no 'citizenship' either."[46] Likewise, higher education may be one of the few remaining sites in which students can learn about the limits of commercial values, address what it means to learn the skills of social citizenship, and work to deepen and expand the possibilities of collective agency and democratic life. I think Toni Morrison is right in arguing that "[i]f the university does not take seriously and rigorously its role as a guardian of wider civic freedoms, as interrogator of more and more complex ethical problems, as servant and preserver of deeper democratic practices, then some other regime or menage of regimes will do it for us, in spite of us, and without us."[47]

Defending higher education as a vital public sphere is necessary to develop and nourish the proper mediation between civil society and corporate power, between identities founded on democratic principles and identities steeped in forms of competitive, self-interested individualism that celebrate selfishness, profit-making, and greed. This view suggests that higher education should be defended through intellectual work that self-consciously recalls the tension between the democratic imperatives or possibilities of public institutions and their everyday realization within a society dominated by market principles. Education is not training, and learning at its best is connected to the imperatives of social responsibility—though we must recognize that political agency does not reduce the citizen to a mere consumer.

I believe that academics and others bear an enormous responsibility in opposing neoliberalism by bringing democratic political culture back to life. As part of this challenge, educators, students, and others must begin to organize individually and collectively against those corporate forces that increasingly define the university less as a social institution than as a business, less as a public good than as a private benefit. As higher education is reduced to the sovereignty of the market, academic labor is being reconfigured in ways that not only remove faculty from issues of governance but increasingly replace faculty with part-time workers and full-time careers with fixed term appointments. For example, in "2001 only about one-quarter of new faculty appointments were to full-tenure track positions (i.e., half were part-time, and more than half of the remaining full-time positions were 'off' the tenure track."[48] Resisting this ongoing assault on higher education demands that educators take seriously the importance of sustained political education and critical pedagogy as a necessary step in redefining the meaning and purpose of higher education as a public sphere essential to creating a democratic society. Radical pedagogy as a form of resistance might be premised on the assumption that educators vigorously oppose any attempt on the part of liberals and conservatives in conjunction with corporate forces to reduce them to the role of either technicians or multinational operatives. But equally important, such issues need to be addressed as part of a broader concern for renewing the struggle for social justice and democracy. Such a struggle, as the writer Arundhati Roy points out, demands that as intellectuals we ask ourselves some very "uncomfortable questions about our values and traditions, our vision for the future, our responsibilities as citizens, the legitimacy of our 'democratic institutions,' the role of the state, the police, the army, the judiciary, and the intellectual community."[49]

Edward Said argued that the public intellectual must function within institutions, in part, as an exile, as someone whose "place it is publicly to raise embarrassing questions, to confront orthodoxy and dogma, to be someone who cannot easily be co-opted by governments or corporations."[50] From this perspective, the educator as public intellectual becomes responsible for linking the diverse experiences that produce knowledge, identities, and social values in the university to the quality of moral and political life in the wider society; and he or she does so by entering into public conversations unafraid of controversy or of taking a critical stand.

The issue is not whether public or higher education has become contaminated with politics; it is more importantly about recognizing that education is already a space of politics, power, and authority. The crucial matter at stake is how to appropriate, invent, direct, and control the multiple layers of power and politics that constitute both the institutional formation of education and the pedagogies that are often an outcome of deliberate struggles to put into place particular notions of knowledge, values, and identity. As committed educators, we cannot eliminate politics, but we can work against a politics of certainty, a pedagogy of censorship, and an institutional formation that closes down rather than opens up democratic relations. This requires that we work diligently to construct a politics without guarantees, one that perpetually questions itself as well as all those forms of knowledge, values, and practices that appear beyond the process of interrogation, debate, and deliberation. Against a pedagogy and politics of certainty, it is crucial for educators to develop pedagogical practices that problematize considerations of institutional location, mechanisms of transmission, and social effects.

Public intellectuals need to approach social issues mindful of the multiple connections and desires that tie humanity together; but they need to do so as border intellectuals moving within and across diverse sites of learning as part of an engaged and practical politics that recognizes the importance of "asking questions, making distinctions, restoring to memory all those things that tend to be overlooked or walked past in the rush to collective judgment and action."[51] If educators are to function as public intellectuals, they need to provide the opportunities for students to learn that the relationship between knowledge and power can be emancipatory, that their histories and experiences matter, and that what students say and do counts in their struggle to unlearn privileges, productively reconstruct their relations with others, and transform, when necessary, the world around them. More specifically, such educators need to argue for forms of pedagogy that close the gap between the university and everyday life.

At one level, this suggests pedagogical practices that affirm and critically enrich the meaning, language, and knowledge that students actually use to negotiate and inform their lives. Unfortunately, however, the political, ethical, and social significance of the role that popular culture plays as the primary pedagogical medium for young people remains largely unexamined. Educators need to challenge the assumption that popular cultural texts cannot be as profoundly important as traditional sources of learning in teaching about important issues framed through, for example, the social lens of poverty, racial conflict, and gender discrimination. This is not a matter of pitting popular culture against traditional curricular sources. More importantly, it is a matter of using both in a mutually informative way, always mindful of how these spheres of knowledge might be employed to teach students how to be skilled citizens, whether that means learning how to use the Freedom of Information Act, knowing one's constitutional rights, building coalitions, writing policy papers, learning the tools of democracy, analyzing social problems, or learning how to make a difference in one's life through individual and social engagements.

As I have said throughout this book, intellectuals bear a special ethical and political responsibility at a time when the forces of mass persuasion and power assault all things democratic and noncommercial on this planet. The urgency of the current historical moment demands that intellectuals discard the professionalism, careerism, and isolation that make them largely irrelevant. Intellectuals inside and outside the university have an important obligation to offer alternative critical analyses, dismantle the illusory discourse of power, and work with others in creating an international social movement for social justice and radical change. In short, educators need to become provocateurs; they need to take a stand while refusing to be involved in either a cynical relativism or doctrinaire politics. Central to intellectual life is the pedagogical and political imperative that academics engage in rigorous social criticism while becoming a stubborn force for challenging false prophets, deflating the claims of triumphalism, and critically engaging all those social relations that promote material and symbolic violence.

At the same time, intellectuals must be deeply critical of their own authority and understand how it structures classroom relations and cultural practices. In this way, the authority they legitimate in the classroom (as well as in other public spheres) would become both an object of self-critique and a critical referent for expressing a more "fundamental dispute with authority itself."[52] This is not to say that teachers should abandon authority or simply equate all forms of authority with the practice of domination, as some radical educators have suggested. On the contrary, authority in the sense I am describing here follows Gramsci in calling upon educators to assert authority in the service of encouraging students to think beyond the conventions of common sense, to expand the horizons of what they know, and to discover their own sense of political agency and what it means to appropriate education as a critical function. Crucial here is the recognition that while the teacher "is an actor on the social and political stage, the educator's task is to encourage human agency, not mold it in the manner of Pygmalion."[53] As Said mentions in a different context, "the role of the intellectual is not to consolidate authority, but to understand, interpret, and question it: this is another version of speaking truth to power."[54]

Conclusion

There is a lot of talk among academics in the United States and elsewhere about the death of politics and the inability of human beings to imagine a more equitable and just world in order to make it better. I would hope that of all groups, educators would be the most vocal and militant in challenging this assumption by reclaiming the university's subversive role—specifically, by combining critiques of dominant discourses and the institutional formations that support and reproduce them with the goal of limiting human suffering while at the same time attempting to create the concrete economic, political, social, and pedagogical conditions necessary for an inclusive and substantive democracy. Critical scholarship is crucial to such a task, but it is not enough. Individual and social agency becomes meaningful as part of the willingness to imagine otherwise in order to act otherwise. Scholarship has a civic and public function, and it is precisely the connection between knowledge and the larger society that makes visible its ethical and political function. Knowledge can and should be used for amplifying human freedom and promoting social justice, and not simply for creating profits or future careers. Intellectuals need to take a position, and, as Said argues, they have an obligation to "remind audiences of the moral questions that may be hidden in the clamour of public debates ... and deflate the claims of [neoliberal] triumphalism."[55] Combining theoretical rigor with social relevance may be risky politically and pedagogically, but the promise of a substantive democracy far outweighs the security and benefits that accompany a retreat into academic irrelevance and the safe haven of a no-risk professionalism that requires, as Paul Sabin observes, "an isolation from society and vows of political chastity."[56]

To think beyond the given is a central demand of politics, but it is also a condition for individual and collective agency. At the heart of such a task is both the possibility inherent in hope and the knowledge and skills available in a critical education. At this particular moment in the United States, cynicism has become a major tool in the war against democracy. But rather than make despair convincing, I think it is all the more crucial to take seriously Derrida's provocation that "[w]e must do and think the impossible. If only the possible happened, nothing more would happen. If I only did what I can do, I wouldn't do anything."[57] In the next chapter, I want to address both the content of neoliberal common sense and the processes it puts into play through the educational force of the culture to produce particular identities, values, and social practices. At stake here is an attempt to both modify the visible and shatter the maps of meaning through which neoliberal ideology works to secure consent and banish any element of indeterminacy, agency, justice, and struggle.

6
Against Neoliberal Common Sense: Rethinking Cultural Politics and Public Pedagogy in Dark Times

Neoliberalism and the New Gilded Age

In his State of the Union address in 1935, President Franklin Delano Roosevelt did what might seem unthinkable today. Note well his words:

> We find our population suffering from old inequalities, little changed by vast sporadic remedies. In spite of our efforts and in spite of our talk, we have not weeded out the over privileged and we have not effectively lifted up the underprivileged. Both of these manifestations of injustice have retarded happiness.... We have, however, a clear mandate from the people, that Americans must forswear that conception of the acquisition of wealth which, through excessive profits, creates undue private power over private affairs and, to our misfortune, over public affairs as well. In building toward this end we do not destroy ambition ... [b]ut we do assert that the ambition of the individual to obtain for him and his a proper security, a reasonable leisure, and a decent living throughout life, is an ambition to be preferred to the appetite for great wealth and great power.[1]

Roosevelt insisted that the struggle against inequality, excessive wealth, and limitless power was inextricably linked to the struggle for democracy. Moreover, he believed that the federal government should play a crucial role in providing the social rights that enabled members of the polity to be political and civic agents in all facets of their lives. Rather than eliminating state-sponsored protections against individual misfortunes and debilitating insecurities, Roosevelt recognized that for democracy and justice to flourish, individuals had to be protected from the existential tremors and material deprivations that disabled the possibility of politics as a matter of public commitment, thoughtfulness, and critical engagement.[2] In this instance, democracy as both an ethical and a political practice became meaningful only through the creation of social provisions and federal policies that enabled existing and future generations to gain access to the knowledge, skills, jobs, housing, education, and security that made possible their active participation in the civic and political life of the larger society. The challenges facing the nation under FDR were addressed neither through the discourses of fear, jingoistic nationalism, and empire-building nor through the reduction of the state to a punishing regime. On the contrary, FDR exercised political leadership and mobilized the government to provide the social spending and federal legislation necessary to offer Americans a decent livelihood, a defense against the major hazards and vicissitudes of life, and government policies that enabled everyone to procure decent work, homes, and an adequate retirement income.[3] Roosevelt's conception of democracy was a corrective to the immediacy of the Great Depression of the 1930s and a political refusal to reproduce the politics of the nineteenth-century Gilded Age "with its minimal taxation, absence of regulation and reliance on faith-based charity rather than government social programs."[4] Unfortunately, the legacies of the New Deal and its ideological successor, the Great Society, initiated by President Lyndon Johnson in the 1960s, have been removed from both the rhetoric of politics and the very meaning of governance in the last few decades. I am not suggesting here that either Roosevelt or Johnson fully addressed the related principles of equality, public welfare, and political citizenship. In fact, despite their eloquent rhetoric, neither moved close in policy to an espousal of equality capable of challenging the radically unequal and frequently polarizing nature of the structural forces of capitalism—let alone taking the lead in promoting the economic, social, and cultural conditions in which people can live a just and dignified existence. Moreover, neither president balked at instituting policies that restricted working-class radicalization while keeping in check those forces that would have challenged, if not dismantled, consolidated corporate power. Where they did succeed was in keeping alive, at least rhetorically, the notion that the primary measure of a government's responsibility in upholding the social contract was the degree to which it took seriously its commitment to "the broad welfare of society, rather than the narrow interests of particular elites."[5]

In this chapter, I take up in explicit terms the challenge of addressing the politics and pedagogy of neoliberal common sense and the crucial role it has played implicitly in securing a new and powerful form of neoliberal hegemony—a project that has animated the entirety of *Against the Terror of Neoliberalism.* But I am concerned not only with trying to understand how neoliberalism became the reigning ideology of the new millennium but also with determining how the construction of neoliberal common sense gains explanatory force through its reliance on the educational force of the culture in securing widespread consent from the American people. At the same time, I call for individuals and social movements to challenge neoliberal common sense by rethinking both the meaning of cultural politics for the twenty-first century and what is involved in making an active and ongoing pedagogical engagement across a wide variety of public spheres central to any viable notion of democratic politics. At the risk of appearing merely descriptive, I would like to map a series of not-readily-connectable, discrete cultural snapshots and moments that speak to the broader crisis not only of democratic politics but also of the existential conundrums that mark efforts to live as human beings in such debased times. I begin thus not with abstractions but with concrete specifics that embody both the rationality and logic of neoliberal common sense while largely operating beneath the radar of critical analysis. In this case, I commence with the everyday or small change of neoliberal cultural politics and proceed to draw out its implications in theoretical, political, and pedagogical terms. Theory in this context becomes a resource and a basis for a form of critical analysis that hopefully makes clear that the consequences of neoliberal common sense deserve the kind of careful consideration a thoughtful public might render, were it not for the imposition of such things as slick advertising, entertainment news, and celebrity culture on the time/space coordinates of our everyday consciousness. One of the key arguments in this chapter is that neoliberalism has not simply led to a redirection in the functions of the state. Rather, it has changed both the function and the idea of the state from one committed to social welfare to one narrowly committed to regulating the global movements of capital and expanding the policing, punishing, and militarizing functions of society.[6] By extending the domain of economics into politics, market rationality now organizes, regulates, and defines the basic principles and workings of the state. Gone are the days when the state "assumed responsibility for a range of social needs."[7] Instead, the state now pursues a wide range of "'deregulations,' privatizations, and abdications of responsibility to the market and private philanthropy."[8] What's more, it has accomplished these shifts through a pedagogical practice that teaches society to understand the world via market mentalities and corporate paradigms. In what follows I will call for attention to the neoliberal state and its complementary pedagogical practices in an effort to reclaim the political and discerning force of pedagogy as a critical tool necessary to the rebuilding of a socially committed state.

Under the regime of neoliberalism[9] that has been put into play since the fiscal crisis of the 1970s, big government is considered the enemy of democracy, social provisions of the kind vouchsafed by FDR and Johnson are dismissed as socialistic, politics is entirely subordinated to the imperatives of the rediscovered "free-market economy," and those institutions that make a mockery of a substantive democracy are deemed the greatest beneficiary of government power. Grover Norquist, the president of Americans for Tax Reform, and arguably Washington's leading strategist for neoliberal policy during George W. Bush's presidency, reveals in the following comment the utter disdain many right-wing politicians and ideologues hold for government policies that operate to uphold the social contract and support the public infrastructure. He states: "My goal is to cut government in half in twenty-five years, to get it down to the size where we can drown it in the bathtub."[10] Without apology, Norquist and his neoliberal ilk target some parts of government for downsizing a little more energetically than others. They are most concerned with dismantling the parts of the public sector that serve the social and democratic needs of the nonaffluent majority of the American populace. The parts that provide corporate subsidies, military contracts to corporations, and welfare to the opulent minority while doling out punishment to the poor are preserved from that great domestic war tool, the budgetary axe. The primary strategy of the neoliberal statecraft used since the Reagan administration has been to "starve-the-beast" by producing large budget deficits in order to force reductions in various social programs such as Medicare, Medicaid, education, food stamps, and community development block grants. For instance, in the Bush administration's federal budget for 2007, "the hardest-hit government programs are those that provide food, child care, health care, and affordable housing to the neediest in our society,"[11] and yet these cuts are being implemented at a time when the poverty rate has risen, with "over 37 million Americans living below the official poverty line" and millions more struggling to pay for basic necessities.[12] Despite the fact that the number of poor Americans has grown by five million since 2001,[13] the Bush administration diverts money from social programs in order to provide handsome tax cuts for the rich and to allocate $626 billion for a bloated 2007 military budget, increasingly tied to massive expenditures for conducting the wars in Iraq and Afghanistan.

Bush's neoliberal policies redistribute income upward to the rich, especially those in "the top 1 percent of earnings, [who] had an average income of $1.25 million, [and] saw their effective individual tax rates drop to 19.6 percent in 2004 from 24.2 percent in 2000."[14] His tax cuts have done more than benefit the rich; they have also resulted in the cutting of crucial social programs and the deepening of race and class inequalities. One need only recall the Bush administration's utter indifference to the plight of poor blacks who were victimized first by Hurricane Katrina and then by the government's initial, shocking indifference to the tragedy. In spite of the catastrophe wrought by "starving the beast," federal policy continued to reproduce, expand, and celebrate a market-driven society in which "top executives now make more in a day than the average worker makes in a year."[15] The politics of neoliberal inequality is also evident in the salaries and bonuses now handed out to top executives. For example, James Simmons, a leading hedge fund manager, earned $1.7 billion in 2006 while the combined income "of the top 25 hedge fund managers ... [totaled] $14 billion—enough to pay New York City's 80,000 public school teachers for nearly three years."[16] It gets worse. The Associated Press reports that compensation for half of America's CEOs in the Standard & Poor's top 500 firms averaged more than $8.3 million in 2006.[17] In some cases, top executives got bonuses and huge salaries while their employees not only had to take cutbacks on their salaries, retirement packages, and health benefits but also worked longer hours. What is especially disconcerting ethically and politically is that some industries, such as the airline industry, are using postbankruptcy initiatives to pay exorbitant salaries and bonuses to their top executives while airline employees are being asked to make excessive concessions. For example, Northwest Airlines will pay $26.6 million in equity to CEO Doug Steenland and divide over $40 million among four executive vice presidents[18] while the "new labor contracts lock workers into lower pay rates and more company-friendly work rules. ... [F]light attendants, for instance, now see their pay top out at about $35,400 a year, down from $44,190 before Northwest filed for bankruptcy protection."[19] In some cases, workers are being asked to make a choice between putting food on the table and paying for crucial medical services. Such disparities in income, wealth, and opportunity in the richest country on earth should be viewed as an outrage.

At the dawn of the new millennium, the Gilded Age with its "'dream-worlds' of consumption, property, and power"[20] has returned with a vengeance. Democracy now either functions as a transparent legitimation for empire abroad or is invoked at home under the conceit of political expediency in the "war on terror" and staged as a performance that mimics the tawdriness and deceit of a rampant culture of corruption and secrecy at the highest levels of government. The war on terror has produced a culture of fear and a battered citizenry increasingly powerless to defend the ideals of democracy and freedom that have been largely gutted in the name of security, privatization, deregulation, and what David Harvey calls the "accumulation of capital by dispossession."[21] As Michael Hardt and Antonio Negri have argued, war has become "the organizing principle of society, and politics merely one of its means or guises."[22] Indeed, as the matrix for all relations of power, war has become the foundation for politics itself and marks a historical transition from the social state to the punishing state. War, fear, death, violence, and greed are now the primary forces shaping

American life and add up to what is unique about the current regime of neoliberalism: its hatred of democracy and dissent.[23] The possibilities of democracy are now answered not with the rule of law, however illegitimate, but with the threat or actuality of violence.[24]

The collapse of the social state, state-administered securities, and the ideal of collective insurance cannot be blamed entirely on neoliberalism, whose success constitutes a related but different narrative. The short list of some of the more general factors in their demise might include the emergence of the military-industrial complex in the post–World War II period; the corporate tax revolt of the 1960s; the tax revolt, in turn, of the middle-class that began in California amid growing economic crises in the 1970s; skyrocketing interest rates and recession in the '70s; Reagan's union-busting policies; the rise of rapacious free-trade agreements; and the general backlash against the social and cultural gains of the civil rights movement, particularly the liberal and radical ideals of the '60s. Access to formal education, at all levels, which had been at the center of civil rights struggles, came under considerable attack from the 1970s to the present. But this is not to suggest that the Right was uninterested in education per se. In some sense, it actually took Raymond Williams' notion of the long revolution more seriously than did the Left, which found itself stunned and disorganized in the face of such assault. Having thoroughly defunded or corporatized those institutions devoted to enhancing the intellectual capacities, cosmopolitanism, and thoughtfulness of its citizenry—namely, the mass media, from news services to book publishing, as well as formal educational sites—the Right developed its own pedagogical spheres for engaging the public. The result of such efforts was the wildly successful rise and dominance of right-wing talk radio by the early '90s; the emergence of a powerful network of neoconservative think tanks and public intellectuals; the takeover of the media by corporate interests, coupled with the Foxification of many of its outlets; the transformation of the public schools into testing centers or prototypes for the nation's prison system, with its surveillance mechanisms and zero-tolerance policies; and the corporatization and militarization of higher education.[25] All of these forces played a role in undermining the social state and its governing apparatuses.

As the welfare state came apart, a market ideology and morality emerged that narrowed not only the meaning of freedom but also the very nature of the public good, public institutions, social security, safety nets—and with these transitions, so too the more abstract concepts of individual agency and citizenship. Economic discourse now trumped social justice, reinforced by the popularizing of a neoliberal discourse in which "all human activities and spaces can and should be absorbed into economic systems"[26] in the interests of consumer choice, market efficiency, and the kind of excellence procured only through rigorous competition (how any of this happened in an era of consolidated corporatism is a theme for another paper). At stake here was an "argument against politics, or at least against a politics that attempts to govern society in social rather than economic terms."[27] Freedom was now decoupled from any vestige of the social, and most welfare provisions were seen as benefiting those deemed immoral and lazy, if not utterly unworthy. At the same time, those who opposed the notion of welfare and social state provision now viewed themselves as being unduly taxed and victimized precisely because of their hard work, thrift, and good fortune.[28] Underlying this shrinking of the ethic of solidarity and equality was a wilting of not only politically active citizenship but, it cannot be repeated often enough, also the modes of critical education that provided the fundamental condition for its existence. And this ongoing assault on public and higher education, as well as on those critical public spheres that are at the heart of educating and informing the culture at large, can be seen in the triumph of the construction of a notion of common sense that provided the conditions both for neoliberalism to take root and for citizens willingly to embrace the enormous risks as well as the comforts, for the lucky few, of consumer society rather than embrace the responsibilities and long-term commitments of a viable democratic state.[29]

One of the most distinctive features of politics in the United States in the last thirty years has been the inexorable move away from the social state and the promise of equality, human dignity, racial justice, and freedom—upon which its conception of democracy rests—to the narrow and stripped down assumption that equates democracy with market identities, values, and relations. Hollowed out under a regime of politics that celebrates the trinity of privatization, deregulation, and financialization, democracy has turned dystopian. Consumption has become the authentic mark of citizenship, while individual competition and personal responsibility are elevated to the new gospel of wealth and material salvation. Driven by the imperative to accumulate capital, neoliberal ideology determines definitions of value, rewarding those who participate in consumer society with the protections of citizenship while those who can't take part as consumers are seen as "failed" and "ever more disposable."[30] In this scenario, freedom is transformed into its opposite for the vast majority of the population as a small, privileged minority can purchase time, goods, services, and security while the vast majority increasingly are relegated to a life without protections, benefits, and support. For those populations considered expendable, redundant, and invisible by virtue of their race, class, and youth, life becomes increasingly precarious.

Mounting signs of increasing redundancy, dispensability, and social homelessness are evident in the depression-level jobless rates among black youth, ranging "at various times over the past few years ... from 59 percent to a breathtaking 72 percent."[31] Such statistics give new meaning to the slogan "Live free or die." The cost of this politics of war and expenditure[32] becomes clear in heartbreaking stories about young people who literally die because they lack health insurance and live in extreme poverty. In one recent case, Deamonte Driver, a seventh-grader in Prince George's County, Maryland, died because his mother did not have the health insurance to cover an $80 tooth extraction. Owing to a lack of insurance, his mother was unable to find an oral surgeon willing to treat her son. By the time he was admitted and diagnosed in a hospital emergency room, the bacteria from the abscessed tooth had spread to his brain and, in spite of the high-quality intensive treatment he finally received, he eventually died.[33] As Jean Comaroff points out in a different context, "the prevention of ... pain and death ... seems insufficient an incentive" to advocates of neoliberal market fundamentalism "in a world in which some 'children are ... consigned to the coffins of history.'"[34] The United States is one of the few industrialized countries in the world that does not provide universal health care for its children, millions of whom are at risk of dying because of a health-care system that doles out services and access on the basis of wealth and privilege rather than human need. Shamelessly, despite the growing number of horror stories about children dying in America for lack of health insurance, the Bush administration vetoed, as I mentioned earlier, the State Children's Health Insurance Program, putting hundreds of thousands of children nationwide at risk.[35] Referring to the 2008 presidential campaign, *New York Times* columnist Bob Herbert argues that "American children are dying because of a lack of access to health care, and we're worried about Mitt Romney's religion and asking candidates to raise their hands to show whether they believe in evolution. I am starting to believe in time travel because there's no doubt this nation is moving backward."[36] TV stock-picker James Cramer makes Herbert's point all the more relevant, if not terrifying, by insisting unapologetically that "the pursuit of wealth is our true national pastime."[37]

What Cramer and others ignore in this homage to market relations as the essence of our national spirit is the implication of bodies, despair, death, and disposability under a regime of neoliberal discourses and policies that support the irrational belief that the market can solve all problems. The collateral damage that reveals the lie of this allegedly unassailable form of common sense can be glimpsed not only in the fate of millions of children who lack health insurance but also in uncomfortable truths that emerge daily in narratives of despair and neglect that haunt those few public spheres that serve the needs of society's most vulnerable.

Chip Ward, a thoughtful administrator at the Salt Lake City Public Library, writes about the growing plight of homelessness in the United States and the enormous strain it puts on libraries as the services once provided by the social state evaporate. He writes poignantly about a homeless person named Ophelia, who retreats to the library because like many of the homeless she has nowhere else to go to use the bathroom, secure temporary relief from bad weather, or simply be able to rest. Excluded from the American dream and treated as both expendable and a threat, Ophelia, in spite of her obvious mental illness, defines her existence in terms that offer a chilling metaphor that extends far beyond her plight. Ward describes Ophelia's presence and actions in the following way:

> Ophelia sits by the fireplace and mumbles softly, smiling and gesturing at no one in particular. She gazes out the large window through the two pairs of glasses she wears, one windshield-sized pair over a smaller set perched precariously on her small nose. Perhaps four lenses help her see the invisible other she is addressing. When her "nobody there" conversation disturbs the reader seated beside her, Ophelia turns, chuckles at the woman's discomfort, and explains, *"Don't mind me, I'm dead. It's okay. I've been dead for some time now." She pauses, then adds reassuringly, "It's not so bad. You get used to it."* Not at all reassured, the woman gathers her belongings and moves quickly away. Ophelia shrugs. Verbal communication is tricky. She prefers telepathy, but that's hard to do since the rest of us, she informs me, "don't know the rules."[38]

Ophelia represents just one of the 200,000 chronically homeless who now use public libraries and any other accessible public space to find shelter. Many are often sick, disoriented, high on drugs, intoxicated, or mentally disabled and close to a nervous breakdown because of the stress, insecurity, and danger that they face every day. Increasingly, along with the 3.5 million human beings who experience homelessness each year in the United States, they are treated like criminals, as if punishment were the appropriate civic response to poverty, mental illness, and human suffering. In what has become standard practice, many cities now either fine the homeless for begging or, as in Key West, Florida, enact punitive legislation in which "panhandlers can be sentenced to 60 days in jail and fined $500."[39] Some jails have entire wings devoted to the mentally ill, the majority of whom are indigent and homeless. Of course, criminalizing and incarcerating the homeless is not only unethical but also financially wasteful. Ward estimates that what it costs to jail a mentally ill person in Utah is the "yearly equivalent of tuition at an Ivy League college."[40] While human resources are being wasted in such scenarios, what is really at stake is an abuse of politics, law, and power, the skewed rationalities of which promote social injustice and needless human suffering. And while Ophelia's comments may be dismissed as the rambling of a "crazy" woman, they speak to something much deeper about the current state of American society and its abandonment of entire populations that are now considered the human waste of a neoliberal social order. Ward's understanding of Ophelia's plight as a public issue is instructive:

> Ophelia is not so far off after all—in a sense she is dead and has been for some time. Hers is a kind of social death from shunning. She is neglected, avoided, ignored, denied, overlooked, feared, detested, pitied, and dismissed. She exists alone in a kind of social purgatory. She waits in the library, day after day, gazing at us through multiple lenses and mumbling to her invisible friends. She does not expect to be rescued or redeemed. She is, as she says, "used to it." She is our shame. What do you think about a culture that abandons suffering people and expects them to fend for themselves on the street, then criminalizes them for expressing the symptoms of illnesses they cannot control? We pay lip service to this tragedy—then look away fast.[41]

Social death becomes the fate of more and more people as the socially strangulating politics of competitive individualism, self-interest, and consumerism become the organizing principles of everyday life. Solutions for social problems are now framed in the depoliticizing vocabularies of the therapeutic and emotional, often enmeshed in the rigid political and moral certainties of bigotry, intolerance, racism, ideological purity, and religious fundamentalism. As the market becomes the template for solving all of society's problems by simply canceling them out, the discourse of self-help, personal responsibility, and self-reliance operate under the conceit of neutrality and efficiency, effectively erasing everything required to understand and address the major social issues of our time. As Jean and John Comaroff put it:

> Gone is any official speak of egalitarian futures, work for all or the paternal government envisioned by the various freedom movements. These ideas have given way to a spirit of deregulation, with its taunting mix of emancipation and limitation. Individual citizens, a lot of them marooned by a rudderless ship of state, try to clamber about the good ship enterprise.[42]

Under current circumstances, the legacy of FDR's social state is largely dismantled and the relationship between politics and life takes on an ominous importance for those populations considered disposable. With its indifference to social justice and democracy, neoliberal rationality ushers in a stage of late modernity in which terror, death, and human suffering mutually inform one another.[43] It is no wonder that conservative Republicans wanted to replace FDR's image on the dime with that of Ronald Reagan, the avatar of neoliberal fundamentalism.[44]

Militarizing the Neoliberal State

> Today as never before in their history Americans are enthralled with military power. The global military supremacy that the United States presently enjoys—and is bent on perpetuating—has become central to our national identity. More than America's matchless material abundance or even the effusions of its pop

culture, the nation's arsenal of high-tech weaponry and the soldiers who employ that arsenal have come to signify who we are and what we stand for.[45]

Rather than simply fading away in keeping with the shrinking and drowning fantasies of some, the state has actually increased its policing and militarizing functions.[46] As decades of social benefits are dismantled, the state refashions itself by rewriting the nature and meaning of its power to increase what Zygmunt Bauman calls "its order-protective policing function."[47] This is particularly true for the United States, which after the events of 9/11 accelerated its militarizing agenda, enacting what Hardt and Negri call "the passage from a welfare state to a warfare state."[48] While militarization is a deeply historical and contingent process, taking many different forms over time and space, it became the mechanism of first choice under the administration of George W. Bush and Dick Cheney. Their administration has been enthralled with military symbols and power, and has worked tirelessly to further solidify "America's marriage of a militaristic mission with utopian ends ... as the distinguishing element of contemporary U.S. policy."[49] Similarly, Bush's militaristic cast of mind was matched by policies that blurred the line between military and civilian functions, diverted funding from social programs for the poor to funds that support the "war on terror," furthered the interests of the national security state, and increasingly relied upon military rather than political solutions to solve both domestic and foreign problems. Under such circumstances, militarized rhetoric, parlance, and practices have become so much a part of our lives that we hardly recognize "that the fields of politics and violence ... are no longer separated," even as the Bush government insisted that it acted in the interests of spreading democracy.[50] With the dawn of a more militarized millennium, violence becomes inaudible in its senseless repetition and unrecognizable in its ever-expanding spectacle. Militarized metaphors become more commonplace, used to describe the multiple wars on drugs, urban crime, poverty, even obesity, and a number of other social problems.[51]

A highly charged example of the ongoing militarization of American society is evident in the way in which military experience, knowledge, values, and discourses increasingly provide the template for organizing many public schools. Military-like discipline and zero-tolerance policies exemplify the structuring principles that are turning many schools, urban ones in particular, into prison-like institutions, largely controlled, regulated, and monitored by armed guards and increasingly characterized by lock-downs, invasive surveillance techniques, and the erosion of student rights. Numerous reports such as *Criminalizing the Classroom*, *Education on Lockdown*, and *Derailed* document the increasing over-policing of public schools, the incarceration of students for petty acts that in an earlier era would have been effectively handled with a stern admonishment from the principal, and the expulsion of students who are perceived as troublemakers (largely youth of color).[52] The increasing tendency to view children as trouble in American society rather than as a social investment for a democratic future means that more and more young people are being abandoned and brutalized by the schools, the police, and other social agencies. *Education on Lockdown* provides numerous examples of the detrimental impact on students as a consequence of the increasing militarization of public schools. The report cites one particular event in a Chicago public school in February 2003, in which "a 7-year-old boy was cuffed, shackled, and forced to lie face down for more than an hour while being restrained by a security officer.... Neither the principal nor the assistant principal came to the aid of the first grader, who was so traumatized by the event he was not able to return to school."[53]

As the criminalization of social problems and the war on youth intensify under the neoliberal state, youth are subject to a growing number of indiscriminate, cruel, and potentially illegal practices by the criminal justice system.[54] Bob Herbert recently expressed his own concerns about the social justice of a system that is "criminalizing children and teenagers all over the country, arresting them and throwing them in jail for behavior that in years past would never have led to the intervention of law enforcement." He insists that "this is an aspect of the justice system that is seldom seen. But the consequences of ushering young people into the bowels of police precincts and jail cells without a good reason for doing so are profound."[55] Youth seem especially vulnerable at a time when they face massive unemployment and inhabit public schools and other public spheres that are undergoing massive disinvestment, especially in the urban centers. Racialized violence and punitive measures are often the first recourse of the state in dealing with brown and black youth.[56]

Instead of offering poor and disenfranchised youth decent schools and potential employment, the militarized state offers them the promise of incarceration; instead of providing the homeless with decent shelter and food, the state issues them fines that they cannot possibly pay or simply imprisons them; instead of providing people with decent health care, the state passes legislation that makes it more difficult to file for bankruptcy and easier to end up in a criminal court; instead of treating new immigrants with dignity, the government supports policies and practices advocated by right-wing militia groups and fortifies borders with walls, not unlike the infamous Berlin Wall that divided East and West Berlin for twenty-eight years or the wall that the Israeli government has built inside the Occupied Territories.[57] In a post-9/11 world, neoliberalism has been weaponized and the high-intensity warfare it promotes abroad is replicated in low-intensity warfare at home. While both militarism and neoliberalism have a long history in the United States, the symbiotic relationship into which they have entered and the way in which it has become normalized constitutes a distinct historical moment.

Moreover, the ever-expanding militarized neoliberal state marked by the interdependence of finance capital, authoritarian order, and a vast war machine now serves as a powerful pedagogical force that shapes our lives, memories, and daily experiences, while effacing everything we thought we knew about history, justice, and the meaning of democracy.[58]

Neoliberalism and the Politics of Disposability

> Is the notion of biopower sufficient to account for the contemporary ways in which the political, under the guise of war, of resistance, or of the fight against terror, makes the murder of the enemy its primary and absolute objective? War, after all, is as much a means of achieving sovereignty as a way of exercising the right to kill. Imagining politics as a form of war, we must ask: What place is given to life, death, and the human body (in particular the wounded or slain body)? How are they inscribed in the order of power?[59]

Politics is never simply about elections. The distribution of material and cultural resources, producing willing subjects of the state, protecting state interests, regulating and disciplining the body, maintaining loyal consuming subjects, and punishing those who are not so loyal—all of these are state projects. More recently, another power has been added to the list of the prerogatives of state power: the ability to condemn entire populations of its own citizens as disposable, and to make life and death the most crucial and relevant objects of political control. As states no longer rely on such domestic populations for many forms of labor, a new politics of disposability now governs American domestic and foreign policy. Within this discourse, those citizens and residents deemed unproductive (the poor, weak, and racially marginalized) are regarded as useless and therefore expendable. This is a politics in which entire populations are considered disposable, an unnecessary burden on state coffers, and as such are consigned to fend for themselves.[60] The punishing state now produces Gitmos not only abroad but also at home as thousands of immigrants disappear and in some cases die "in a secretive detention system, a patchwork of federal centers, private prisons and local jails."[61] As Naomi Klein argues, the politics of disposability travels and is now a worldwide phenomenon.

> Mass privatization and deregulation have bred armies of locked-out people, whose services are no longer needed, whose lifestyles are written off as "backward," whose basic needs go unmet. These fences of social exclusion can discard an entire industry, and they can also write off an entire country, as has happened to Argentina. In the case of Africa, essentially an entire continent can find itself exiled to the global shadow world, off the map and off the news, appearing only during wartime when its citizens are looked on with suspicion as potential militia members, would-be terrorists or anti-American fanatics.[62]

Like the consumer goods that flood American society, immigrants, refugees, the unemployed, the homeless, the poor, young people, and the disabled are relegated to a frontier-zone of invisibility created by a combination of economic inequality, racism, the collapse of the welfare state, and the brutality of a militarized society, all of which "designates and constitutes a production line of human waste or wasted humans."[63]

The daily consequences of neoliberal rationality and negative globalization go beyond the often analyzed power of finance capital, the separation of nation-state-based politics from the power of global corporations, the deregulation of corporations, an emerging militarism, and other economically driven registers of governmental and corporate power. Neoliberal policies also employ a shifting, yet deadly, cultural politics that normalizes its own values and decouples ethics and social responsibility from the consequences of ever-expanding market relations and ever-foreclosing human ones. Neoliberalism as a form of biocapital reaches into all aspects of the global social order and "when deployed as a form of governmentality"[64] attempts to regulate, shape, guide, construct, and affect the conduct of people. Under neoliberalism, economic and political power expand far beyond the production of goods and the legislating of laws. As neoliberalism becomes biopolitical, the boundaries of the cultural, economic, and political become porous and leak into each other, sharing the task, though in different ways, of producing identities, goods, knowledge, modes of communication, affective investments, and all other aspects of social life and the social order.[65] Neoliberalism produces a particular view of the world and mobilizes an array of pedagogical practices in a variety of sites in order to normalize its modes of governance, subject positions, forms of citizenship, and rationality.[66] Under the reign of neoliberal ideology, "The Rising Tide of Free Markets" is now embraced as the precondition for freedom, and "[e]conomic development is understood as preceding human development."[67] Moreover, as a mode of oppressive public pedagogy, neoliberalism extends and disseminates "market values to all institutions and social action, [and] prescribes the citizen-subject of a neoliberal order."[68] Central to the construction of the neoliberal subject is the acceptance of what Lynda Cheshire and Geoffrey Lawrence call the "individualization of risk, whereby responsibility for managing the risks of contemporary life have been redistributed from the state and the economy to the individual. ... [S]uch moves are synonymous with the emergence of an advanced liberal mode of rule that relies upon the construction of self-governing individuals who accept that the responsibility for improving the conditions of their existence lies in their own hands."[69]

The oppressive public pedagogy at work in neoliberal discourse is one that claims that all public difficulties are individually determined and all social problems can be reduced to biographical solutions. And as Zygmunt Bauman points out, "In our 'society of individuals' all the messes into which one can get are assumed to be self-made and all the hot water into which one can fall is proclaimed to have been boiled by the hapless failures [of those] who have fallen into it. For the good and the bad that fill one's life a person has only himself or herself to thank or to blame. And the way the 'whole-life-story' is told raises this assumption to the rank of an axiom."[70] Similarly, any notion of collective goals designed to deepen and expand the meaning of freedom and democracy as part of the vocabulary of the public good is entirely lost in neoliberal discourse. That is, "[c]ollective goals such as redistribution, public health and the wider public good have no place in this landscape of individual preferences."[71] Instead, neoliberal theory and practice give rise to the replacement of the social contract with a market contract in which political rights are strictly limited, economic rights are deregulated and privatized, and social rights are replaced by individual duty and self-reliance. Within the impoverished vocabulary of privatization, getting ahead, and exaggerated materialism that promises to maximize choice and to minimize taxation, the new citizen-consumer bids a hasty retreat from those public spheres that view critique as a democratic value, collective responsibility as fundamental to the nurturing of a democracy, and the deepening and expanding of collective protections as a legitimate function of the state. Defined largely by "the exaggerated and quite irrational belief in the ability of markets to solve all problems," the public domain is emptied of the democratic ideals, discourses, and identities needed to address important considerations such as "universal health care, mass transit, affordable housing, trains across the nation, subsidized care for the young and elderly, and government efforts to reduce carbon emissions. The list, of course, is endless."[72] Underlying these elements of neoliberal rationality is a pedagogical practice, parading as common sense—produced, located, and disseminated from many institutional and cultural sites ranging from the shrill noise of largely conservative talk radio to the halls of academia and the screen culture of popular media.

As a distinct form of governmentality, neoliberalism has not only vitiated democracy, gutted the social state, reinforced the conditions for the emergence of the punishing state, and undermined any viable notion of the common good, it has also produced a hardening of the culture.[73] Public and private policies of investing in the public good are dismissed as bad business, just as the notion of protecting people from the dire misfortunes of poverty, sickness, or the random blows of fate is viewed as an act of bad faith. Long-term commitments are considered a trap and weakness is now a sin, punishable by social exclusion. The state's message to unwanted populations: Society neither wants nor cares about nor needs you. An unchecked form of social Darwinism rages throughout the culture, demonizing the most vulnerable, treating misfortune with scorn, and granting legitimacy to a fiercely competitive ethos that offers big prizes to society's winners while reproducing a growing insensitivity to the plight and suffering of others, especially those now considered redundant in a world where market values determine one's worth. Hollywood and Reality TV, among other cultural sites, unapologetically provide in the name of entertainment the ideological undercurrents of a neoliberal politics of disposability.[74] Defined primarily through a discourse of "lack" in the face of the social imperatives of good character, personal responsibility, and hyper-individualism coupled with the drive toward cultural homogeneity, entire populations are expelled from the index of moral concerns. Defined as neither producers nor consumers, they are reified as products without value and then disposed of like "leftovers in the most radical and effective way: we make them invisible by not looking and unthinkable by not thinking."[75]

Keeping disposable bodies and populations invisible is not always easy, especially when the registers of class and race become intertwined with matters of war, national honor, and patriotism. An obvious example is when young black and brown youth try to escape the politics of disposability by joining the military with the hopes of attaining job skills and some measure of economic security. But such hopes are overridden by their status as cannon fodder smashed daily by the violence in the streets and on the battlefields in Iraq and Afghanistan and by the body bags, mangled bodies, and amputated limbs that offer all that is left of broken bodies and dreams—sights rarely seen in the narrow ocular vision of the dominant media. When it becomes impossible to relegate disposable populations to the space of the not-seen, neoliberal ideology offers up endless representations that dehumanize and reify their presence in society. A few examples will suffice. Long after the tragedy of Hurricane Katrina, and after the government incompetence that produced it had been exposed, the victims were rendered not only unworthy of state protections but also dangerous and disposable. What kind of politics is at work when, for instance, Anderson Cooper on his CNN *360°* television program returns a year later to the scene of the crime named Katrina and, rather than connecting the Bush administration's contempt for social programs and the social state to the failed attempts to reconstruct New Orleans, focuses instead on the increasing crime and lawlessness that have emerged in the wake of the Katrina tragedy? What forces are at work in a culture where Juan Williams, a senior correspondent for National Public Radio, writes in a *New York Times* op-ed that the real lesson of Katrina is that the poor "cause problems for themselves" and that they should be condemned for not "confronting the poverty of spirit"?[76] Williams invokes the ghost of personal responsibility and self-reliance to demonize those populations for whom the very economic, educational, political, and social conditions that make agency possible barely exist.

The hardening of the culture can also be seen in the 2007 film *The Condemned,* which gives new meaning to the marriage of casino capitalism and the redundancy of certain disposable groups. The plot is organized around the sinister machinations of a wealthy television mogul who purchases ten inmates from different countries and puts them on an island as part of a contest in which they have to plot to kill each other with the promise that the last person alive in thirty hours will be set free. The killings are broadcast live on the Internet, with the hope of drawing millions of viewers. Sally Kohn, commenting on the film and the current state of hyper-violence in the culture, claims that if this type of program were to take place in real life "streaming live internet deaths would probably bring in more viewers than *American Idol* on elimination night."[77] In 2007, a Dutch television network traded on the receptive currency of casino capitalism when it said that it would produce a Reality TV program called *The Big Donor Show*.[78] The show was to be organized around three patients competing for a kidney from a terminally ill woman who would make her choice after viewers sent in text messages to the program. In the end, the show was revealed to be a hoax, which the sponsors claimed was orchestrated in order "to raise consciousness about the desperate shortage of organ donors."[79] Many people thought the hoax was a good idea because it called attention to the plight of people needing such organs. Others thought it was not too far removed from the scenario whereby people are already trying to buy organs through personal appeals on the Internet. Not addressed in the corporate media was how the program resonated with prevailing market values that foster a narrow sense of social responsibility, agency, and public values. Also neglected was how neoliberalism functioning as a form of biocapital has established the conditions in which serious medical decisions involving life and death are reduced to the logic and spectacle of a game show, the promise of high television ratings, and utterly privatized choices organized, in this case, around which individual recipient the kidney donor might find most appealing.

As public spaces disappear under the weight of commercial and narrowly privatized concerns, we lose those public spaces where individuals have access to a language for developing democratic identities and nonmarket values such as trust, fidelity, love, compassion, respect, decency, courage, and civility. As neoliberalism refigures the relationship between space and capital, it eliminates those public spheres where individuals can develop vocabularies for the political in a seemingly apolitical world of market and increasingly military relations. Moreover, as the boundaries between public culture and commercial interests collapse, commodified public and private spaces provide neither a context for moral considerations nor a language for defending vital social institutions as a collective good. One consequence is that neoliberalism as both an ideology and a practice represents the disturbing victory of military aspirations, structural power, and commercial values over those competing public spheres and value systems that are critical to a just and democratic society. Under the existing regime of neoliberalism, commercialized spheres appear to be the only places left where one can dream about winning a chance at living a decent life or mediating the difficult decisions that often make the difference between living and dying.

Commodified pleasures, hyper-competitiveness, greed, a growing divide between the rich and poor, and horrific suffering commingle in a society that has stopped questioning itself, allowing public issues to dissolve into a sea of talk shows, advertisements, and celebrity culture. Important issues about politics, power, war, life, and death get either trivialized or excluded from public discourse as a market-driven media culture strives to please its corporate sponsors and attract the audiences it has rendered illiterate. While the corporate media either trivialize, misrepresent, or exclude important social issues, the American government continues to dismiss the critical role of dissent as either unpatriotic, un-American or, even worse, a condition of treason.[80]

The representations and by-products of a neoliberal assault on a democratic imaginary are everywhere. As the punishing society increasingly fills its jails, prisons, and penitentiaries, approaching a total of more than 2 million people,[81] mostly poor people of color, the role of the punishing state and the public and private world of prison culture are largely addressed by the media through their habit of reporting news as entertainment, as when celebrity starlet Paris Hilton was ordered to jail for a short period of time in the summer of 2007. The hardening of the culture is also evident in the visual representations that are pervasive among the culture industry. I offer two telling examples. In Chicago, a lawyer puts up a billboard with photographs of a sexy and scantily clad young woman and a buff, bare-chested young man with a text between the photos proclaiming "Life's short. Get a divorce." Rather than discuss what such an ad says about the narratives that contemporary culture legitimates—in this case, the devaluing of any notion of intimacy as well as of long-term commitment to spouses and children—the corporate media focus largely on discussions that the ad promoted in "bars, shops and offices [over] whether it is okay to get divorced—just because you feel like it."[82] Indifferent to the national shame of over 9 million children who lack health insurance and the millions more living in poverty, the dominant media report without critical comment on the boom in kiddie birthday parties, some single events costing as much as $50,000. Instead of addressing the state of impoverishment and deprivation experienced by millions of children in America, the corporate media focus on how "[a] spiraling level of competitiveness to keep up with the 'baby Joneses' is driving parents across the nation to pull out all the stops and their checkbooks to make sure that Junior's birthday party becomes the talk of the town."[83]

In the 1987 movie *Wall Street,* the central character, Gordon Gekko, offered a commentary on the unchecked greed that captured the reckless and dehumanizing spirit of investment banking that permeated the 1980s. As

Gekko put it, "The point is, ladies and gentleman, that "greed"—for lack of a better word—is good. Greed is right. Greed works. Greed clarifies, cuts through, and captures the essence of the evolutionary spirit. Greed, in all of its forms—greed for life, for money, for love, knowledge—has marked the upward surge of mankind." The character of Gekko was meant to be shocking and provocative. He was portrayed as a power-hungry scoundrel and his speech provided a warning against a possible future dominated by corporate power and values. Unfortunately, Gekko's embrace of greed as the most fundamental human value appears to be in the new millennium not only a source of inspiration for many people but *central* to a set of neoliberal commitments that are now utterly normalized. As the market runs rampant, shaping every aspect of the social order, nothing escapes the reach of investment and commerce. Human lives and broad public values are largely ignored in favor of private financial gain and market determinism as matters concerning the public good, art, and intellectual culture are entirely subordinated to private interests and market values. Every aspect of daily existence is mediated through the lens of commodification, and one's sense of purpose and agency is largely measured by the presupposition that in a market society one's highest calling is to make a profit. Stories abound in the press and media about the lifestyles of the rich and famous, and corporate executives are held up as models of business culture, their leadership skills largely indexed by the obscene bonuses they often receive. Power and greed under the Bush administration have gained a position in what can only be described as a public posture that is not only arrogant and unapologetic but also characteristic of a certain measure of contempt and vengeance for those excluded from the realm of power. Abdicating their responsibility to facilitate the formation of a participating and informed citizenry, the dominant media no longer hold corporate and government power accountable. Instead, they function as an advertisement and a powerful pedagogical force both in legitimizing the culture and values of neoliberalism and in producing the citizen-consumer. It is difficult to believe that the dominant media, eager to be rewarded by the wealthy and powerful, have any goal other than making money for shareholders. This is revealed not only in the kind of stories they tell about politics and power but also in how they define what counts as knowledge, art, and public culture.

One telling example of what sort of country the United States has become under the reign of neoliberal fundamentalism can be glimpsed in the prominent and widespread coverage the corporate media gave to Damien Hirst's new artwork *For the Love of God,* a life-size platinum skull covered in 8,601 high-quality diamonds, with an estimated selling value of around $100 million. The *New York Times* covered the story, focusing largely on the fact that the diamond skull cost Hirst $23.6 million to make and that, given the $100 million asking price in a poor art market, he might have a hard time finding a buyer.[84] Treated largely as a market issue, the story sidestepped any substantive criticism of Hirst by specifying that all of the diamonds set in the skull were "ethically sourced," as if this self-righteous public relations revelation either served to cancel out the broader consequences and dynamics behind neoliberal global capital and its politics of disposability or laid to rest the necessity to address *For the Love of God* as an utterly depraved example of commodification and a grossly shallow representation of the meaning of art. The irony of how a fascist aesthetic and capitalist rationality merge in a narrative that connects the blood diamonds and a skull that symbolize the disposable bodies of Africans, many of whom are children forced into a form of slavery, is almost entirely missed in commentaries that simply regale Hirst as "the world's most extravagant artist."[85] While the materialistic excess of Hirst's work may be obvious to most of the corporate media and general public—a point of pride for him—what is completely ignored is the way in which both the art product and its surrounding representations become complicit with what Achille Mbembe calls a racist economy of neoliberal biopolitics, whose function is not only to accumulate capital but also "to regulate the distribution of death and to make possible the murderous functions of the state."[86]

Meanwhile, the social order becomes even more depoliticized, removed from the realm of power and producing a politics that is banal, registering little if any public outrage even when a sitting president lies to justify a war in Iraq, undermines civil liberties through the creation of a warrantless spying program, abolishes habeas corpus with the passing of the Military Commissions Act of 2006, admits to abducting "enemies of the state" and holding them in secret prisons, and defies international law by holding "enemy combatants" in Guantanamo—the American Gulag that symbolizes both our hypocrisy in claiming to uphold human rights and the willingness of the U.S. government to abandon any pretense to international law, the American constitution, and democracy itself.[87]

As a form of oppressive public pedagogy, neoliberal ideology has, especially under the second Bush administration, transformed the meaning of freedom, agency, and the very nature of governmentality. Coupled with the protracted "war on terrorism," neoliberalism provides the conditions for a new mode of governmentality that is not only more global, but also more frightening in its recourse to violence, military force, war, and suppression of all those defined as "others" because they deny its claim to universal legitimacy.[88] An imperial presidency now extends market values and practices to all institutions and social relations, creating a form of politics in which insecurity, flexibility, deprivation, extreme poverty, ill health, and hyper-commodification have become routine. The signs are written less in the history of economic theories extending from Adam Smith to Friedrich Hayek to Milton Friedman, though the influence of such ideas and the institutions that disseminate them should not be underestimated, than in the diverse details of daily life that embody a representation of politics in which the most important choices—structured within the unchecked dynamics of inequality, uncertainty, and insecurity—are often between life and death, between either getting by or retreating into gated communities. And yet, behind the misrepresentations and social amnesia lies a range of global problems fueled by egregious corporate corruption and a deadly inequality of wealth and resources. According to Jeremy Rifkin:

> Today, while corporate profits are soaring around the world, 89 countries find themselves worse off economically than they were in the early 1990s. Capitalism promised that globalization would narrow the gap between rich and poor. Instead the divide has widened. The 356 richest families on the planet enjoy a combined wealth that now exceeds the annual income of 40% of the human race. Two-thirds of the world's population have never made a phone call and one-third have no access to electricity.[89]

Ethical and political arguments against the vast inequalities that neoliberalism produces do not take on the urgency that they should in the United States. Economic, political, and social issues now merge in a world in which subjectivities and identifications are produced largely through a cultural politics in which the public good and social justice are disparaged because they carry not just a financial burden but also the burden of intimacy, non-commodified values, and long-standing commitments. David Kotz is right to argue that neoliberalism as the dominant theory, practice, and politics of our time has within the last three decades "affected practically every dimension of social life, including the gap between the rich and the poor, the nature of work, the role of big money in politics, the quantity and quality of public services, and the character of family life."[90] What is important to recognize regarding what is new about neoliberalism is both its ability to normalize its set of core beliefs and its successful pedagogical efforts at grounding its theories and practices in a persuasive notion of common sense. In doing so, it manages to equate big government with monopoly, waste, and incompetency, portray individualism and freedom as strictly market concepts determined through choice, and make market relations and democracy synonymous. Corporate power now sets the terms for government regulation and allows the development of industry to be left to the wisdom of the market while the "assault on big government" becomes a rallying cry by neoliberals to liquidate all remnants of the social state. And as Bauman points out, "Ethical arguments for the public good do not cut much worth in a society in which competitiveness, cost-and-effect calculations, profitability and other free market commandments rule."[91] Democracy has never appeared more fragile and endangered in the United States than at this time of civic and political crisis.

Against the commodification, deregulation, and privatization of everything, democratic public spheres disappear and with them any vestige of democratic values, discourse, and social relations. One example of the neoliberal rush to sell off public goods through privatization can be found in the person of Mitch Daniels, who previously served in the Bush White House as budget director and is now the governor of Indiana. Daniels has been dubbed by his critics as "Governor Privatize," and rightly so. He has already handed over to private companies "some welfare-applicant screening, running a prison, and, most notably, operating the 157-mile Indiana Toll Road ... [and] has also called for new privately operated roads and for leasing the state's lottery." Daniels defends his mania for privatization with the endlessly repeated argument by advocates of neoliberalism that "[g]overnment is the last monopoly" and is not as efficient as the "benefits of competition."[92] This is truly an odd, if not incomprehensible, position when posing as an unproblematic truism, especially after the debacle, as I have noted, of a bungled federal response to the tragedy of Katrina, largely attributed to the neoliberal penchant for gutting valuable government aid programs.[93]

Rethinking the Political in the Age of Neoliberalism

> I would argue that no account of biopolitics in the modern world ... can neglect this imploding history of biocapital. It is integral to the ways in which the substance of human existence itself can be objectified, regulated, and struggled over.[94]

As neoliberal rationality spreads throughout the United States, it undercuts the tension between democratic values and the needs of capital while instituting the foundation for a new form of authoritarianism, raising the fundamental questions about where a democratic politics might take place and how neoliberalism might be resisted in pedagogical and political terms. In what follows, I want to briefly analyze the work of David Harvey and Wendy Brown, who provide different but important analyses of the nature, influence, and threat of neoliberalism to any substantive democratic politics. Their respective books are significant both for their attempts to understand neoliberalism as an ideology, politics, and mode of rationality and for what they suggest about theorizing a pedagogy about and against neoliberalism. Pedagogy in this instance takes on a dialectical character, grounded in different forms of knowledge, social relations, subject positions, and ethical values. Pedagogical projects and practices tied to the production of prevailing arrangements of power tend to be disabling politically and work in the favor of dominant interests, whereas critical pedagogy makes the operations of politics and power visible, recognizes that "knowledge has its very conditions of possibility in power relations,"[95] critically addresses major social issues, and extends and deepens the conditions necessary for democratic public life.

David Harvey argues that neoliberalism has become the new common sense, and if it is to be resisted not only its major theoretical assumptions but also its history must be clearly understood and delimited. In taking on this task, he performs a major theoretical service by tracing neoliberalism's roots in eighteenth-century liberal doctrines about freedom and individual liberties and their connection to the emergence of a vastly more ruthless model of economics that first appeared in Chile, the United States, England, and China in the 1970s and 1980s. For Harvey, there is a direct line between the application of neoliberal principles in these countries, ruled by highly conservative, market-oriented politicians, and the restructuring of the World Bank and IMF in 1982 along neoliberal principles, the instituting of educational blueprints for sustaining mass consent for neoliberal policies, and the restoration of class power. With meticulous attention, Harvey addresses the historical transformations of wealth, power, and institutions in the service of neoliberal ideology. He provides a detailed analysis of how neoliberal principles were put to work in restructuring the debt in New York City in the 1970s; how Chile under Pinochet became a petri dish for Milton Friedman's neoliberal ideas; how Ronald Reagan and Margaret Thatcher attempted to dismantle the welfare state, disempower unions, let markets set prices, and liberalize trade and finance; and how the Bush administration represents the terminal point in neoliberal statecraft. Harvey is especially convincing about the merging of neoliberal policies and militarism, particularly when he points to the attempt by Paul Bremer, head of the Coalition Provisional Authority in Iraq, who, on September 19, 2003, issued a number of orders that provided the Bush administration's model for the neoliberal state. According to Harvey, Bremer's order included "the full privatization of public enterprises, full ownership rights by foreign forms of Iraqi business, full repatriation of foreign profits ... the opening of Iraq's banks to foreign control, national treatment for foreign companies ... and the elimination of nearly all trade barriers."[96] Harvey makes a strong case that neoliberalism wages a war against democracy on a number of fronts that range from a battle for ideas to its ruthless attempts as a "political project to re-establish the conditions for capital accumulation and to restore the power of economic elites"—that is, the restoration of what he unequivocally calls class power.[97]

Harvey gestures toward the importance of neoliberalism as a hegemonic mode of cultural politics when he argues that "[i]t has pervasive effects on ways of thought to the point where it has become incorporated into the common-sense way many of us interpret, live in, and understand the world."[98] While he mentions the emergence of right-wing think tanks, the increasing corporatization of higher education, the rise of new information technologies, and the role of the media in making neoliberalism a mode of hegemonic discourse, Harvey never fully theorizes how pedagogy as a form of cultural politics actually constructs particular modes of address, modes of identification, affective investments, and social relations that produce consent and complicity in the ethos and practice of neoliberalism. Hence, Harvey never refutes seriously the notion that neoliberal hegemony can be explained simply through an economic optic and consequently gives the relationship of politics, culture, and class scant analysis. If neoliberalism as theory and practice is deeply indebted to furthering a market economy and its power structures, then it also recognizes the value of a cultural politics that has successfully mobilized a hegemonic discourse based on the assumption that the market is in a better position to decide matters than any genuine democracy. What is missing here is the notion of neoliberalism as a form of governmentality that couples "forms of knowledge, strategies of power and technologies of self"[99] as part of its effort to transform politics, restructure power relations, and produce an array of narratives and disciplinary measures that normalizes its view of citizenship, the state, and the supremacy of market relations. Given its profound appeal to the American public in the last thirty years, the success of neoliberal ideology raises fundamental questions about how it is capable of enlisting in such a compelling way the consent of so many Americans, ordinarily dismissed by many leftists who argue "that working-class people do not, under normal circumstances, care deeply about anything beyond the size of their paychecks."[100]As Lawrence Grossberg has argued, the popular imaginary is far too important as part of a larger political and educational struggle not be taken seriously by progressives. He writes:

> The struggle to win hegemony has to be anchored in people's everyday consciousness and popular cultures. Those seeking power have to struggle with and within the contradictory realms of common sense and popular culture, with the languages and logics that people use to calculate what is right and what is wrong, what can be done and what cannot, what should be done and what has to be done. The popular is where social imagination is defined and changed, where people construct personal identities, identifications, priorities, and possibilities, where people form moral and political agendas for themselves and their societies, and where they decide whether and in what (or whom) to invest the power to speak for them. It is where people construct their hopes for the future in the light of their sense of the present. It is where they decide what matters, what is worth caring about, and what they are committed to.[101]

Unfortunately, we have no sense from Harvey about how the educational force of the culture actually works pedagogically to produce neoliberal ideology, values, and consent—how the popular imagination both deploys power and is influenced by power. This is particularly ironic since Harvey relies heavily on Antonio Gramsci's interrelated notions of hegemony and common sense, but renders them devoid of their pedagogical dimensions. Gramsci famously claimed that "[e]very relationship of 'hegemony' is necessarily an educational relationship,"[102] and in doing so he refused to separate culture from economic relations of power, or politics and pedagogy from the production of knowledge, identities, and social formations. While Harvey does not repeat the mistake made by many leftists of treating culture as merely superstructural, ornamental, or a burden on class-based politics, he undertheorizes the important interrelationships between cultural politics and pedagogy involved in the production of neoliberal consent. In doing so, he fails to connect the primacy of the pedagogical as part of a broader politics that mediates the ever-shifting and dynamic modes of common sense that legitimate the institutional arrangements of capitalism, the changing politics of class formations, and the creation of the neoliberal state. Similarly, the primacy of material relations in his analysis cannot adequately register the changing consequences of neoliberal ideology as the nature of labor and production itself is radically transformed in late modernity. Hence, Harvey provides little critical commentary on how the rationality of exchange and exploitation might not quite capture the fate of those populations—refugees, jobless youth, the poor elderly, immigrants, poor minorities of color—increasingly rendered disposable because they exist outside any productive notion of what it means to be a citizen-consumer, or how such groups might be mobilized to collectively resist the fact of their social, economic, and political exclusion as an alleged matter of destiny. In spite of the crucial connection between hegemony and pedagogy, we have no sense from Harvey—or, for that matter, many progressive social theorists—of what it might mean both to learn from young people about their appropriation of education, pedagogy, and culture as a tool of resistance to neoliberal ideology and to understand how we might employ the pedagogical as part of a broader effort to educate them to be critical and engaged agents in a world that increasingly views them as a problem or simply as a market for raking in lucrative profits.[103]

Wendy Brown takes a different route analytically in trying to critically engage neoliberalism as a form of governmentality. She argues that while many theorists capture the "important effects of neoliberalism, they also reduce neoliberalism to a bundle of economic policies with inadvertent political and social consequences: they fail to address the political rationality that both organizes these policies and reaches beyond the market."[104] For Brown, neoliberalism is not merely a set of economic policies but "a social analysis that, when deployed as a form of governmentality, reaches from the soul of the citizen-subject to education policy to practices of empire. As a regulating strategy of governance, neoliberal rationality exercises its hegemony as an administrative project that defines all aspects of life through the economy of cost-benefit analysis. Neoliberal rationality, while foregrounding the market, is not only or even primarily focused on the economy; it involves extending and disseminating market values to all institutions and social action, even as the market itself remains a distinctive player."[105] Governmentality becomes important as an operational concept to the degree that it complicates power as the reciprocal constitution of technologies of intervention aimed at governing others and those pedagogical technologies of representation whose purpose is to produce forms of self-governing in which the exercise of power is rationalized and consent is momentarily achieved.[106] In developing this theoretical insight, Brown attempts to identify the basic elements that constitute such a rationality and to explain how it shapes different realms of the social order. For example, she points to how, among other things, neoliberalism tends to cast all dimensions of human life in terms of economic relations; defines "the market as the organizing and regulative principle of the state"; attempts to develop institutions in accordance with neoliberal principles; "interpellates individuals as entrepreneurial subjects in every sphere of life"; and shifts the responsibilities of the social state on to "free" and "responsible" individuals.[107] Taking a somewhat different position from Harvey, Brown engages neoliberalism as a calculating and market-based rationality that reaches into every aspect of the social order, representing a powerful threat both to the very idea of democracy in the United States and to its practice. She expresses particular concern about the ways in which neoliberal governmentality cloaks itself in the language of freedom and democracy in order to further its own narrow economic interests. To her credit, Brown not only analyzes the workings of the neoliberal state and the elements of neoliberal rationality, she furthers our understanding of how neoliberal ideology undertakes in social, economic, and political terms an assault on civil liberties and democratic values. In particular, she argues that neoliberalism

> is a formation that is developing a domestic imperium correlative with a global one, achieved through a secretive and remarkably agentic state; through corporatized media, schools, and prisons; and through a variety of technologies for intensified local administrative, regulatory, and police powers. It is a formation made possible by the production of citizens as individual entrepreneurial actors across all dimensions of their lives, by the reduction of civil society to a domain for exercising this entrepreneurship, and by the figuration of the state as a firm whose products are rational individual subjects, and expanding economy, national security, and global power.[108]

Ironically, it is precisely Brown's notion of governmentality, defined exclusively by neoliberal rationality and policies, that prevents her from acknowledging various other and equally important anti-democratic forces—such as religious fundamentalism, militarism, and the assault on higher education and a critical media—that suggest the emergence of a new form of authoritarianism in the United States. In addition, while calling for both resistance to neoliberalism as a form of governmentality and a radical restructuring of the neoliberal state, she fails to advance any critical understanding of the kind of pedagogical interventions and cultural politics that would be central to such a task. Neglected in such an analysis are central issues concerning how the intertwining of culture, politics, and meaning provide the social forms through which neoliberal rationality is legitimated and lived. Moreover, she has nothing to say about what pedagogical apparatuses, locations, and spaces "provide the particular detailed methods through which competing or dissenting rationalities are disqualified and dismissed,"[109] or the methods through which hegemonic neoliberal pedagogies organize affective investments, desires, and identities into a web of common sense, social control, and consent. Any viable theory of governmentality must address not merely the diffuse operations of power throughout civil society but also what it would mean to engage those pedagogical sites producing and legitimating neoliberal rationality. In addition, it is crucial to examine what role public intellectuals, think tanks, the media, and universities actually play pedagogically in constructing and legitimating a neoliberal notion of common sense, and how the latter works pedagogically in producing neoliberal subjects and securing hegemonic consent. There is little sense in Brown's analysis of how neoliberal rationality is lived through diverse social, racial, and class formations, or what Jean Baudrillard has called "a sorcery of social relations."[110] Nor is there any acknowledgment of the fundamental importance of how neoliberal discourses, values, and ideas are taken up in ongoing struggles over culture, meaning, and identity as they bear down on people's daily lives.[111] And while her call for an alternative "vision in which justice would center not on maximizing individual wealth or rights but on developing and enhancing the capacity of citizens to share power and hence to collaboratively govern themselves"[112] is important, she offers few insights as to how such a task would be engaged pedagogically, under what conditions, and in what public or private spheres. If pedagogy anchors governmentality in the "domain of cognition," functioning largely as "a grid of insistent calculation, experimentation, and evaluation concerned with the conduct of conduct,"[113] it becomes crucial to understand the pedagogical challenges at work in such an ordering project. For example, what pedagogical challenges would have to be addressed in overcoming the deeply felt view in American culture that criticism is destructive or, for that matter, the deeply rooted anti-intellectualism reinforced daily through various forms of public pedagogy as in talk radio and the televisual infotainment sectors?[114] How might we engage pedagogical practices that open up spaces of resistance to neoliberal governance and authority through a culture of questioning that enables people to resist and reject neoliberal assumptions that reduce citizenship to consumerism and a mode of calculating self-ambition? What are the implications of theorizing pedagogy and the practice of learning as essential to social change, and where might such interventions take place? How might the related matters of experience and learning, knowledge and authority, and history and cultural capital be theorized as part of a broader pedagogy of critique and possibility? What kind of pedagogical practice might be appropriate in providing the tools to unsettle hegemonic "domains of cognition"[115] and break apart the continuity of consensus and common sense as part of a broader political and pedagogical attempt to provide people with a critical sense of social responsibility and agency? How might it be possible to theorize the pedagogical importance of the new media and the new modes of political literacy and cultural production they employ, or to analyze the circuits of power, translation, and distribution that make up neoliberalism's vast apparatus or public pedagogy—extending from talk radio and screen culture to the Internet and newspapers? At stake here is both recognizing the importance of the media as a site of public pedagogy and breaking the monopoly of information that is a central pillar of neoliberal common sense. As Hardt and Negri point out, challenging the information monopoly of the corporate media must include becoming "actively involved in the production and distribution of information."[116] Moreover, such a project must be viewed as part of a larger effort to democratize the media "through equal access and active expression," examples of which can be found on numerous websites where people not only have access to alternative discourses but also can upload their own stories, commentaries, and narratives.[117] These are only some of the concerns that would be central to any viable recognition of what it would mean to theorize pedagogy as a condition that enables both critique, understood as more than a struggle against incomprehension, and social responsibility as the foundation for forms of intervention that are oppositional and empowering.

Cultural Politics and Public Pedagogy

> The point is not to inculcate perfect ideas, it is to make people become self-critical, reflexive, critical of others—though not critical in an irritating sort of way—to open their eyes, especially about their own motives, and to encourage them to be autonomous. I think this is both the main aim of analysis and the prerequisite for social change.[118]

Both Harvey and Brown make important contributions to our understanding of neoliberalism, and we need to build on these by theorizing more fully a notion of pedagogy that expands our understanding of how the educational force of the culture has become harnessed to neoliberalism as both a mode of common sense and a dangerous form of rationality. Such a recognition presents the challenge of what it means to address the pedagogical conditions at work in the reproduction of both neoliberalism and negative globalization. Engaging pedagogy as a form of cultural politics requires a concern with analyses of the production and representation of meaning and how these practices and the practices they provoke are implicated in the dynamics of social power. Pedagogy as a form of cultural politics raises the issue of how education might be understood as a moral and political practice that takes place in a variety of sites outside schools. Pedagogy as defined here is fundamentally concerned with the relations among politics, subjectivities, and cultural and material production. As a form of cultural production, pedagogy is implicated in the construction and organization of knowledge, desires, emotional investments, values, and social practices. What is significant here is developing a notion of public pedagogy, in particular, that is capable of contesting the various forms of symbolic production that secure individuals to the affective and ideological investments that produce the neoliberal subject. As Gramsci reminds us, every hegemonic relationship is an educational one, and hegemony as an educational practice is always necessarily part of a pedagogy of persuasion,[119] one that, as Ellen Willis points out, makes a claim to "speak to vital human needs, interests, and desires, and therefore will be persuasive to many and ultimately most people."[120]

Neoliberal hegemony is partly secured as a result of the crisis of agency that now characterizes much of American politics. As neoliberal ideology successfully normalizes and depoliticizes its basic assumptions and its market-based view of the world, people find it increasingly difficult to recognize that neoliberal rationality is a historical and political construction, and that there are alternatives to its conceptions of democracy as an extension of market principles and citizens as hyper-consumers or unthinking patriots. Challenging neoliberal hegemony means exposing its historical character and its flimsy claims to promoting freedom through choice while making visible how it operates in the service of class and corporate power. But the ideology and structures of neoliberal domination must be analyzed not merely within economic discourses but also as an oppressive form of public pedagogy and cultural politics—as a practice of political persuasion, actively responsible for systematic forms of misrepresentation, distortion, and the mangling of public discourse by commercial interests.[121]

The institutions and sites that constitute the machinery of persuasion are at the heart of any system of culture and thus represent crucial sites of what I have called spheres of and about public pedagogy. Recognizing this means treating conflicts of culture, power, and politics, in part, as pedagogical issues and recognizing cultural education as a project related to democracy.[122] The concern that animates this book is to address precisely how neoliberalism constitutes what Imre Szeman has called "a problem of and for pedagogy."[123] If neoliberalism requires a supporting political culture, it is crucial to recognize that culture is the place where deeply held meanings and values are produced, internalized, identified with, and fought over. Culture under the regulating hand of the market is not simply about texts, commodities, consumption, or the creation of the utterly privatized subject; it is also about how various people take up and invest in various symbolic representations in the ongoing and daily practices of comprehension and communication. Culture has become a form of capital for economic investment, but it has little to do with the power of self-definition or the capacities needed to expand the scope of justice and human freedom. And it is precisely the challenge of education to provide a liminal space where knowledge, values, and desires can become meaningful in order to be both critical and transformative. If neoliberalism is to be challenged as a new mode of governmentality, it will have to be engaged as both a form of cultural politics and a pedagogical force, and not merely as a political and economic theory or mode of common sense or rationality.

As democratic institutions are downsized and public goods are offered up for corporate plunder, those of us who take seriously the related issues of equality, human rights, justice, and freedom face the crucial challenge of formulating a connection between the political and pedagogical that is suitable for addressing the urgent problems facing the twenty-first century—a politics that, as Bauman argues, "never stops criticizing the level of justice already achieved [while] seeking more justice and better justice."[124] Part of the problem to be addressed is that neoliberal ideology and practice will have to be challenged as part of an ongoing effort to open up new national and global spaces of education—employing a vast array of old and new media and delivery platforms, including free radio stations, digital video, the Internet, digital technologies, and cable television. This means not only making critical pedagogy central to any viable notion of politics but also struggling to expand the "spaces for public life, democratic debate and cultural expression."[125] At its best, critical pedagogy makes the operations of power visible and enables people to act on their beliefs; it should not only "shift the way people think about the moment but potentially energize them to do something differently in that moment."[126] Pedagogy is political in that it modifies the visible, rearticulates the coordinates of the possible, and thwarts dominant and official expectations. Such a pedagogy has the potential to turn theory into a resource and to analyze how power deploys culture and how culture produces power. Moreover, critical pedagogy is deeply concerned with matters of specificity and context, and demands a certain ability to listen, witness, make public connections, and be open to others and the conditions that give meaning to their lives.[127] As Nick Couldry points out, pedagogy for democracy requires more than an obsession with abstractions, rhetoric, instrumentalization, and the jargon of specialization; it demands an "engagement with the claims of others, with questions of justice [and] justice requires always an engagement with the concrete other, not merely an abstract other. For justice and, therefore, for an adequate notion of citizenship, there must be a commitment to dialogue with concrete others."[128]

Democracy and the Crisis of the Social State

> The conception of politics that we defend is far from the idea that "everything is possible." In fact, it's an immense task to try to propose a few possibilities, in the plural—a few possibilities other than what we are told is possible. It is a matter of showing how the space of the possible is larger than the one assigned—that something else is possible, but not that everything is possible. In any case, it is essential that politics renounce the category of totality, which is perhaps another change with respect to the previous period.[129]

We live at a time when the advocates of neoliberalism have no use for democracy except to view it as a rationale for expanding empires, opening trade barriers, and pursuing new markets. But democracy as both an ethical referent and a promise for a better future is much too important to cede to a slick new mode of authoritarianism advanced by advocates of neoliberalism and other fundamentalists. Democracy as theory, practice, and promise for a better future must be critically engaged, struggled over, and reclaimed if it is to be used in the interests of social justice and the renewal of the labor movement as well as the building of national and international social movements, the struggle for the social state, and the confrontation of hierarchy, inequality, and power as ruling principles in an era of rampant neoliberalism.[130] While many of the latter issues are central to most critiques of neoliberalism, the importance of the social state is often dismissed as either a throwback to the liberal dreams of the New Deal and a mainstay of state bureaucracy or simply dead on arrival—an indisputable by-product of the separation of nation-based politics from the rise of mobile, global economic power. All of these positions are theoretically flawed and, when taken too far, provide ammunition for advocates of neoliberalism to define big government as wasteful, incompetent, and the cause of all of our problems.[131] Against the notion of the vanishing state it is more accurate to say, as Stanley Aronowitz points out, that, rather than disappearing, the state's "core functions have shifted from the legitimating institutions such as those of social welfare to, on the one hand, providing the monetary and fiscal conditions for the internal, but spurious, expansion of capital ... and on the other to supplying a vastly expanded regime of coercion, that is, the growth of the police powers of government at home and abroad directed against the insurgencies that object to the growing phenomenon of an authoritarian form of democracy."[132] Intellectuals, social movements, academics, and others concerned with nurturing a radical democracy must confront the coercive power of the punishing state under neoliberalism while simultaneously arguing for the renewal of a social state.

The dismantling of the social state through deregulation, privatization, and individualization transforms broader forms of community, solidarity, and equality into a theater of war legitimated by a new "order of egoism" and the ruthless and annihilating principles of an updated social Darwinism with its "devastating competitive 'war of all against all.'"[133] The reconfiguring of the social state into the corporate and militarized state also promotes a massive exodus from politics and undermines the conditions that make political enlightenment and agency possible. As Zygmunt Bauman puts it, "Without collective insurance [there is] no stimulus for political engagement—and certainly not for participation in a democratic game of elections. No salvation is likely to arrive from a political state that is not, and refuses to be, a social state. Without social rights for all, a large and in all probability growing number of people would find their political rights useless and unworthy of their attention."[134] The idea and importance of a radically democratic social state cannot be overstated. Not only does it "protect men and women from the plague of poverty[, it also] stands a chance of becoming a profuse source of solidarity able to recycle 'society' into a common, communal good, thanks to the defense it provides against the horror of misery, that is of the terror of being excluded, of falling or being pushed over the board of a fast accelerating vehicle of progress, of being condemned to 'social redundancy' and otherwise designated as 'human waste.'"[135] At the same time, the social state is now the central foundation of governance, social justice, and freedom. In other words, the state becomes important less for its control of goods, services, and industries than for its regulatory power in ensuring the emergence of social provisions, noncommodified public spheres, and a larger commons that makes matters of critical agency and substantive democracy possible at both the local and global levels.

The struggle for the social state also foregrounds another important consideration for developing an emergent theory of democratic politics to address the current threat of neoliberal authoritarianism. The central issues of power and politics can lead to cynicism and despair if capitalism is not addressed as a system of social relations that diminishes—through its cultural politics, modes of commodification, and market pedagogies—the capacities and possibilities of individuals and groups to move beyond the vicissitudes of necessity and survival in order to fully participate in exercising some control over the myriad forces that shape their daily lives. The social state can provide a living wage, decent health care, public works, investment in schools, child care, housing for the poor, and a range of other crucial social resources that can make a difference between living and dying. The rebuilding of the social state and the renewal of the social contract should be a central goal of any broad-based radical social movement for democracy. I want to emphasize that I am not suggesting that rebuilding the social state be understood as simply a pragmatic adjustment of the institutions of liberal democracy. On the contrary, the emergence of the social state can be comprehended as part of a radical break from liberalism and formalistic politics only if there is to be any move toward a genuine democracy in which matters of equality, power, and justice are central to what Aronowitz calls the constitution of a radical democratic politics.[136] Such a task necessitates a politics and pedagogy that not only expand critical awareness and promote critical modes of inquiry but also sustain public connections. As Edward Said reminds us, if such a politics is to make any difference, it must be worldly;[137] that is, it must incorporate a critical pedagogy and an understanding of cultural politics that not only contemplates social problems but also addresses the conditions for new forms of democratic political exchange and enables new forms of agency, power, and collective struggle. This is a pedagogy that embraces a global politics in its reach and vision, in its call for the democratic sharing of power and in the elimination of those conditions that promote needless human suffering and imperil the biosystems of the earth itself.

Part of the task of developing a new understanding of the social and a new model of democratic politics rests with the demand to make the political more pedagogical while resisting at every turn the neoliberalization of public and higher education, creating new alliances between students and faculty, and rethinking the potential connections that might be deployed between those of us who work in education and the vast array of cultural workers outside schools. As Stanley Aronowitz, Howard Zinn, Roger Simon, Susan Giroux, and others have stressed repeatedly, academics have a responsibility to view the academy as a contested site, a site where the spread of neoliberal ideas must be challenged.[138] Contesting the neoliberalization of the university must be defended as important political work[139] and viewed as a central element in theorizing the role of public intellectuals as part of a larger project of defining the meaning and purpose of the university as a democratic public sphere. In connecting the work that is done in educational institutions with the larger society, educators and academics also face the important task of supporting, as Judith Butler argues, other public spheres "where thoughtful considerations can take place."[140] There is a long legacy among educators and academics to engage in forms of criticism that appear unconnected to the discourse of possibility and hope. This approach to critique and social criticism should be modified so that while we should continue to defend critique as a democratic value and "dissent as a basis for a politics that diminishes human suffering,"[141] we have a responsibility to go beyond criticism. Transcending this space requires combining a discourse of critique and possibility, one that enables others to recast themselves as agents who can forge new democratic visions against a fractured social, racial, and economic reality while speaking in the name of a desirable democratic future. Fortunately, although neoliberalism has achieved considerable dominance over political and economic discourse, there are a number of countervailing forces both at home and abroad that are challenging the politics and common sense assumptions that drive its rationality and practices. From Seattle and Davos to Genoa and Rostok, people are engaging in various modes of popular struggle, collectively challenging the ethos, values, and relations of neoliberalism and resuscitating the meaning of politics, resistance, and the spaces where the latter becomes possible and takes place. Indeed, signs of resistance are evident in grassroots and local movements to reclaim public education, the varied movements against neoliberal globalization, various struggles on behalf of people who are HIV-positive, workers' rights movements, and those diverse groups fighting for environmental justice and public goods, among other struggles.[142] Under the reign of neoliberal globalization, it is crucial for intellectuals and others to develop better theoretical frameworks for understanding how power, politics, and pedagogy as a political and moral practice work in the service of neoliberalism to secure consent, to normalize authoritarian policies and practices, and to erase a history of struggle and injustice. The stakes are too high to ignore such a task. We live in dark times, and the specter of neoliberalism and other modes of authoritarianism are gaining ground throughout the globe. We need to rethink the meaning of politics, take risks, and exercise the courage necessary to reclaim the pedagogical conditions, visions, and economic projects that make the promise of a democracy and a different future worth fighting for.

Notes

Notes to Introduction

1. Susan George, "A Short History of Neo-Liberalism: Twenty Years of Elite Economics and Emerging Opportunities for Structural Change," *Conference on Economic Sovereignty in a Globalizing World* (March 24–26, 1999). Available online at http://www.globalexchange.org/campaigns/econ101/neoliberalism.html.

2. Thomas Lemke, "Foucault, Governmentality, and Critique," *Rethinking Marxism* 14:3 (Fall 2007), pp. 49–64.

3. Nick Couldry, "Reality TV, or the Secret Theatre of Neoliberalism," *The Review of Education, Pedagogy, and Cultural Studies* (forthcoming), p. 1.

4. Wendy Brown, *Edgework: Critical Essays on Knowledge and Politics* (Princeton: Princeton University Press 2005), p. 40.

5. William K. Tabb, "Race to the Bottom?" in Stanley Aronowitz and Heather Gautney, eds., *Implicating Empire: Globalization and Resistance in the 21st Century World Order* (New York: Basic Books, 2003), p. 153.

6. Richard L. Harris, "Popular Resistance to Globalization and Neoliberalism in Latin America," *Journal of Developing Societies* 19:2–3 (2003), pp. 365–426; Naomi Kein, *The Shock Doctrine: The Rise of Disaster Capitalism* (New York: Metropolitan Books, 2007).

7. Lewis Lapham, "Buffalo Dances," *Harper's Magazine* (May 2004), pp. 9, 11.

8. Randy Martin, "War, by All Means," *Social Text* 25:2 (Summer 2007), p. 17.

9. For an excellent analysis of the profound impact the World Bank has on global politics and culture, see Bret Benjamin, *Invested Interest: Capital, Culture, and the World Bank* (Minneapolis: University of Minnesota Press, 2007).

10. Stanley Aronowitz and Heather Gautney, "The Debate About Globalization: An Introduction," in Stanley Aronowitz and Heather Gautney, eds., *Implicating Empire: Globalization & Resistance in the 21st Century World Order* (New York: Basic Books, 2003), p. 3.

11. Stanley Aronowitz, *How Class Works* (New Haven, CT: Yale University Press, 2003), p. 30.

12. Vincent Lloyd and Robert Weissman, "Against the Workers: How IMF and World Bank Policies Undermine Labour Power and Rights," *The Multinational Monitor* (September 2001), pp. 7–8. See also David Moberg, "Plunder and Profit," *In These Times* (March 29, 2004), pp. 20–21.

13. Sean Gonsalves, "How to Skin a Rabbit," *Cape Cod Times* (April 20, 2004). Available online at www.commondreams.org/views04/0420-05.htm (accessed on April 24, 2004).

14. Cheryl Woodard. "Who Really Pays Taxes in America? Taxes and Politics in 2004," *AskQuestions.org* (April 15, 2004). Available online at http://www.askquestions.org/articles/taxes/ (accessed on April 24, 2004).

15. Martin Wolk, "Cost of Iraq Could Surpass $1 Trillion," *MSNBC* (March 17, 2006). Available online at http://www.msnbc.msn.com/id/11880954/.

16. Lisa Duggan, *The Twilight of Equality: Neoliberalism, Cultural Politics, and the Attack on Democracy* (Boston: Beacon Press, 2003), p. 16.

17. For some informative commentaries on the S-chip program and Bush's veto, see Amy Goodman, "Children's Defense Fund Marian Wright Edelman Calls on Congress & Bush Administration to Help the Country's Nine Million Children Without Health Insurance," *Democracy Now* (July 24, 2007). Available online at www.democracynow.org/print.pl?sid=o7/07/24/1431211; Paul Krugman, "Children Versus Insures," *New York Times* (April 6, 2007), p. A21; Editorial, "Misleading Spin on Children's Health," *New York Times* (October 5, 2007), p. A26; Paul Krugman, "Conservatives Are Such Jokers," *New York Times* (October 5, 2007), p. A27.

18. Cited in Kellie Bean, "Coulter's Right-Wing Drag," *The Free Press* (October 29, 2003). Available online at www.freepress.org/departments/display/20/2003/441.

19. Report by the Center for American Progress and Free Press, *The Structural Imbalance of Political Talk Radio* (Washington, DC: Center for American Progress and Free Press, 2007).

20. Editorial, "Savage Anti-Semitism: Radio Host Targets Jewish Foes with Ethnic Derision," *Fairness and Accuracy in Reporting* (July/August 2003). Available online at http://www.fair.org/extra/0307/savage-anti-semitism.html.

21. Fredric Jameson, *The Seeds of Time* (New York: Columbia University Press, 1994), p. xii.

22. Susan Buck-Morss, *Thinking Past Terror: Islamism and Critical Theory on the Left* (London: Verso, 2003), pp. 65–66.

23. George Soros, *The Bubble of American Supremacy* (New York: Public Affairs, 2004), p. 10.

24. Christopher Newfield, "The Culture of Force," *The South Atlantic Quarterly*, 105:1 (2006), p. 244.

25. Here I am quoting David Frum and Richard Perle, cited in Lewis H. Lapham, "Dar al-Harb," *Harper's Magazine* (March 2004), p. 8. Such fascistically inspired triumphalism can also be found in three recent books churned out to gratify the demands of a much-celebrated jingoism: Joseph Farah, *Taking America Back* (New York: WND Books, 2003); Michelle Malkin, *Invasion: How America Still Welcomes Terrorists, Criminals, and Other Foreign Menaces to Our Shores* (New York: Regnery, 2002);

and William J. Bennett, *Why We Fight: Moral Clarity and the War on Terrorism* (New York: Regnery, 2003).

26. Michael Foessel, "Legitimations of the State: The Weakening of Authority and the Restoration of Power," *Constellations* 13:3 (2006), pp. 313–314.

27. Cited in Lapham, "Dar al-Harb," p. 8. The full exposition of this position can be found in David Frum and Richard Perle, *An End to Evil: How to Win the War on Terror* (New York: Random House, 2004).

28. For a rather vivid example of how dissent is criminalized, see the *NOW with Bill Moyers* transcript of "Going Undercover/Criminalizing Dissent," which aired on March 5, 2004. The program documents how undercover agents from all levels of government are infiltrating and documenting peaceful protests in the United States.

29. Chalmers Johnson, *Nemesis: The Last Days of the American Republic* (New York: Metropolitan Books, 2006); Andrew Bacevich, *The New American Militarism: How Americans Are Seduced by War* (New York: Oxford University Press, 2005).

30. For the latest revelation about the refusal of the Bush administration to take responsibility for the abuse and torture perpetrated at Abu Ghraib and other U.S. prisons, see Seymour M. Hersh, "The General's Report," *New Yorker* (June 25, 2007), pp. 58–69. See also Tara McKelvey, *Monstering: Inside America's Policy of Secret Interrogations and Torture in the Terror War* (New York: Carroll & Graf, 2007).

31. Editorial, "On Torture and American Values," *New York Times* (October 7, 2007), p. 13.

32. Zygmunt Bauman, *Globalization: The Human Consequences* (New York: Columbia University Press, 1998), pp. 9–10.

33. George, "A Short History of Neo-Liberalism."

34. David Kotz, "Neoliberalism and the U.S. Economic Expansion of the '90s," *Monthly Review* 54:11 (April 2003), p. 16.

35. On neoliberalism as a form of governmentality or politics of conduct, see Michel Foucault, *Society Must Be Defended: Lectures at the College de France 1975–1976* (New York: Picador, 2003).

36. David Harvey, *A Brief History of Neoliberalism* (New York: Oxford University Press, 2005).

37. See, for instance, Friedrich Hayek, *The Road to Serfdom* (Chicago: University of Chicago Press, 1994, 50th edition), and Milton Friedman, *Capitalism and Freedom: Fortieth Anniversary Issue* (Chicago: University of Chicago Press, 2002).

38. See David Harvey, *A Brief History of Neoliberalism* (New York: Oxford University Press, 2005).

39. For a comprehensive critical analysis of the New Gilded Age, see Michael McHugh, *The Second Gilded Age: The Great Reaction in the United States, 1973–2001* (Boulder: University Press of America, 2006).

40. Pierre Bourdieu, *Acts of Resistance* (New York: Free Press, 1989), p. 35.

41. Colin Leys, *Market-Driven Politics* (London: Verso, 2001), p. 2.

42. Lisa Duggan, *The Twilight of Equality: Neoliberalism, Cultural Politics, and the Attack on Democracy* (Boston: Beacon Press, 2003), p. 34.

43. Ibid., p. xvi.

44. Bill Moyers, "The Media, Politics, and Censorship," *Common Dreams News Center* (May 10, 2004). Available online at www.commondreams.org/cgi-bin/print.

cgi?file=/views04/0510-10.htm. See also Eric Alterman, "Is Koppel a Commie," *The Nation* (May 24, 2004), p. 10.

45. Buck-Morss, *Thinking Past Terror,* p. 103.

46. Alain Touraine, *Beyond Neoliberalism* (London: Polity Press, 2001), p. 2.

47. Alex Callinicos, "The Anti-Capitalist Movement After Genoa and New York," in Stanley Aronowitz and Heather Gautney, eds., *Implicating Empire: Globalization & Resistance in the 21st Century World Order* (New York: Basic Books, 2003), p. 147.

48. Buck-Morss, *Thinking Past Terror,* pp. 4–5.

Notes to Chapter 1

1. Bob Herbert, "America the Fearful," *New York Times* (May 15 2006), p. A25.

2. See Philip Roth, *The Plot Against America* (New York: Vintage, 2004).

3. George Soros, "The US Is Now in the Hands of a Group of Extremists," *The Guardian* (January 26, 2004). Available online at www.commondreams.org/views04/0126-01.htm.

4. Cited in Aaron Glantz, "Bush and Saddam Should Both Stand Trial, Says Nuremberg Prosecutor," *OneWorld.Net* (August 25, 2006). Available online at http://us.oneworld.net/article/view/138319/1/.

5. James Traub, "Weimar Whiners," *New York Times Magazine* (June 1, 2003), p. 11.

6. Elisabeth Young-Bruehl, *Why Arendt Matters* (New Haven: Yale University Press, 2006), p. 46. Of course, this issue is taken up by Hannah Arendt in her classic *Origins of Totalitarianism,* rev. ed. (New York: Schocken, 2004; originally published in 1951).

7. Sidney Blumenthal, "Bush's War on Professionals," *Salon.com* (January 5, 2006). Available online at www.salon.com/opinion/blumenthal/2006/01/05/spying/index. html?x.

8. Herbert, "America the Fearful," p. A25.

9. The sources here are too numerous to cite in full, but I can recommend three insightful analyses in particular: Andrew J. Bacevich, *The New American Militarism* (New York: Oxford University Press, 2005); Carl Boggs, *Imperial Delusions: American Militarism and Endless War* (Lanham: Rowman and Littlefield, 2005); and Chalmers Johnson, *Nemesis: The Last Days of the American Republic* (New York: Metropolitan Books, 2006).

10. Achille Mbembe, "Necropolitics," translated by Libby Meintjes, *Public Culture* 15:1 (Winter 2003), pp. 11–40. Additional discussions of disposable populations can be found in Zygmunt Bauman, *Wasted Lives* (London: Polity, 2004) and, especially, Giorgio Agamben, *Homer Sacer,* translated by Daniel Heller-Roazen (Stanford: Stanford University Press, 1998).

11. Paul Gilroy, *Against Race: Imagining Political Culture Beyond the Color Line* (Cambridge, MA: Harvard University Press, 2000), p. 148.

12. See Bruce Western, *Punishment and Inequality in America* (New York: Russell Sage Foundation, 2007); Jeff Manza and Christopher Uggen, *Locked Out: Felon Disenfranchisement and American Democracy* (New York: Oxford University Press, 2007); Angela Y. Davis, *Abolition Democracy: Beyond Empire, Prisons, and Torture* (New

York: Seven Stories Press, 2005); David Cole, *No Equal Justice: Race and Class in the American Criminal Justice System* (New York: The New Press, 1999); Christian Parenti, *Lockdown America: Police and Prisons in the Age of Crisis* (London: Verso Press, 1999); Mark Mauer, *Race to Incarcerate* (New York: The New Press, 1999); and Marc Mauer and Meda Chesney-Lind, *Invisible Punishment: The Collateral Consequences of Mass Imprisonment* (New York: The New Press, 2002).

13. See Pierre Tristam, "One Man's Clarity in America's Totalitarian Time Warp," *Daytona Beach News-Journal* (January 27, 2004). Available online at www.commondreams.org/views40/0127-08.htm.

14. Nina Bernstein, "New Scrutiny as Immigrants Die in Custody," *New York Times* (June 26, 2007), pp. A1, A19.

15. Editorial, "Gitmos Across America," *New York Times* (June 27, 2007), p. A22.

16. See Bertram Gross, *Friendly Fascism: The New Face of Power in America* (Montreal: Black Rose Books, 1985).

17. Umberto Eco, "Eternal Fascism: Fourteen Ways of Looking at a Blackshirt," *New York Review of Books* (November–December 1995), p. 15.

18. Kevin Passmore, *Fascism* (London: Oxford University Press, 2002), p. 90.

19. Ibid., p. 19.

20. Alexander Stille, "The Latest Obscenity Has Seven Letters," *New York Times* (September 13, 2003), p. 19.

21. Robert O. Paxton, *The Anatomy of Fascism* (New York: Knopf, 2004), p. 218.

22. Mark Neocleous, *Fascism* (Minneapolis: University of Minnesota Press, 1997), p. 91.

23. Bill Moyers, "This is Your Story—The Progressive Story of America. Pass It On," conference paper, *Take Back America* Conference (June 4, 2003). Available online at www.utoronto.ca/csus/pm/moyers.htm.

24. William Greider, "The Right's Grand Ambition: Rolling Back the Twentieth Century," *The Nation* (May 12, 2003). There has been a drastic increase in income and wealth inequality in the last few decades. For example, Paul Krugman, using data from the Congressional Budget Office, has pointed out that "between 1973 and 2000 the average real income of the bottom 90 percent of American taxpayers actually fell by 7 percent. Meanwhile, the income of the top 1 percent rose by 148 percent, the income of the top 0.1 percent rose by 343 percent and the income of the top 0.01 percent rose 599 percent." See Krugman, "The Death of Horatio Alger," *The Nation* (January 5, 2004), pp. 16–17.

25. David Harvey, *A Brief History of Neoliberalism* (New York: Oxford University Press, 2005); Stanley Aronowitz, *How Class Works: Power and Social Movements* (New Haven, CT: Yale University Press, 2003).

26. Zygmunt Bauman, *The Individualized Society* (London: Polity Press, 2001); see also Zygmunt Bauman, *Consuming Life* (London: Polity Press, 2007).

27. Jürgen Habermas, *The Structural Transformation of the Public Sphere* (Cambridge: MIT Press, 1991); David Harvey, *Justice, Nature, and the Geography of Difference* (Malden, MA: Blackwell, 1997). Beyond these two works, the literature on the politics of space is far too extensive to cite, but of special interest are Michael Keith and Steve Pile, eds., *Place and the Politics of Identity* (New York: Routledge, 1993); Do-

reen Massey, *Space, Place, and Gender* (Minneapolis: University of Minnesota, 1994); and Margaret Kohn, *Radical Space: Building the House of the People* (Ithaca: Cornell University Press, 2003).

28. Jo Ellen Green Kaiser, "A Politics of Time and Space," *Tikkun* 18:6 (2003), pp. 17–19.

29. Margaret Kohn, *Radical Space: Building the House of the People* (Ithaca: Cornell University Press, 2003), p. 7.

30. Kaiser, pp. 17–18.

31. Zygmunt Bauman, *Globalization: The Human Consequences* (New York: Columbia University Press, 1998), pp. 25–26.

32. Lawrence Grossberg, *Caught in the Crossfire: Kids, Politics, and America's Future* (Boulder: Paradigm Publishers, 2005), p. 112.

33. I take this theme up in detail in Henry A. Giroux, *The University in Chains: Confronting the Military-Industrial-Academic Complex* (Boulder: Paradigm Publishers, 2007). See also Zygmunt Bauman, *Liquid Fear* (London: Polity, 2006); Robert Stam and Ella Shohat, *Flagging Patriotism: Crises of Narcissism and Anti-Americanism* (New York: Routledge, 2007).

34. Susan Buck-Morss, *Thinking Past Terror: Islamism and Critical Theory on the Left* (New York: Verso, 2003), p. 29.

35. Stanley Aronowitz, *The Last Good Job in America* (Lanham, MD: Rowman and Littlefield, 2001), p. 160.

36. Richard Falk, "Will the Empire Be Fascist?" Transnational Foundation for Peace and Future Research (March 24, 2003). Available online at www.transnational.org/forum/meet/2003/Falk_FascistEmpire.html.

37. Victoria de Grazia, *The Culture of Consent: Mass Organization of Leisure in Fascist Italy* (New York: Cambridge University Press, 2002), p. 22.

38. Robert McChesney and John Nichols, *Our Media, Not Theirs: The Democratic Struggle Against Corporate Media* (New York: Seven Stories Press, 2002), pp. 48–49. See also, Robert McChesney, *Communication Revolution: Critical Junctures and the Future of the Media* (New York: New Press, 2007); Robert McChesney, *The Political Economy of the Media* (New York: Monthly Review Press, 2008).

39. Source Watch, "Clear Channel Worldwide," *Center for Media and Democracy* (January 2007), available online at http://www.sourcewatch.org/index.php?title=Clear_Channel_Worldwide; Jeff Sharlet, "Big World: How Clear Channel Programs America," *Harper's Magazine* (December 2003), pp. 38–39; G. R. Anderson, Jr., "Clear Channel Rules the World," *City Pages* 26:1263 (February 16, 2005), available online at http://www.citypages.com/databank/26/1263/article12961.asp.

40. *NOW with Bill Moyers,* PBS, February 13, 2004. Transcript available online at www.pbs.org /now/transcript/.

41. David Barstow and Robin Stein, "The Message Machine: How the Government Makes News," *New York Times* (March 13, 2005). Available online at http://select.nytimes.com/search/restricted/article?res=F50914FC3E580C708DDDAA0894DD404482.

42. McChesney and Nichols, *Our Media, Not Theirs,* pp. 52–53.

43. I address the assault on academic freedom in Giroux, *The University in Chains.*

44. Frank Rich, "The Swift Boating of Cindy Sheehan," *New York Times* (August 21, 2005). Available online at http://www.nytimes.com/2005/08/21/opinion/21rich.html?ei=5090&en=6c0b54b3c1bcba20&ex=1282276800&adxnnl=1&partner=rssuserland&emc=rss&adxnnlx=1124637090-/6pGluHeUZjJ/ES9/qnIvQ.

45. Ibid.

46. Editorial, *The Nation,* "Bush's High Crimes" (January 9–16, 2006), p. 3.

47. Rory O'Conner, "United States of Fear," *AlterNet* (January 13, 2005). Available online at www.alternet.org/story/03801. To understand this issue in a larger context, see Nafeez Mosaddeo Ahmed, *Behind the War on Terror* (New York: New Society Publishers, 2003).

48. Richard Bernstein, *The Abuse of Evil: The Corruption of Politics and Religion Since 9/11* (London: Polity, 2005), p. 26.

49. Eco, "Eternal Fascism," p. 15.

50. See Paul O'Neill, "Bush Sought Way to Invade Iraq," *60 Minutes,* CBS News, June 11, 2004. Transcript available online at www.cbsnews.com/stories/2004/01/09/60minutes/main592330.shtml.

51. Abbott Gleason, "The Hard Road to Fascism," *Boston Review* (Summer 2003). Available online at www.bostonreview.net/BR28.3/gleason.html.

52. Bob Herbert, "Casualties at Home," *New York Times* (March 27, 2003), p. A27.

53. Robert Parry, "Bush Lies . . . And Knows He's Lying," *Consortium News* (October 31, 2006). Available online at www.alternet.org/module/printversion/43686.

54. Ibid.

55. Frank Rich, "Bush of a Thousand Days," *New York Times* (April 30, 2006). Available online at http://select.nytimes.com/search/restricted/article?res=F60711F83B5B0C738FDDAD0894DE404482. Rich develops this theme and the selling of the Bush administration in Frank Rich, *The Greatest Story Ever Told* (New York: Penguin Press, 2006).

56. Terry Gross, "Millions and Millions Lost," *Harper's Magazine* (January 2004), p. 16.

57. Juan Stam, "Bush's Religious Language," *The Nation* (December 22, 2003), p. 27.

58. Bush's use of doublespeak is so pronounced that the National Council of Teachers of English awarded him its 2003 Doublespeak Award. See online at www.govst.edu/users/ghrank/Introduction/bush2003.htm.

59. Ruth Rosen, "Bush Doublespeak," *San Francisco Chronicle* (July 14, 2003). Available online at www.commondreams.org/views03/0714-10.htm. In January 2004, former vice president Al Gore, in a major speech on Bush's environmental policies, said: "Indeed, they often use Orwellian language to disguise their true purposes. For example, a policy that opens national forests to destructive logging of old-growth trees is labeled Healthy Forest Initiative. A policy that vastly increases the amount of pollution that can be dumped into the air is called the Clear Skies Initiative." Cited in Bob Herbert, "Masters of Deception," *New York Times* (January 16, 2004), p. A21.

60. Cited in Jennifer Lee, "U.S. Proposes Easing Rules on Emissions of Mercury," *New York Times* (December 3, 2003), p. A20.

61. Eric Pianin, "Clean Air Rules to Be Relaxed," *Washington Post* (August 23, 2003). Available online at www.washingtonpost.com/ac2/wp-dyn/A34334-2003Aug22.

62. The *New York Times* reported that the Environmental Protection Agency actually eliminated references to any studies that "concluded that warming is at least partly caused by rising concentrations of smokestack and tail pipe emissions and could threaten health and ecosystems." See Huck Gutman, "On Science, War, and the Prevalence of Lies," *The Statesman* (June 28, 2003). Available online at www.commondreams.org/views03/0628-04.htm.

63. For all of the direct government sources for these lies, see *One Thousand Reasons to Dump George Bush,* especially the section titled "Honesty." This information is available online at thousandreasons.org/the_top_ten.html.

64. David Corn, *The Lies of George W. Bush* (New York: Crown, 2003), pp. 228–230.

65. Paul Krugman, "Standard Operating Procedure," *New York Times* (June 3, 2004), p. A17.

66. See Lloyd Grove, "Lowdown," *New York Daily News* (January 11, 2004). Available online at www.unknownnews.net/insanity011404.html.

67. Cited in Paul Krugman, "Going for Broke," *New York Times* (January 20, 2004), p. A21.

68. Bob Herbert, "America the Fearful," *New York Times* (May 12, 2006), p. A25.

69. The poverty rate in the United States rose to 12.5 percent (35.9 million people) in 2004. For African Americans the poverty rate was twice the national rate. Over 45 million people are uninsured in the United States, a number that increased by 6 million since 2000, the year George W. Bush was first appointed to the presidency. See the report by the Center of Budget and Policy Priorities, "Economic Recovery Failed to Benefit Much of the Population in 2004" (August 30, 2005), available online at www.cbpp.org/8-30-05pov.htm. The rate of child poverty in the United States rose in 2004 to 17.6 percent, boosting the number of poor children to 12.9 million. Children make up a disproportionate share of the poor: Though only 26 percent of the total population, they constitute 39 percent of the poor. As Cesar Chelala points out, "UNICEF states that although the U.S. is still the wealthiest country on Earth, with income levels higher than any other country, it also has one of highest incidences of child poverty among the rich, industrialized nations. Denmark and Finland have child-poverty levels of less than 3 percent, and are closely followed by Norway and Sweden, thanks to higher levels of social spending." See Chelala, "Rich Man, Poor Man: Hungry Children in America," *Seattle Times* (January 4, 2006), available online at www.commondreams.org/views060104-24.htm.

70. Cited in Grey Myre, "Israelis' Anger at Evangelist May Delay Christian Center," *New York Times* (January 12, 2006), p. A12.

71. Esther Kaplan, *With God on Their Side: How Christian Fundamentalists Trampled Science, Policy, and Democracy in George W. Bush's White House* (New York: The New Press, 2004), p. 13.

72. Grossberg, *Caught in the Crossfire,* p. 229.

73. Heather Wokusch, "Make War Not Love: Abstinence, Aggression and the Bush White House," *Common Dreams News Center* (October 23, 2003). Available online at www.commondreams.org/views03/1026-01.htm.

74. Cited in Laura Flanders, "Bush's Hit List: Teens and Kids," *Common Dreams News Center* (February 13, 2005). Available online at www.commondreams.org/views05/0213-11.htm.

75. Frank Rich, "The Year of Living Indecently," *New York Times* (February 6, 2005), p. AR1.

76. Dana Milibank, "Religious Right Finds Its Center in Oval Office," *Washington Post* (December 24, 2001), p. A02.

77. Cited in ibid.

78. Ibid.

79. Jill Lawrence, "Bush's Agenda Walks the Church-State Line," *USA Today* (January 29, 2003). Available online at www.usatoday.com/news/washington/2003-01-29-bush-religion_x.htm.

80. Cited in Sydney H. Schanberg, "The Widening Crusade," *Village Voice* (October 15–21, 2003). Available online at www.villagevoice.com.issues/0342/schanberg.phb.

81. Robyn E. Blumner, "Religiosity as Social Policy," *St. Petersburg Times* (September 28, 2003). Available online at www.sptimes.com/2003/09/28/news_pf/Columns/religiosity_as_social.shtml.

82. Paul Harris, "Bush Says God Chose Him to Lead His Nation," *The Guardian* (November 1, 2003). Available online at www.observer.co.uk.

83. Joseph L. Conn, "Faith-Based Fiat," *Americans United for Separation of Church and State,* January 2002. Available online at www.au.org/churchstate/cs01031.htm.

84. Blumner, "Religiosity as Social Policy."

85. Jonathan Turley, "Raze the Church/State Wall? Heaven Help Us!" *Los Angeles Times* (February 24, 2003). Available online at www.enrongate.com/news/index.asp?id=169632.

86. Cited in Alan Cooperman, "Paige's Remarks on Religion in Schools Decried," *Washington Post* (April 9, 2003). Available online at www.washingtonpost.com/wp-dyn/articles/A59692-2003Apr8.html.

87. Jeremy Brecher, "Globalization Today," in Stanley Aronowitz and Heather Gautney, eds., *Implicating Empire: Globalization & Resistance in the 21st Century World Order* (New York: Basic Books, 2003), p. 202.

88. Graydon Carter, "The President? Go Figure," *Vanity Fair* (December 2003), p. 70.

89. Elizabeth Amon, "Name Withheld," *Harper's Magazine* (August 2003), p. 59.

90. Cited in Blumner, "Religiosity as Social Policy."

91. Cited in William M. Arkin, "The Pentagon Unleashes a Holy Warrior," *Los Angeles Times* (October 16, 2003). Available online at http://pqasb.pqarchiver.com/latimes/results.html? QryTxt=William+Arkin.

92. Cited in *NOW with Bill Moyers,* PBS, December 26, 2003. Transcript available online at www.pbs.org/now/transcript/transcript248_full.html.

93. Gary Wills, "With God On His Side," *New York Times Sunday Magazine* (March 30, 2003), p. 26.

94. Cited in "Bill Moyers Interviews Joseph Hough," *NOW with Bill Moyers,* PBS, October 24, 2003. Transcript available online at www.pbs.org/now/transcript/transcript_hough.html.

95. Kevin Phillips, *American Theocracy: The Peril and Politics of Radical Religion, Oil, and Borrowed Money in the 21st Century* (New York: Viking, 2006), p. xv; and Kevin Phillips, "How the GOP Became God's Own Party," *Washington Post* (April 2, 2006), p. B03.

96. Chris Hedges, *American Fascists: The Christian Right and the War on America* (New York: Free Press, 2006), p. 207.

97. Paul Gilroy, *Postcolonial Melancholia* (New York: Columbia University Press, 2005), p. 142.

98. Cited in Esther Kaplan, p. 13.

99. Maureen Dowd, "The Red Zone," *New York Times* (November 4, 2004), p. A27.

100. Cited in Susan Searls Giroux, "Interview with David Theo Goldberg," *JAC: The Journal of Advanced Composition* 26: 112 (2006), pp. 11–66.

101. How this obsession affects domestic and foreign policy in the United States can be seen in Noam Chomsky, *Hegemony or Survival: America's Quest for Global Dominance* (New York: Metropolitan Books, 2003).

102. Christopher Hellman, "The Runaway Military Budget: An Analysis," *FCNL Washington Newsletter* (March 2006). Available online at http://www.fcnl.org/now/pdf/2006/mar06.pdf.

103. Ibid.

104. Anap Shah, "High Military Expenditures in Some Places," *Global Issues* (November 9, 2006). Available online at http://www.globalissues.org/Geopolitics/ArmsTrade/Spending.asp?p=1.

105. Richard Falk, "Will the Empire Be Fascist?" *Transnational.org.* Available online at http://www.transnational.org/forum/meet/2003/Falk_FascistEmpire.html.

106. James Sterngold, "After 9/11 U.S. Policy Built on World," *San Francisco Chronicle* (March 21, 2004). Available online at http://www.sfgate.com/cgi-bin/article.cgi?file=/c/a/2004/03/21/MNGJ65OS4J1.DTL&type=printable.

107. See Johnson, *Nemesis,* p. 138.

108. Jim Wolf, "US Predicts Bumper Year in Arms Sales," *Reuters* (December 4, 2006). Available online at http://news.yahoo.com/s/nm/20061204/pl_nm/aero_arms_summit_arms_sales_usa_dc.

109. C. Wright Mills, *The Power Elite* (New York: Oxford University Press, 1956), p. 222.

110. Bacevich, *The New American Militarism,* p. 2.

111. Michael Hardt and Antonio Negri, *Multitude: War and Democracy in the Age of Empire* (New York: Penguin, 2004), pp. 12–13. See also Chris Hedges, *War is a Force That Gives Us Meaning* (New York: Anchor Books, 2003).

112. Chris Hedges, *War Is a Force That Gives Us Meaning* (New York: Anchor Books, 2003), p. 22.

113. John R. Gillis, ed., *The Militarization of the Western World* (New Brunswick: Rutgers University Press, 1989). On the militarization of urban space, see Mike Davis, *City of Quartz* (New York: Vintage, 1992), and Kenneth Saltman and David Gabbard, eds., *Education as Enforcement: The Militarization and Corporatization of Schools* (New York: Routledge, 2003). And for a discussion of the current neoconservative influence on militarizing American foreign policy, see Thomas Donnelly, Donald Kagen, and Gary Schmidt's *Rebuilding America's Defenses,* which was developed under the auspices of The Project for the New American Century (www.newamericancentury.org) and is one of many reports outlining this issue.

114. Catherine Lutz, "Making War at Home in the United States: Militarization and the Current Crisis," *American Anthropologist* 104 (Sept. 2002), p. 723.

115. Kevin Baker, "We're in the Army Now: The G.O.P.'s Plan to Militarize Our Culture," *Harper's Magazine* (October 2003), p. 40.

116. Jorge Mariscal, "'Lethal and Compassionate': The Militarization of US Culture," *CounterPunch* (May 5, 2003). Available online at www.counterpunch.org/mariscal05052003.html.

117. George Monbiot, "States of War," *The Guardian* (October 14, 2003). Available online at www.commondreams.org/views03/1014-09.htm.

118. Mariscal, "'Lethal and Compassionate': The Militarization of US Culture."

119. Baker, "We're in the Army Now," p. 48.

120. Ibid., p. 37. This view has been dealt with in substantial detail by Chalmers Johnson in a number of books as well as by Andrew Bacevich in *The New American Militarism* (New York: Oxford University Press, 2005).

121. Baker, ibid.

122. Piper Fogg, "Independent Alumni Group Offers $100 Bounties to Ferret Out Classroom Bias," *Chronicle of Higher Education* (January 19, 2006). Available online at www.chronicle.com/daily/2006/01/2006011904n.htm.

123. This charge comes from a report by the conservative group American Council of Trustees and Alumni (ACTA), founded by Lynne Cheney and Joseph Lieberman. ACTA also posted on its website a list of 115 statements made by allegedly "un-American professors." See Jerry L. Martin and Anne D. Neal, *Defending Civilization: How Our Universities Are Failing America and What Can Be Done About It.* Available online at www.goacta.org/publications/Reports/defciv.pdg.

124. Ruth Rosen, "Politics of Fear," *San Francisco Chronicle* (December 30, 2002). Available online at www.commondreams.org/views02/1230-02.htm.

125. *Time Magazine,* "The American Soldier" (December 29, 2003).

126. Richard H. Kohn, "Using the Military at Home: Yesterday, Today, and Tomorrow," *Chicago Journal of International Law* 94:1 (Spring 2003), pp. 174–175.

127. Ibid.

128. Pennsylvania State University, "Penn State's Spanier to Chair National Security Board," News Release, September 16, 2005.

129. David Goodman, "Covertly Recruiting Kids," *Baltimore Sun* (September 29, 2003). Available online at www.commondreams.org/views03/1001-11.htm.

130. Elissa Gootman, "Metal Detectors and Pep Rallies: Spirit Helps Tame a Bronx School," *New York Times* (February 4, 2004), p. C14.

131. Gail R. Chaddock, "Safe Schools at a Price," *Christian Science Monitor* (August 24, 1999), p. 15.

132. Tamar Lewin, "Raid at High School Leads to Racial Divide, Not Drugs," *New York Times* (December 9, 2003), p. A16.

133. "Kindergarten Girl Handcuffed, Arrested at Fla. School," *WFTV.com* (March 30, 2007). Available online at http://www.wftv.com/news/11455199/detail.html.

134. Randall Beger, "Expansion of Police Power in the Public Schools and the Vanishing Rights of Students," *Social Justice* 29:1–2 (2002), p. 124.

135. Advancement Project, *Education on Lockdown: The Schoolhouse to Jailhouse Track* (Washington, DC: Advancement Project Publishing, 2005).

136. Sara Rimer, "Unruly Students Facing Arrest, Not Detention," *New York Times* (January 4, 2004), p. 15.

137. Ibid.

138. David Garland, "Men and Jewelry; Prison as Exile: Unifying Laughter and Darkness," *Chronicle of Higher Education* (July 6, 2001), p. B4.

139. Howard Witt, "School Discipline Tougher on African Americans," *Chicago Tribune* (September 25, 2007). Available online at http://www.chicagotribune.com/news/nationworld/chi-070924discipline,0,22104.story?coll=chi_tab01_layout.

140. Bob Herbert, "Arrested While Grieving," *New York Times* (May 26, 2007), p. A27. See, for example, Elora Mukheree and Marvin Karpatikin, *Criminalizing the Classroom: The Over-Policing of New York City Schools* (Washington, DC: American Civil Liberties Union, 2007); Advancement Project, *Education on Lockdown* (Washington, DC: Advancement Project Publishing, 2005).

141. Peter B. Kraska, "The Military-Criminal Justice Blur: An Introduction," in Peter B. Kraska, ed., *Militarizing the American Criminal Justice System* (Boston: Northeastern University Press, 2001), p. 3.

142. See Christian Parenti, *Lockdown America: Police and Prisons in the Age of Crisis* (London: Verso Press, 1999).

143. Kraska, "The Military-Criminal Justice Blur," p. 10.

144. Jonathan Simon, "Sacrificing Private Ryan: The Military Model and the New Penology," in Peter B. Kraska, ed., *Militarizing the American Criminal Justice System* (Boston: Northeastern University Press, 2001), p. 113.

145. Gary Delgado, "'Mo' Prisons Equals Mo' Money," *ColorLines* (Winter 1999–2000), p. 18; CBS News, "Largest Prison Increase Since 2000," (June 27, 2007). Online: http://www.cbsnews.com/stories/2007/06/27/national/main2987952.shtml?source=search_story.

146. Sanho Tree, "The War at Home," *Sojourner's Magazine* (May–June 2003), p. 5.

147. For some extensive analyses of the devastating effects the criminal justice system is having on black males, see Michael Tonry, *Malign Neglect: Race, Crime, and Punishment in America* (New York: Oxford University Press, 1995), and Jerome Miller, *Search and Destroy: African-American Males in the Criminal Justice System* (Cambridge: Cambridge University Press, 1996).

148. Arianna Huffington, "The War on Drugs is Really a War on Minorities," *AlterNet* (March 31, 2007), available online: www.alternet.org/story/49782/. See also Jason Deparle, "The American Prison Nightmare," *The New York Review of Books* 54:6 (April 12, 2007), pp. 33–36.

149. Steven R. Donziger, ed., *The Real War on Crime: The Report of the National Criminal Justice Commission* (New York: Harper Perennial, 1996), p. 101.

150. Lisa Featherstone, "A Common Enemy: Students Fight Private Prisons," *Dissent* (Fall 2000), p. 78.

151. Carl Chery, "U.S. Army Targets Black Hip-Hop Fans," *The Wire/Daily Hip-Hop News* (October 21, 2003). Available online at www.sohh.com/article_print.php?content_ ID=5162.

152. Ibid.

153. Mariscal, "'Lethal and Compassionate': The Militarization of US Culture."

154. Nicholas Turse, "Have Yourself a Pentagon Xmas," *The Nation* (January 5, 2004), p. 8, available online at www.tomdispatch.com; Matt Slagle, "Military Recruits Video-Game Makers," *Chicago Tribune* (October 8, 2003), p. 4.

155. R. Lee Sullivan, "Firefight on Floppy Disk," *Forbes Magazine* (May 20, 1996), pp. 39–40.

156. Cited in Gloria Goodale, "Video Game Offers Young Recruits a Peek at Military Life," *Christian Science Monitor* (May 31, 2003), p. 18.

157. Wayne Woolley, "From 'An Army of One' to Army of Fun: Online Video Game Helps Build Ranks," *Times-Picayune* (September 7, 2003), p. 26.

158. "Gaming News—October 2003," *The Gamer's Temple* (October 10, 2003). Available online at www.gamerstemple.com/news/1003/100331.asp.

159. Ibid.

160. Nicholas Turse, "The Pentagon Invades Your Xbox," *Dissident Voice* (December 15, 2003). Available online at www.dissidentvoice.org/Articles9/Turse_Pentagon-Video-Games.htm.

161. See, especially, Carl Boggs and Tom Pollard, *The Hollywood War Machine* (Boulder: Paradigm Publishers, 2006).

162. Ibid.

163. Maureen Tkacik, "Military Toys Spark Conflict on Home Front," *Wall Street Journal* (March 31, 2003), p. B1.

164. Amy C. Sims, "Just Child's Play," *Fox News Network* (August 21, 2003). Available online at www.wmsa.net/news/FoxNews/fn-030822_childs_ play.htm.

165. Mike Conklin, "Selling War at Retail," *Chicago Tribune* (May 1, 2003), p. 1.

166. Cathy Horyn, "Macho America Storms Europe's Runways," *New York Times* (July 3, 2003), p. A1.

167. Baker, "We're in the Army Now," p. 38.

168. This quotation from Coulter has been cited extensively. It can be found online at www.coulterwatch.com/files/BW_2-003-bin_Coulter.pdf.

169. Susan George, "A Short History of Neoliberalism: Twenty Years of Elite Economics and Emerging Opportunities for Structural Change," *Global Policy Forum*, March 24–26, 1999. Available online at www.globalpolicy.org/globaliz/econ/histneol.htm.

170. There are a number of important works on the politics of neoliberalism. I have found the following particularly useful: Pierre Bourdieu, *Acts of Resistance: Against the Tyranny of the Market* (New York: The New Press, 1998); Pierre Bourdieu, "The Essence of Neoliberalism," *Le Monde Diplomatique* (December 1998), available online at www.en.monde-diplomatique.fr/1998/12/08bourdieu; Zygmunt Bauman,

Work, Consumerism and the New Poor (London: Polity, 1998); Noam Chomsky, *Profit over People: Neoliberalism and the Global Order* (New York: Seven Stories Press, 1999); Jean Comaroff and John L. Comaroff, *Millennial Capitalism and the Culture of Neoliberalism* (Durham: Duke University Press, 2000); Anatole Anton, Milton Fisk, and Nancy Holmstrom, eds., *Not for Sale: In Defense of Public Goods* (Boulder: Westview Press, 2000); Alain Touraine, *Beyond Neoliberalism* (London: Polity, 2001); Colin Leys, *Market-Driven Politics* (London: Verso, 2001); Randy Martin, *Financialization of Daily Life* (Philadelphia: Temple University Press, 2002); Ulrich Beck, *Individualization: Institutionalized Individualism and Its Social and Political Consequences* (London: Sage, 2002); Doug Henwood, *After the New Economy* (New York: The New Press, 2003); Lisa Duggan, *The Twilight of Equality: Neoliberalism, Cultural Politics, and the Attack on Democracy* (Boston: Beacon Press, 2003); Pierre Bourdieu, *Firing Back: Against the Tyranny of the Market 2,* translated by Loic Wacquant (New York: The New Press, 2003); David Harvey, *A Brief History of Neoliberalsim* (New York: Duke University Press, 2005); Aihwa Ong, *Neoliberalism as Exception* (Durham: Duke University Press, 2006); and Neil Smith, *The End Game of Globalization* (New York: Routledge, 2005).

171. Minqi Li provides an important summary of neoliberal policies and their effects: "A neoliberal regime typically includes monetarist policies to lower inflation and maintain fiscal balance (often achieved by reducing public expenditures and raising the interest rate), 'flexible' labor markets (meaning removing labor market regulations and cutting social welfare), trade and financial liberalization, and privatization. These policies are an attack by the global ruling elites (primarily with the finance capital of the leading capitalist states) on the working people of the world. Under neoliberal capitalism decades of social progress and developmental efforts have been reversed. Global inequality in income and wealth has reached unprecedented levels. In much of the world, working people have suffered pauperization. Entire countries have been reduced to misery." See Li, "After Neoliberalism," *Monthly Review* (January 2004), p. 21.

172. For instance, a United Nations Human Development Report states that "the world's richest 1 percent receive as much income as the poorest 57 percent. The income gap between the richest 20 percent and the poorest 20 percent in the world rose from 30:1 in 1960 to 60:1 in 1990, and to 74:1 in 1999, and is projected to reach 100:1 in 2015. In 1999–2000, 2.8 billion people lived on less than $3 a day, 840 million were undernourished, 2.4 billion did not have access to any form of improved sanitation services, and one in every six children in the world of primary school age were not in school. About 50 percent of the global nonagricultural labor force is estimated to be either unemployed or underemployed." Cited in ibid.

173. George Steinmetz, "The State of Emergency and the Revival of American Imperialism: Toward an Authoritarian Post-Fordism," *Public Culture* 15:2 (Spring 2003), p. 337.

174. Barry Bluestone and Bennett Harrison, *The Deindustrialization of America: Plant Closings, Community Abandonment and the Dismantling of Basic Industry* (New York: Basic Books, 1982), p. 6.

175. Stanley Aronowitz, *How Class Works* (New Haven: Yale University Press, 2003), p. 21.

176. Ibid., p. 101.

177. See Bret Benjamin, *Invested Interest: Capital, Culture, and the World Bank* (Minneapolis: University of Minnesota Press, 2007).

178. Stanley Aronowitz, "Introduction," in Paulo Freire, *Pedagogy of Freedom: Ethics, Democracy and Civic Courage* (Lanham, MD: Rowman and Littlefield, 1998), p. 7.

179. Bourdieu, *Firing Back,* p. 38.

180. See Henwood, *After the New Economy*; Kevin Phillips, *Wealth and Democracy: A Political History of the American Rich* (New York: Broadway, 2003); and Paul Krugman, *The Great Unraveling: Losing Our Way in the New Century* (New York: W. W. Norton, 2003).

181. Aronowitz, *How Class Works,* p. 102.

182. Gar Alperovitz, "Another World Is Possible," *Mother Jones* (January/February 2006), p. 68.

183. William Greider, "The Right's Grand Ambition: Rolling Back the 20th Century," *The Nation* (May 12, 2003), p. 18.

184. Edward S. Herman and Robert W. McChesney, *The Global Media: The New Missionaries of Global Capitalism* (Washington, DC/London: Cassell, 1997), p. 3.

185. I address this issue in Henry A. Giroux, *Public Spaces, Private Lives: Democracy Beyond 9/11* (Lanham: Rowman and Littlefield, 2003).

186. James Rule, "Markets, in Their Place," *Dissent* (Winter 1998), p. 31.

187. Bauman, *The Individualized Society,* p. 107.

188. Alan Bryman, *Disney and His Worlds* (New York: Routledge, 1995), p. 154.

189. Of course, there is widespread resistance to neoliberalism and its institutional enforcers, as voiced by the WTO, the IMF, and many intellectuals, students, and members of global justice movements; but this resistance rarely gets aired in the dominant media, and when it does it is often dismissed as irrelevant or tainted by Marxist ideology.

190. Soros, "The US Is Now in the Hands of a Group of Extremists." Soros provides a scorching critique of the Bush administration in George Soros, *The Age of Fallibility: Consequences of the War on Terror* (New York: PublicAffairs, 2006).

191. Paul Tolme, "Criminalizing the Homeless," *In These Times* (April 14, 2003), pp. 6–7.

192. Democracy Now, "Uncharitable Care: How Hospitals Are Gouging and Even Arresting the Uninsured," *Common Dreams News Center* (January 8, 2004). Available online at http://www.commondreams.org/headlines04/0108-07.htm.

193. Bourdieu, *Acts of Resistance,* p. 4.

194. Comaroff and Comaroff, *Millennial Capitalism,* p. 305.

195. Ibid., p. 332.

196. Ibid.

197. See Scott Lash, *Critique of Information* (Thousand Oaks, CA: Sage, 2002).

Notes to Chapter 2

1. W.E.B. Du Bois, *The Souls of Black Folk,* in *Three Negro Classics* (New York: Avon Books, 1965), p. 221.

2. It is important to note that while such covert modes of expression may be true of anti-black racism, they certainly do not characterize the racist policies

being enacted by the United States against immigrants and nationals from the Middle East. The racial profiling, harassment, and outright use of unconstitutional means to intimidate, deport, and jail members of the Arab and Muslim populations in the United States represent a most shameful period in this country's ongoing history of state-sanctioned racist practices. Thus, while the focus of this chapter is on black-white relations, I am not suggesting that racism encompasses only the latter. Obviously, any full account of racism would have to be applied to the wide range of groups who constitute diverse peoples of color and ethnic origin.

3. Howard Winant, "Race in the Twenty-First Century," *Tikkun* 17:1 (2002), p. 33.

4. Cited in David Shipler, "Reflections on Race," *Tikkun* 13:1 (1998), p. 59.

5. Dinesh D'Souza, *The End of Racism* (New York: The Free Press, 1995); Jim Sleeper, *Liberal Racism: How Fixating on Race Subverts the American Dream* (Lanham, MD: Rowman and Littlefield, 2002); Stephan and Abigail Thernstrom, *America in Black and White: One Nation, Indivisible* (New York: Simon and Schuster, 1999).

6. Cited in Tim Wise, "See No Evil: Perception and Reality in Black and White," *ZNet Commentary* (August 2, 2001). Available online at www.zmag.org. The Gallup Poll on "Black-White Relations in the United States—2001 Update" is available online at http://www.gallup.com/poll/specialReports/.

7. As Greg Winter points out, the Center for Equal Opportunity and the American Civil Rights Institute, two groups that oppose affirmative action, have launched a new offensive "against scholarships and summer programs intended to ease minority students into college life." See Winter, "Colleges See Broader Attack on Their Aid to Minorities," *New York Times* (March 30, 2003), p. A15.

8. Following is a representative sample of works that point to the pervasive racism at work in American life: Howard Winant, *The World Is a Ghetto: Race and Democracy Since World War II* (New York: Basic Books, 2001); Manning Marable, *The Great Wells of Democracy: The Meaning of Race in American Life* (New York: BasicCivitas Books, 2002); David Theo Goldberg, *The Racial State* (Malden, MA: Blackwell Books, 2002); Steve Martinot, *The Rule of Racialization: Class, Identity, Governance* (Philadelphia: Temple University Press, 2003).

9. Michael Omi, "Racialization in the Post-Civil Rights Era," in Avery Gordon and Christopher Newfield, eds., *Mapping Multiculturalism* (Minneapolis: University of Minnesota Press, 1996), p. 183.

10. Jack Geiger, "The Real World of Race," *The Nation* (December 1, 1997), p. 27.

11. See, for instance, Shelby Steele, "The Age of White Guilt," *Harper's Magazine* (November 2002), pp. 33–42.

12. This position is fully developed in Shelby Steele, *The Content of Our Character* (New York: Harper, 1990).

13. John McWhorter, "Don't Do Me Any Favors," *American Enterprise Magazine* (April/May 2003). Available on line at www.theamericanenterprise.org/taeam03d.htm.

14. Zygmunt Bauman, *The Individualized Society* (London: Polity Press, 2001), p. 205.

15. Charles Murray, *Losing Ground: American Social Policy, 1950–1980* (New York: Basic Books, 1985).

16. For excellent analyses of this shift in race relations, see Eduardo Bonilla-Silva, *White Supremacy and Racism in the Post-Civil Rights Era* (Boulder: Lynne Rienner Publishers, 2001); and Amy Elizabeth Ansell, *New Right, New Racism: Race and Reaction in the United States and Britain* (New York: New York University Press, 1997).

17. Douglas Kellner, "Globalization and New Social Movements: Lessons for Critical Theory and Pedagogy," in Nicholas Burbules and Carlos Torres, eds., *Globalization and Education* (New York: Routledge/Falmer, 2000), p. 307.

18. Bauman, *The Individualized Society,* p. 159.

19. Lewis H. Lapham, "Res Publica," *Harper's Magazine* (December 2001), p. 8.

20. Zygmunt Bauman, *Globalization: The Human Consequences* (New York: Columbia University Press, 1998), p. 47.

21. Ansell, *New Right, New Racism,* p. 111.

22. Ibid., pp. 20–21.

23. Charles Gallagher, "Color-Blind Privilege: The Social and Political Functions of Erasing the Color Line in Post Race America," unpublished essay, p. 12.

24. Ibid., p. 11.

25. This issue is taken up brilliantly in David Theo Goldberg, *The Racial State* (Malden, MA: Blackwell Books, 2002), especially on pp. 200–238.

26. Manning Marable, "Beyond Color-Blindness," *The Nation* (December 14, 1998), p. 29.

27. For specific figures in all areas of life, see Bonilla-Silva, *White Supremacy and Racism in the Post-Civil Rights Era,* especially the chapter titled "White Supremacy in the Post–Civil Rights Era," pp. 89–120.

28. Paul Street, "A Whole Lott Missing: Rituals of Purification and Racism Denial," *Z Magazine* (December 22, 2002). Available online at www.zmag.org/content/print_article.cfm?itemID=2784§ion.

29. I address these issues in detail in Henry A. Giroux, *Public Spaces, Private Lives: Democracy Beyond 9/11* (Lanham, MD: Rowman and Littlefield, 2002).

30. Loic Wacquant, "From Slavery to Mass Incarceration: Rethinking the 'Race Question' in the U.S.," in *New Left Review* (January–February 2002), p. 44.

31. Paul Street, "Mass Incarceration and Racist State Priorities at Home and Abroad," *DissidentVoice* (March 11, 2003), pp. 6–7. Available online at http://www.dissidentvoice.org/Articles2/Street_MassIncarceration.htm.

32. Richard J. Herrnstein and Charles Murray, *The Bell Curve: Intelligence and Class Structure in American Life* (New York: The Free Press, 1994), pp. 533–534, 551.

33. Nikhil Aziz, "Moving Right On! Fairness, Family, and Faith," *The Public Eye* 16:2 (Summer 2002), p. 5.

34. See "Civil Rights" within the Mission section of the CIR's website, at http://www.cir-usa.org/civil_rights_theme.html.

35. For an excellent summary and analysis of many of these legal cases, see Aziz, "Moving Right On!"

36. Ibid., p. 15.

37. Zsuza Ferge, "What Are the State Functions That Neoliberalism Wants to Eliminate?" in Antole Anaton, Milton Fisk, and Nancy Holmstrom, eds., *Not for Sale: In Defense of Public Goods* (Boulder: Westview Press, 2000), p. 183.

38. David Theo Goldberg, *The Racial State* (Malden, MA: Blackwell, 2002), p. 217. The ideas in the sentence prior to this quote are also taken from Goldberg's text.

39. Jean Comaroff and John L. Comaroff, "Millennial Capitalism: First Thoughts on a Second Coming," *Public Culture* 12:2 (2000), pp. 305–306.

40. Aziz, "Moving Right On!" p. 6.

41. Cited in Philip Klinker, "The 'Racial Realism' Hoax," *The Nation* (December 14, 1998), p. 37.

42. Dinesh D'Souza, *The End of Racism: Principles for a Multiracial Society* (New York: The Free Press, 1995), p. 268.

43. Patricia J. Williams, *Seeing a Color-Blind Future: The Paradox of Race* (New York: Noonday Press, 1997), pp. 18, 26.

44. John Meacham, "A Man Out of Time," *Newsweek* (December 23, 2003), p. 27.

45. Ibid.

46. On Trent Lott's voting record on matters of race, see Derrick Z. Jackson, "Brother Lott's Real Record," *Boston Globe* (December 18, 2002). Available online at www.commondreams.org/views02/1218-09.htm.

47. See Robert Kuttner, "A Candid Conversation About Race in America," *Boston Globe* (December 25, 2002). Available online at www.commondreams.org/views02/1225-02.htm.

48. David Brooks, "We Don't Talk This Way," *Newsweek* (December 23, 2002), p. 31.

49. Cited in David Roediger, *Toward the Abolition of Whiteness* (London: Verso Press, 1994), p. 8.

50. Frank Rich, "Bonfire of the Vanities," *New York Times* (December 21, 2002), p. A35.

51. Ibid.

52. I have taken this idea from David Theo Goldberg, *Racial Subjects: Writing on Race in America* (New York: Routledge, 1997), pp. 17–26.

53. Ellis Cose, "Lessons of the Trent Lott Mess," *Newsweek* (December 23, 2002), p. 37.

54. Ibid.

55. David Theo Goldberg, "Racialized Discourse," in *Racist Culture* (Malden, MA: Blackwell, 1993), pp. 54, 55, 56.

56. Teun A. Van Dijk, "Denying Racism: Elite Discourse and Racism," in Philomena Essed and David Theo Goldberg, eds., *Race Critical Theories: Texts and Contexts* (Malden, MA: Blackwell, 2002), pp. 323–324.

57. Jean Comaroff and John L. Comaroff, "Millennial Capitalism," p. 322.

58. James Rule, "Markets, in Their Place," *Dissent* (Winter 1998), p. 31.

59. Bauman, *The Individualized Society*, p. 107.

60. Ibid.

61. Leerom Medovoi, "Globalization as Narrative and Its Three Critiques," *Review of Education/Pedagogy/Cultural Studies* 24:1–2 (2002), p. 66.

62. D'Souza, *The End of Racism*, p. 545.

63. David Theo Goldberg, *The Racial State* (Malden, MA: Blackwell, 2002), p. 229.

64. Pierre Bourdieu and Günter Grass, "The 'Progressive' Restoration: A Franco-German Dialogue," *New Left Review* 14 (March–April 2002), p. 71.

65. John Brenkman, "Race Publics: Civic Illiberalism, or Race After Reagan," *Transition* 5:2 (Summer 1995), p. 8.

66. On this subject, see Robert W. McChesney and John Nichols, *Our Media, Not Theirs* (New York: Seven Stories Press, 2002).

67. David Goldberg and John Solomos, "Introduction to Part III," in David Goldberg and John Solomos, eds., *A Companion to Ethnic and Racial Studies* (Malden, MA: Blackwell, 2002), p. 231.

Notes to Chapter 3

1. On the move to what can be called the punishing state or a notion of governmentality based on criminalization, see Jonathan Simon, *Governing Through Crime* (New York: Oxford University Press, 2007).

2. Bernadine Dohrn, "Look Out, Kid, It's Something You Did," in Valerie Polakow, ed., *The Public's Assault on America's Children* (New York: Teachers College Press, 2000), p. 161.

3. Paul Street, "Race, Prison, and Poverty: The Race to Incarcerate in the Age of Correctional Keynesianism," *Z Magazine* (May 2001), p. 26. For an excellent analysis of the disenfranchisement of prisoners, see Jeff Manza, *Locked Out: Felon Disenfranchisement and American Democracy* (New York: Oxford University Press, 2006).

4. Lisa Featherstone, "A Common Enemy: Students Fight for Private Prisons," *Dissent* (Fall 2000), p. 78.

5. James Sterngold, "Prisons' Budget to Trump Colleges,'" *San Francisco Chronicle* (May 21, 2007) p. 1.

6. Randall Beger, "Expansion of Police Power in Public Schools and the Vanishing Rights of Students," *Social Justice* 29:1/2 (2002), p. 121.

7. For a moving narrative of the devastating effects of the juvenile justice system on teens, see Edward Humes, *No Matter How Loud I Shout: A Year in the Life of Juvenile Court* (New York: Touchstone, 1996).

8. Margaret Talbot, "The Maximum Security Adolescent," *New York Times Magazine* (September 10, 2000), p. 42.

9. Evelyn Nieves, "California Proposal Toughens Penalties for Young Criminals," *New York Times* (March 6, 2000), pp. A1, A15.

10. Sara Rimer and Raymond Bonner, "Whether to Kill Those Who Killed as Youths," *New York Times* (August 22, 2000), p. A16.

11. Ann Patchett, "The Age of Innocence," *New York Times Sunday Magazine* (September 29, 2002), p. 17.

12. I have taken up this critique in great detail in Henry A. Giroux, *The Abandoned Generation* (Boulder: Paradigm Publishers, 2004).

13. Center for American Progress Task Force on Poverty, *From Poverty to Prosperity* (Washington, DC: Center for American Progress, 2007), p. 1.

14. Paul Krugman, "Gilded Once More," *New York Times* (April 27, 2007). Available online at http://www.truthout.org/docs_2006/042707F.shtml.

15. Jenny Anderson and Julie Creswell, "Top Hedge Fund Managers Earn Over $240 million," *New York Times* (April 24, 2007), p. 1; Council on International and Public Affairs, "Too Much Executive Pay Scorecard," *Too Much Online Weekly* (May 1, 2007). Available online at www.cipa-apex.org/toomuch/ExecPayScoreboard.html.

16. Paul Krugman, "Bush's Class-War Budget," *New York Times* (February 11, 2005). Available online at www.nytimes.com/2005/02/11/opinion/11krugman.html?ex=1265864400&en=c5baff37424e2a5d&ei=5088&.

17. Elisabeth Young-Bruehl, *Why Arendt Matters* (New Haven: Yale University Press, 2006), pp. 53–54.

18. Jacques Derrida, "The Future of the Profession or the Unconditional University," in Laurence Simmons and Heather Worth, eds., *Derrida Down Under* (Auckland, New Zealand: Dunmarra Press, 2001), p. 253.

19. Lawrence Grossberg, *Caught in the Crossfire* (Boulder: Paradigm Publishers, 2005), p. 16.

20. Bob Herbert, "Arrested While Grieving," *New York Times* (May 26, 2007), p. A25.

21. Lawrence Grossberg, "Why Does Neo-Liberalism Hate Kids? The War on Youth and the Culture of Politics," *Review of Education/Pedagogy/Cultural Studies* 23:2 (2001), p. 133.

22. For an analysis of the drop in youth crime in the 1990s, see S. D. Levitt, "Understanding Why Crime Fell in the 1990s: Four Factors That Explain the Decline and Six That Do Not," *Journal of Economic Perspectives* 18:1 (Winter 2004), pp. 163–190.

23. Beger, "Expansion of Police Power in Public Schools," p. 127.

24. Peter Cassidy, "Last Brick in the Kindergulag," *AlterNet* (May 12, 2003). Available online at alternet.org/print.hgml?Storyld=13616.

25. Gail R. Chaddock, "Safe Schools at a Price," *Christian Science Monitor* (August 24, 1999), p. 15.

26. "Kindergarten Girl Handcuffed, Arrested at Fla. School," *WFTV.com* (March 30, 2007). Available online at www.wftv.com/news/11455199/detail.html.

27. Andrew Gumbel, "America Has 2,000 Young Offenders Serving Life Terms in Jail," *The Independent* (October 12, 2005). Available online at www.commondreams.org/headlines05/1012-02.htm.

28. I have taken up a detailed critique of No Child Left Behind in Henry A. Giroux, *America on the Edge* (New York: Palgrave, 2006). For a devastating critique of No Child Left Behind, see Jonathan Kozol, *Letters to a Young Teacher* (New York: Crown, 2007).

29. Sara Rimer, "Unruly Students Facing Arrests, Not Detention," *New York Times* (January 4, 2004), p. 1.

30. Ibid., p. 15.

31. Ibid.

32. American Bar Association, "Report on Zero Tolerance Laws" (May 28, 2003), p. 3. Available online at www.abanet.org/crimjust/juvius/zerotolreport.html.

33. Kate Zernike, "Crackdown on Threats in School Fails a Test," *New York Times* (May 17, 2001), p. A21.

34. Tyson Lewis, "The Surveillance Economy of Post-Columbine Schools," *Review of Education/Pedagogy/Cultural Studies* 25:4 (October–December 2003), p. 336.

35. Brian Moore, "Letting Software Make the Call," *Chicago Reader* 29:49 (2000), p. 18.

36. Editorial, "Zero Tolerance Takes Student Discipline to Harsh Extremes," *USA Today* (January 2, 2004), p. A11.

37. Ellen Goodman, "'Zero Tolerance' Means Zero Chance for Troubled Kids," *Centre Daily Times* (January 4, 2000), p. 8.

38. These examples are taken from a report on zero-tolerance laws by the American Bar Association, May 28, 2003. Available online at www.abanet.org/crimjust/juvius/zerotolreport.html.

39. Beger, "Expansion of Police Power in Public Schools," p. 123.

40. Goodman, "'Zero Tolerance' Means Zero Chance," p. 8.

41. Steven Drizin, "Arturo's Case," in William Ayers, Bernadine Dohrn, and Rick Ayers, eds., *Zero Tolerance* (New York: The New Press, 2001), p. 32.

42. Editorial, "Zero Tolerance Is the Policy," *Denver Rocky Mountain News* (June 22, 1999), p. A38.

43. Gregory Michie, "One Strike and You're Out: Does Zero Tolerance Work? Or Does Kicking Kids Out of School Just Make Things Worse?" *Chicago Reader* 29:49 (2000), p. 24.

44. Jane Gordon, "In Schools, Bad Behavior Is Shown the Door," *New York Times* (November 16, 2003), p. C14.

45. Annette Fuentes, "Discipline and Punish," *The Nation* (December 15, 2003), pp. 17–20. More recent studies suggest the trend is increasing; see Howard Witt, "School Discipline Tougher on African Americans," *Chicago Tribune* (September 25, 2007). Available online at http://www.chicagotribune.com/news/nationworld/chi-070924discipline,0,22104.story?coll=chi_tab01_layout.

46. Editorial, "Zero Tolerance," *USA Today* (January 2, 2004), p. A11.

47. Cited in Gordon, "In Schools," p. 2.

48. Tamar Lewin and Jennifer Medina, "To Cut Failure Rate, Schools Shed Students," *New York Times* (July 31, 2003), p. A1. For more recent studies, see Elora Mukheree and Marvin Karpatikin, *Criminalizing the Classroom: The Over-Policing of New York City Schools* (Washington, DC: American Civil Liberties Union, 2007) and the Advancement Project, *Education on Lockdown* (Washington, DC: Advancement Project Publishing, 2005).

49. It was reported in the *New York Times* that in responding to the spate of recent school shootings, the FBI has provided educators across the country with a list of behaviors that could identify "students likely to commit an act of lethal violence." One such behavior is "resentment over real or perceived injustices." The reach of domestic militarization becomes more evident not only as the FBI takes on the role of monitoring potentially disruptive student behavior but also in the degree to which teachers are positioned to become adjuncts of the criminal justice system. The story and quotes appear in the editorial "F.B.I. Caution Signs for Violence in Classroom," *New York Times* (September 7, 2000), p. A18.

50. Tamar Lewin, "Study Finds Racial Bias in Public Schools," *New York Times* (March 11, 2000), p. A14.

51. Libero Della Piana, "Crime and Punishment in Schools: Students of Color Are Facing More Suspensions Because of Racially Biased Policies," *San Francisco Chronicle* (February 9, 2000), p. A21.

52. Marilyn Elias, "Disparity in Black and White?" *USA Today* (December 11, 2000), p. D9.

53. Editorial, "Zero Tolerance," *USA Today* (January 2, 2004), p. A11.

54. Lewis, "The Surveillance Economy," p. 337.

55. Loic Wacquant, "From Slavery to Mass Incarceration: Rethinking the 'Race Question' in the U.S.," *New Left Review* (January–February 2002), p. 52.

56. For a provocative analysis of the relationship between what Norman Geras calls "the contract of mutual indifference" and neoliberalism's refusal of the social as a condition for contemporary forms of mutual indifference, see Geras, *The Contract of Mutual Indifference* (London: Verso Press, 1998), p. 30.

57. For some illuminating commentaries on the new student movement, see Lisa Featherstone, "The New Student Movement," *The Nation* (May 15, 2000), pp. 11–15; David Samuels, "Notes from Underground: Among the Radicals of the Pacific Northwest," *Harper's Magazine* (May 2000), pp. 35–47; Katazyna Lyson, Monique Murad, and Trevor Stordahl, "Real Reformers, Real Results," *Mother Jones* (October 2000), pp. 20–22; Alexander Cockburn, Jeffrey St. Clair, and Allan Sekula, *5 Days that Shook the World* (London: Verso Press, 2000); and Mark Edelman Boren, *Student Resistance* (New York: Routledge, 2001). See also Imre Szeman, "Learning from Seattle," Special Issue of the *Review of Education/Pedagogy/Cultural Studies* 24:1–2 (January–June 2002) and Henry A. Giroux, *The Abandoned Generation* (New York: Palgrave, 2004).

58. For an insightful commentary on the media as well as on the racial nature of the war on drugs, see Jimmie L. Reeves and Richard Campbell, *Cracked Coverage: Television News, the Anti-Cocaine Crusade, and the Reagan Legacy* (Durham: Duke University Press, 1994).

59. Dohrn, "Look Out, Kid, It's Something You Did," p. 175.

60. Heather Wokusch, "Leaving Our Children Behind," *Common Dreams News Center* (July 8, 2002). Available online at www.commondreams.org/view02/0708-08.htm.

61. Tony Pugh, "US Economy Leaving Record Numbers in Severe Poverty," *McClatchy Newspapers* (February 23, 2007). Available online at www.commondreams.org/headlines07/0223-09.htm.

62. Cesar Chelala, "Rich Man, Poor Man: Hungry Children in America," *Seattle Times* (January 4, 2006). Available online at www.commondreams.org/views06/0104-24.htm.

63. Bob Herbert, "Young, Jobless, Hopeless," *New York Times* (January 6, 2003), p. A35.

64. Childhood Poverty Research Brief 2, "Child Poverty in the States: Levels and Trends from 1979 to 1998," September 13, 2001. Available online at www.nccp.org.

65. Street, "Race, Prison, and Poverty," p. 26.

66. Zygmunt Bauman, *In Search of Politics* (Stanford: Stanford University Press, 1999), p. 2.

67. Bob Herbert, "The Danger Zone," *New York Times* (March 15, 2007), p. A25.

68. As widely reported, the prison industry has become big business, with many states spending more on prison construction than on university construction. See,

for instance, Anthony Lewis, "Punishing the Country," *New York Times* (December 2, 1999), p. A1.

69. Abigail Thernstrom, "Schools Are Responsible for the Main Source of Racial Inequality Today," *Los Angeles Times* (November 13, 2003), p. B17.

70. Robin D.G. Kelley, *Yo' Mama's Disfunktional!: Fighting the Culture Wars in Urban America* (Boston: Beacon Press, 1997), p. 44.

71. Dwight Garner, "The Season of the Heirheads," *New York Times* (November 16, 2003), p. 29.

72. John Leland, "Once You've Seen Paris, Everything Is E=mc2," *New York Times* (Sunday Styles) (November 23, 2003), p. 9.

73. Street, "Race, Prison, and Poverty," p. 26.

74. Even more shameful is the fact that such discrimination against African Americans is often justified from the Olympian heights of institutions such as Harvard University by apologists such as lawyer Randall Kennedy, who argues that such laws, criminal policies, and police practices are necessary to protect "good" blacks from "bad" blacks who commit crimes. See Kennedy, *Race, Crime, and the Law* (New York: Pantheon, 1997).

75. Interview with Jesse Jackson, "First-Class Jails, Second-Class Schools," *Rethinking Schools* (Spring 2000), p. 16.

76. Bill Moyers, "A Time for Anger, a Call to Action," *Common Dreams* (February 7, 2007). Available online at www.commondreams.org/views07/0322-24.htm.

77. I discuss this phenomenon in Henry A. Giroux, *The University in Chains* (Boulder: Paradigm Publishers, 2007).

78. Ibid.

79. See Penn State News Release, "Penn State's Spanier to Chair National Security Board," September 16, 2005.

80. For a much more detailed account of this type of attack on higher education, see Henry A. Giroux and Susan Searls Giroux, *Take Back Higher Education* (New York: Palgrave, 2006).

81. Greg Toppo, "U.S. Students Say Press Freedoms Go Too Far," *USA Today* (January 30, 2005). Available online at www.usatoday.com/news/education/2005-01-30-students-press_x.htm.

82. Wendy Brown, *Regulating Aversion* (Princeton: Princeton University Press, 2006), p. 88.

83. Public time similarly differs from the fragmented model of time implied by the news media, in which catastrophes exist in the time pocket of the news clip; each day, new catastrophes appear, only to be forgotten and replaced the next day with a different set of catastrophes. News stories are seldom followed long enough to suggest that events spring from complex causes and have equally complex repercussions, and the very fact that stories are so quickly dropped implies that, no matter how catastrophic an event, its social importance is minimal.

84. Zygmunt Bauman, *Liquid Times: Living in an Age of Uncertainty* (London: Polity, 2007), p. 5.

85. Cited in Lawrence W. Levine, *The Opening of the American Mind* (Boston: Beacon Press, 1996), p. 19.

86. Bauman, *Liquid Times,* p. 8.

Notes to Chapter 4

1. Zygmunt Bauman, *Work, Consumerism and the New Poor* (Philadelphia: Open University Press, 1998), pp. 97–98.

2. Stanley Aronowitz and Peter Bratsis, "State Power, Global Power," in Stanley Aronowitz and Peter Bratsis, eds., *Paradigm Lost: State Theory Reconsidered* (Minneapolis: University of Minnesota Press, 2002), p. xvii.

3. Pierre Bourdieu, *Language and Symbolic Power* (Cambridge, MA: Harvard University Press, 2001), p. 127.

4. Ibid., p. 128.

5. For some general theoretical principles for addressing the new sites of pedagogy, see Jeffrey R. DiLeo, Walter Jacobs, and Amy Lee, "The Sites of Pedagogy," *Symploke* 10:1–2 (2003), pp. 7–12.

6. William Greider, "The Right's Grand Ambition: Rolling Back the 20th Century," *The Nation* (May 12, 2003), p. 11.

7. One interesting analysis on the contingent nature of democracy and public space can be found in Rosalyn Deutsche, *Evictions: Art and Spatial Politics* (Cambridge, MA: MIT Press, 1998).

8. Cited in Robert Dreyfuss, "Grover Norquist: 'Field Marshal' of the Bush Plan," *The Nation* (May 14, 2001), p. 1. Available online at http://www.thenation.com/doc.mhtml?i=20010514&s=dreyfuss.

9. Raymond Williams, *Communications,* rev. ed. (New York: Barnes & Noble, 1966), p. 15.

10. Benjamin R. Barber, "A Failure of Democracy, Not Capitalism," *New York Times* (July 29, 2002), p. A23.

11. Bob Herbert, "The Art of False Impression," *New York Times* (August 11, 2003), p. A17.

12. W.E.B. Du Bois, *Against Racism: Unpublished Essays, Papers, Addresses, 1887–1961,*" edited by Herbert Aptheker (Amherst: University of Massachusetts Press, 1985).

13. Cornelius Castoriadis, cited in Zygmunt Bauman, *The Individualized Society* (London: Polity Press, 2001), p. 127.

14. Michele Barrett, *Imagination in Theory* (New York: New York University Press, 1999), p. 161.

15. Zygmunt Bauman and Keith Tester, *Conversations with Zygmunt Bauman* (Malden, MA: Polity Press, 2001), p. 32.

16. On the importance of problematizing and pluralizing the political, see Jodi Dean, "The Interface of Political Theory and Cultural Studies," in Jodi Dean, ed., *Cultural Studies and Political Theory* (Ithaca: Cornell University Press, 2000), pp. 1–19.

17. Robert W. McChesney and John Nichols, *Our Media, Not Theirs: The Democratic Struggle Against Corporate Media* (New York: Seven Stories Press, 2002).

18. Zygmunt Bauman, *In Search of Politics* (Stanford: Stanford University Press, 1999).

19. Nick Couldry, "In the Place of a Common Culture, What?" *Review of Education/Pedagogy/Cultural Studies* 26:1 (January 2004), p. 6.

20. Raymond Williams, "Preface to Second Edition," *Communications* (New York: Barnes and Noble, 1967), pp. 15, 16.

21. Raymond Williams, "Preface to Second Edition," *Communications* (New York: Barnes and Noble, 1967), p. 14.

22. See, especially, Raymond Williams, *Marxism and Literature* (New York: Oxford University Press, 1977); and Raymond Williams, *The Year 2000* (New York: Pantheon, 1983).

23. Williams, *Marxism and Literature.*

24. See Tony Bennett, *Culture: A Reformer's Science* (Thousand Oaks, CA: Sage, 1998), p. 223.

25. Antonio Gramsci, *Selections from the Prison Notebooks* (New York: International Press, 1971), p. 350.

26. Cornelius Castoriadis, "Democracy as Procedure and Democracy as Regime," *Constellations* 4:1 (1997), p. 10.

27. Cornelius Castoriadis, "The Problem of Democracy Today," *Democracy and Nature* 8 (April 1996), p. 19.

28. Cornelius Castoriadis, "The Nature and Value of Equity," *Philosophy, Politics, Autonomy: Essays in Political Philosophy* (New York: Oxford University Press, 1991), pp. 124–142.

29. Cornelius Castoriadis, *The World in Fragments,* edited and translated by David Ames Curtis (Stanford: Stanford University Press, 1997), p. 91.

30. Both quotes are taken from Cornelius Castoriadis, "Culture in a Democratic Society," *The Castoriadis Reader,* edited by David Ames Curtis (Malden, MA: Blackwell, 1997), pp. 343, 341.

31. Cornelius Castoriadis, "The Crisis of the Identification Process," *Thesis Eleven* 49 (May 1997), pp. 87–88.

32. Cornelius Castoriadis, "The Anticipated Revolution," *Political and Social Writings, Vol. 3,* edited and translated by David Ames Curtis (Minneapolis: University of Minnesota Press, 1993), pp. 153–154.

33. John Binde, "Toward an Ethic of the Future," *Public Culture* 12:1 (2000), p. 65.

34. Cornelius Castoriadis, "The Greek Polis and the Creation of Democracy," *Philosophy, Politics, Autonomy: Essays in Political Philosophy* (New York: Oxford University Press, 1991), p. 102.

35. Cornelius Castoriadis, "Power, Politics, and Autonomy," *Philosophy, Politics, Autonomy: Essays in Political Philosophy* (New York: Oxford University Press, 1991), pp. 144–145.

36. Castoriadis, "Democracy as Procedure and Democracy as Regime," p. 15. It is crucial here to note that Castoriadis develops his notions of both democracy and the primacy of education in political life directly from his study of ancient Greek democracy.

37. Castoriadis, "The Problem of Democracy Today," p. 24.

38. Bauman and Tester, *Conversations with Zygmunt Bauman,* p. 131.

39. Susan Sontag, "Courage and Resistance," *The Nation* (May 5, 2003), pp. 11–14.

40. Zygmunt Bauman, *Society Under Siege* (Malden, MA: Blackwell, 2002), p. 170.

41. Jacques Derrida, "Intellectual Courage: An Interview," translated by Peter Krapp, *Culture Machine* 2 (2000), pp. 1–15.

42. Zygmunt Bauman, *The Individualized Society* (London: Polity Press, 2001), pp. 54–55.

43. Gerald Graff appears to have made a career out of this issue by either misrepresenting the work of Paulo Freire and others, citing theoretical work by critical educators that is outdated and could be corrected by reading anything they might have written in the last five years, creating caricatures of their work, or holding up extreme and ludicrous examples as characteristic of what is done by people in critical pedagogy (or, more generally, by anyone who links pedagogy and politics). For more recent representations of this position, see Gerald Graff, "Teaching Politically Without Political Correctness," *Radical Teacher* 58 (Fall 2000), pp. 26–30; and Gerald Graff, *Clueless in Academe* (New Haven: Yale University Press, 2003).

44. Lani Guinier, "Democracy Tested," *The Nation* (May 5, 2003), p. 6. Guinier's position is in direct opposition to that of Graff and his acolytes. For instance, see "A Conversation Between Lani Guinier and Anna Deavere Smith: Rethinking Power, Rethinking Theater," *Theater* 31:3 (Winter 2002), pp. 31–45.

45. George Lipsitz, "Academic Politics and Social Change," in Jodi Dean, ed., *Cultural Studies and Political Theory* (Ithaca: Cornell University Press, 2000), pp. 81–82.

46. For a more detailed response to this kind of watered-down pedagogical practice, see Stanley Aronowitz, *The Knowledge Factory* (Boston: Beacon Press, 2000); and Henry A. Giroux, *The Abandoned Generation: Democracy Beyond the Culture of Fear* (New York: Palgrave, 2003).

47. Interview with Julie Ellison, "New Public Scholarship in the Arts and Humanities," *Higher Education Exchange* (2002), p. 20.

48. Amy Gutmann, *Democratic Education* (Princeton: Princeton University Press, 1998), p. 42.

49. Bauman and Tester, *Conversations with Zygmunt Bauman,* p. 63.

Notes to Chapter 5

1. This paraphrase is actually taken from Fredric Jameson's quotation: "It seems to be easier for us today to imagine the thoroughgoing deterioration of the earth and of nature than the breakdown of late capitalism." See Jameson, *The Seeds of Time* (New York: Columbia University Press, 1994), p. xii.

2. Perry Anderson, *A Zone of Engagement* (London: Verso, 1992), p. 335.

3. Zygmunt Bauman, *Work, Consumerism, and the New Poor* (Philadelphia: Open University Press, 1998).

4. Editorial, "Bush's Domestic War," *The Nation* (December 31, 2001), p. 3.

5. Ibid.

6. Molly Ivins, "Bush's Sneak Attack on 'Average' Taxpayers," *Chicago Tribune* (March 27, 2003). Available online at www.commondreams.org/views03/0327-04.htm.

7. Jennifer Lee, "U.S. Proposes Easing Rules on Emissions of Mercury," *New York Times* (December 3, 2003), p. A20.

8. See Jaider Rizvi, "United States: Hunger in a Wealthy Nation," *Tierramerica/Interpress Service* (March 26, 2003). Available online at www.foodfirst.org/media/

news/2003/hungerwealthy.html. Also see Jennifer Egan, "To Be Young and Homeless," *New York Times Magazine* (March 24, 2002), p. 35.

9. Robert McChesney, *Rich Media, Poor Democracy: Communication Politics in Dubious Times* (New York: The New Press, 1999).

10. Ulrich Beck, *Risk Society: Towards a New Modernity* (Thousand Oaks, CA: Sage, 1992), p. 137.

11. Cornelius Castoriadis, "Democracy as Procedure and as Regime," *Constellations* 4:1 (1997), p. 5.

12. Ibid., p. 10.

13. See the work of Manuel Castells, especially his *The Information Age: Economy, Society and Culture, Volume III: End of Millennium* (Malden, MA: Basil Blackwell, 1998).

14. Takis Fotopoulos, *Towards an Inclusive Democracy* (London and New York: Cassell, 1997).

15. Anatole Anton, "Public Goods as Commonstock: Notes on the Receding Commons," in Anatole Anton, Milton Fisk, and Nancy Holmstrom, eds., *Not for Sale: In Defense of Public Goods* (Boulder: Westview Press, 2000), pp. 3–4.

16. See, for example, Todd Gitlin, "The Anti-Political Populism of Cultural Studies," in M. Ferguson and P. Golding, eds., *Cultural Studies in Question* (Thousand Oaks, CA: Sage, 1998), pp. 25–38; Tony Bennett, "Cultural Studies: A Reluctant Discipline," *Cultural Studies* 12:4 (1998), pp. 528–545; and Ian Hunter, *Rethinking the School: Subjectivity, Bureaucracy, Criticism* (New York: St. Martin's Press, 1994).

17. John Brenkman, "Race Publics: Civil Illiberalism, or Race After Reagan," *Transition* 5:2 (Summer 1995), p. 7.

18. Gary Olson and Lynn Worsham, "Changing the Subject: Judith Butler's Politics of Radical Signification," *JAC* 20:4 (2000), p. 741.

19. Cornelius Castoriadis, "Institutions and Autonomy," in Peter Osborne, ed., *A Critical Sense* (New York: Routledge, 1996), p. 8.

20. Noam Chomsky, *Profits Over People: Neoliberalism and Global Order* (New York: Seven Stories Press, 1999), p. 92.

21. Brenkman, "Race Publics," p. 123.

22. Gary Olson and Lynn Worsham, "Rethinking Political Community: Chantal Mouffe's Liberal Socialism," *JAC* 18:3 (1999), p. 178.

23. Ibid., p. 11.

24. Pierre Bourdieu, "For a Scholarship with Commitment," *Profession* (2000), p. 43.

25. John Brenkman, "Extreme Criticism," in J. Butler, J. Guillory, and K. Thomas, eds., *What's Left of Theory* (New York: Routledge, 2000), p. 130.

26. Zygmunt Bauman, *Globalization: The Human Consequences* (New York: Columbia University Press, 1998), p. 5.

27. Simon Critchley, "Ethics, Politics, and Radical Democracy—The History of a Disagreement," *Culture Machine.* Available online at www.culturemachine.tees.ac.uk/frm_f1.htm.

28. This section draws from a chapter on utopian hope in Henry A. Giroux, *Public Spaces, Private Lives* (Lanham, MD: Rowman and Littlefield, 2002).

29. Zygmunt Bauman "The Journey Never Ends: Zygmunt Bauman Talks with Peter Beilharz," in Peter Beilharz, ed., *The Bauman Reader* (Oxford: Blackwell, 2001), p. 342.

30. Jacques Derrida, "The Future of the Profession or the Unconditional University," in *Derrida Downunder,* edited by Laurence Simmons and Heather Worth (Auckland, New Zealand: Dunmore Press, 2001), p. 7.

31. Giroux, *Public Spaces, Private Lives.*

32. Bloch's great contribution in English on the subject of utopianism can be found in his three-volume work, *The Principle of Hope,* Vols. I, II, and III, translated by Neville Plaice, Stephen Plaice, and Paul Knight (Cambridge, MA: MIT Press, 1986; originally published in 1959).

33. Ernst Bloch, "Something's Missing: A Discussion Between Ernst Bloch and Theodor W. Adorno on the Contradictions of Utopian Longing," in Ernst Bloch, *The Utopian Function of Art and Literature: Selected Essays* (Cambridge, MA: MIT Press, 1988), p. 3.

34. Anson Rabinach, "Ernst Bloch's *Heritage of Our Times* and the Theory of Fascism," *New German Critique* 11 (Spring 1977), p. 11.

35. Thomas L. Dunn, "Political Theory for Losers," in Jason A. Frank and John Tambornino, eds., *Vocations of Political Theory* (Minneapolis: University of Minnesota Press, 2000), p. 160.

36. Russell Jacoby, "A Brave Old World," *Harper's Magazine* (December 2000), pp. 72–80; Norman Geras, "Minimum Utopia: Ten Theses," *Socialist Register* (2000), pp. 41–42; Leo Panitch and Sam Gindin, "Transcending Pessimism: Rekindling Socialist Imagination," in Leo Panitch and Sam Gindin, eds., *Necessary and Unnecessary Utopias* (New York: Monthly Review Press, 1999), pp. 1–29; David Harvey, *Spaces of Hope* (University of California Press, 2000); Russell Jacoby, *The End of Utopia: Politics and Culture in an Age of Apathy* (New York: Basic Books, 1999).

37. Jacoby, "A Brave Old World," p. 80.

38. Norman Podhoretz, cited in Ellen Willis, "Buy American," *Dissent* (Fall 2000), p. 110.

39. For a critique of the entrepreneurial populism of this diverse group, see Thomas Frank, *One Market Under God: Extreme Capitalism, Market Populism and the End of Economic Democracy* (New York: Doubleday, 2000).

40. Carl Boggs, *The End of Politics: Corporate Power and the Decline of the Public Sphere* (New York: Guilford Press, 2000), p. 7.

41. Alain Badiou, *Ethics: An Essay on the Understanding of Evil* (London: Verso, 2001), p. 96.

42. Samir Amin, "Imperialization and Globalization," *Monthly Review* (June 2001), p. 12.

43. Antonio Gramsci, *Selections from the Prison Notebooks* (New York: International Press, 1971), p. 350.

44. Edward Said, "Scholarship and Commitment: An Introduction," *Profession* (2000), pp. 8–9.

45. Bill Readings, *The University in Ruins* (Cambridge, MA: Harvard University Press, 1996).

46. Zygmunt Bauman, *In Search of Politics* (Stanford: Stanford University Press, 1999), p. 170.

47. Toni Morrison, "How Can Values Be Taught in the University?" *Michigan Quarterly Review* (Spring 2001), p. 278.

48. Martin Finklestein, "The Morphing of the American Academic Profession," *Liberal Education* 89:4 (2003), p. 1.

49. Arundhati Roy, *Power Politics* (Cambridge, MA: South End Press, 2001), p. 3.

50. Edward Said, *Representations of the Intellectual* (New York: Pantheon, 1994), p. 11.

51. Ibid., p. 52–53.

52. R. Radhakrishnan, "Canonicity and Theory: Toward a Poststructuralist Pedagogy," in Donald Morton and Mas'ud Zavarzadeh, eds., *Theory/Pedagogy/Politics* (Urbana: University of Illinois Press, 1991), pp. 112–135.

53. Stanley Aronowitz, Introduction to Paulo Freire's *Pedagogy of Freedom* (Lanham, MD: Rowman and Littlefield, 1998), pp. 10–11.

54. Edward Said, *Reflections on Exile and Other Essays* (Cambridge, MA: Harvard University Press, 2001), p. 503.

55. Ibid., p. 504.

56. Paul Sabin, "Academe Subverts Young Scholars' Civic Orientation," *Chronicle of Higher Education* (February 8, 2002), p. B24.

57. Jacques Derrida, "No One Is Innocent: A Discussion with Jacques Derrida About Philosophy in the Face of Terror," *The Information Technology, War and Peace Project*. Available online at http://www.watsoninstitute.org/infopeace/911.

Notes to Chapter 6

1. Franklin D. Roosevelt, "State of the Union Address Franklin D. Roosevelt" (January 4, 1935), pp. 9–17. Available online at www.infoplease.com/t/hist/state-of-the-union/146.html. Of course, it must be remembered that FDR's New Deal was exclusively a contract with white America, but it contained within its discourse the promise of a democracy that offered the possibility of correcting that gross injustice.

2. Hannah Arendt, *Responsibility and Judgment* (New York: Schocken, 2005).

3. For a classic work on FDR and the New Deal, see William E. Leuchtenberg, *Franklin D. Roosevelt and the New Deal, 1932–1940* (New York: HarperCollins, 1963).

4. Paul Krugman, "Gilded Once More," *New York Times* (May 27, 2007). Available online at www.truthout.org/docs_2006/042707F.shtml.

5. Erik Olin Wright, "Compass Points: Towards a Socialist Alternative," *New Left Review* (September 26, 2006), p. 93.

6. On the increased role of the state in regulating the global movement of capital, see Michael Hardt and Antonio Negri, *Multitude: War and Democracy in the Age of Empire* (New York: Penguin Press, 2004).

7. George Steinmetz, "The State of Emergency and the Revival of American Imperialism: Toward an Authoritarian Post-Fordism," *Public Culture* 15:2 (Spring 2003), p. 337. The move on the part of the state from investment to punishment is analyzed brilliantly in Jonathan Simon, *Governing Through Crime* (New York: Oxford University Press, 2007).

8. Steinmetz. Ibid., p. 337.

9. As Lawrence Grossberg points out, neoliberalism "describes a political-economic project" whose "supporters are bound together by their fundamental opposition to Keynesian demand-side fiscal policy and to government regulation of business. Second, many neoliberals support laissez-faire and define the free economy as the absence of any regulation or control.... [N]eoliberals tend to believe that, since the free market is the most rational and democratic system of choice, every domain of human life should be open to the forces of the marketplace. At the very least, that means that the government should stop providing services that would be better delivered by opening them up to the marketplace. Third, neoliberals believe that economic freedom is the necessary precondition for political freedom (democracy); they often act as if democracy were nothing but economic freedom or the freedom to choose. Finally neoliberals are radical individualists. Any appeal to larger groups (e.g., gender, racial, ethnic, or class groups) as if they functioned as agents or had rights, or to society itself, is not only meaningless but also a step toward socialism and totalitarianism." See Grossberg, *Caught in the Crossfire: Kids, Politics, and America's Future* (Boulder: Paradigm Publishers, 2005), p. 112.

10. Cited in Robert Dreyfuss, "Grover Norquist: 'Field Marshal' of the Bush Plan," *The Nation* (May 14, 2001), p. 1. Available online at www.thenation.com/doc.mhtml?i=20010514&s=dreyfuss.

11. Editorial, "President Bush's Fiscal Year 2007 Budget Proposal," *Sojourners* (December 2006). Available online at www.sojo.net/index.cfm?action=action.display_c&item=060308_07budget_analysis.

12. Mark Greenberg, Indivar Duta-Gupta, and Elisa Minoff, *From Poverty to Prosperity* (Washington, DC: Center for American Progress, 2007), p. 1.

13. Ibid.

14. Edmund L. Andrews, "Tax Cuts Offer Most for Very Rich, Study Says," *New York Times* (January 8, 2007). Available online at www.nytimes.com/2007/01/08/washington/08tax.html?ei=5090&en=e1dc82f54ac7eacb&ex=1325912400&adxnnl=1&pagewanted=print&adxnnlx=1181590853-PJ6FtoR+IK2IDt0S2zSLFg.

15. Russell Mokhiber and Robert Weissman, "Economic Apartheid in America," *Common Dreams News Center* (November 21, 2005). Available online at www.commondreams.org/views05/1121-21.htm.

16. Jenny Anderson and Julie Creswell, "Top Hedge Fund Managers Earn Over $240 Million," *New York Times* (April 24, 2007), p. 1.

17. Ellen Simon, "Half of S&P CEOs Topped $8.3 Million," *Associated Press* (June 11, 2007). Available online at http://abcnews.go.com/Business/wireStory?id=3266191. See also Council on International and Public Affairs, "Too Much Executive Pay Scorecard," *Too Much Online Weekly* (May 1, 2007). Available online at www.cipa-apex.org/toomuch/ExecPayScoreboard.html.

18. Editorial, "Northwest to Award CEO $26.6 Million in Equity After Bankruptcy," *USA Today* (April 5, 2007). Available online at www.usatoday.com/travel/flights/2007-05-07-nwa-ceo-pay_N.htm.

19. Joshua Freed, "Northwest Exits Bankruptcy Protection," *Washington Post* (May 31, 2007). Available online at www.washingtonpost.com/wp-dyn/content/article/2007/05/30/AR2007053002063_pf.html.

20. Mike Davis and Daniel Bertrand Monk, "Introduction," *Evil Paradises* (New York: The New Press, 2007), p. ix.

21. See David Harvey, *A Brief History of Neoliberalism* (New York: Oxford University Press, 2005), especially pp. 160–164.

22. Hardt and Negri, *Multitude,* p. 12.

23. Jacques Rancière, *Hatred of Democracy* (London: Verso, 2006). I am not suggesting that there was a golden period in American history when war and intervention did not exist. What I am suggesting is that under the imperial presidency of George W. Bush, matters of force and empire have become the regulative principles organizing American foreign policy and establishing the foundation for an utterly militarized society, which is new. On the complicated nature of American history and the culture of force, see Christopher Newfield, "The Culture of Force," *South Atlantic Quarterly* (Winter 2006), pp. 241–263. On the increasing militarization of American society, see Henry A. Giroux, *The University in Chains: Confronting the Military-Industrial-Academic Complex* (Boulder: Paradigm Publishers, 2007); Chalmers Johnson, *Nemesis: The Last Days of the American Republic* (New York: Metropolitan Books, 2006); and Andrew Bacevich, *The New American Militarism: How Americans Are Seduced by War* (New York: Oxford University Press, 2005). For an excellent critique of Bush's imperial presidency, see Fredrick A. O. Schwarz Jr. and Aziz Z. Hug, *Unchecked and Unbalanced: Presidential Power in a Time of Terror* (New York: The New Press, 2007).

24. Hardt and Negri, *Multitude,* p. 341.

25. I take up these issues in more detail in Giroux, *The University in Chains.*

26. Grossberg, *Caught in the Crossfire,* p. 117.

27. Ibid.

28. Zygmunt Bauman, *Work, Consumerism and the New Poor* (Philadelphia: Open University Press, 1998).

29. Ibid.

30. Jean Comaroff and John L. Comaroff, "Millennial Capitalism: First Thoughts on a Second Coming," *Public Culture* 12: 2 (Durham: Duke University Press, 2000), p. 301.

31. Bob Herbert, "The Danger Zone," *New York Times* (March 15, 2007), p. A25.

32. This concept is taken from Achille Mbembe, "On Politics as a Form of Expenditure," in Jean and John Comaroff, eds., *Law and Disorder in the Postcolony* (Chicago: University of Chicago Press, 2006), pp. 299–335.

33. Bob Herbert, "Young, Ill and Uninsured," *New York Times* (May 19, 2007), p. A25.

34. Jean Comaroff, "Beyond Bare Life: AIDS, (Bio)Politics, and the Neoliberal Order," *Public Culture* 19:1 (Winter 2007), p. 213.

35. Jason Reed, "Lots of Kids Left Behind If Bush Cuts Funds for Health-Care Plan," *Hamilton Spectator* (February 24, 2007), p. A3. For a detailed analysis of the failure of the health-care system for poor families in the United States, see Ronald J. Angel, *Poor Families in America's Health Care Crisis* (Cambridge: Cambridge University Press, 2006).

36. Bob Herbert, "The Divide in Caring for Our Kids," *New York Times* (June 12, 2007), p. A23.

37. James Cramer, "Cramer vs. Cramer," *New York Magazine* (June 4, 2007); emphasis added. Available online at http://nymag.com/news/features/32382/.

38. Chip Ward, "America Gone Wrong: A Slashed Safety Net Turns Libraries into Homeless Shelters," *TomDispatch.com* (April 2, 2007). Available online at www.alternet.org/story/50023.

39. Paul Tolme, "Criminalizing the Homeless," *In These Times* (April 14, 2003), p. 6.

40. Ward, "America Gone Wrong."

41. Ibid.

42. Comaroff and Comaroff, "Millennial Capitalism," p. 293.

43. Zygmunt Bauman, *Liquid Times: Living in an Age of Uncertainty* (London: Polity, 2007).

44. Associated Press, "Conservatives Want Reagan to Replace FDR on U.S. Dimes," *USA Today* (December 5, 2003). Available online at www.usatoday.com/news/washington/2003-12-05-reagan-dime_x.htm.

45. Andrew J. Bacevich, *The New American Militarism* (New York: Oxford University Press, 2005), p. 1.

46. Of course, there is some legitimacy here in arguing that George W. Bush's administration suggests that he is as much indebted to military Keynesianism as he is to neoliberalism. Chalmers Johnson, for instance, argues that "[w]ith the coming to power of George W. Bush and the launching of his Global War on Terror, military Keynesianism returned with a vengeance." See Johnson, *Nemesis: The Last Days of the American Republic,* p. 275.

47. Zygmunt Bauman, "Freedom From, In and Through the State: T.H. Marshall's Trinity of Rights Revised," *Theoria* 52:108 (December 2005), p. 16.

48. Hardt and Negri, *Multitude,* p. 17.

49. Bacevich, *The New American Militarism,* p. 3.

50. Étienne Balibar, *We, the People of Europe: Reflections on Transnational Citizenship* (Princeton: Princeton University Press, 2004), p. 125.

51. See, for example, the discussion of the militarized war against the urban poor in Daryl Meeks, "Police Militarization in Urban Areas: The Obscure War Against the Underclass," *The Black Scholar* 35:4 (Winter 2006), pp. 33–41.

52. Ulysses Kalladaryn, *Criminalizing the Classroom: The Over-Policing of New York City Schools* (New York: ACLU, 2007); Advancement Project, *Education on Lockdown: The Schoolhouse to Jailhouse Track* (Washington, DC: Advancement Project, March 2005), available online at www.advancementproject.org/reports/FINALEOLrep.pdf; and Judith Brown, *Derailed! The Schoolhouse to Jailhouse Track* (Washington, DC: Advancement Project, May 2003), available online at www.advancementproject.org/Derailerepcor.pdf.

53. Advancement Project, *Education on Lockdown: The Schoolhouse to Jailhouse Track.*

54. I take up this issue in great detail in Henry A. Giroux, *The Abandoned Generation* (New York: Palgrave, 2004) and *America On the Edge* (New York: Palgrave, 2007). See also Grossberg, *Caught in the Crossfire.*

55. Bob Herbert, "School to Prison Pipeline," *New York Times* (June 9, 2007), p. A29.

56. For an excellent analysis of youth and the militarization of public schools, see Christopher Robbins, *Expelling Hope: The Assault on Youth and the Militarization of Schooling* (Albany: SUNY Press, in press).

57. Amnesty International, "Israel and the Occupied Territories: The Place of the Fence/Wall in International Law" (February 19, 2004). Available online at http://web.amnesty.org/library/index/engmde150162004.

58. I have borrowed this idea from the criticisms made of the Israeli Defense Force by the writer Yitzhak Laor. See Laor, "You Are Terrorists, We Are Virtuous," *London Review of Books* 28:16 (August 17, 2006). Available online at www.lrb.co.uk/v28/n16/print/laor01_.html.

59. Achille Mbembe, "Necropolitics," translated by Libby Meintjes, *Public Culture* 15:1 (2003), p. 12.

60. The most important theorist working on the politics of disposability is Zygmunt Bauman. See Bauman, *Wasted Lives* (London: Polity Press, 2004). See also Ruth Wilson Gilmore, *Golden Gulag: Prisons, Surplus, Crisis, and Opposition in Globalizing California* (Berkeley: University of California Press, 2007); Henry A. Giroux, *Stormy Weather: Katrina and the Politics of Disposability* (Boulder: Paradigm Publishers, 2006); Louis Uchitelle, *The Disposable America: Layoffs and Their Consequences* (New York: Knopf, 2006); and Edwin Black, *War Against the Weak* (New York: Thunder Mouth Press, 2003).

61. Editorial, "Gitmos Across America," *New York Times* (June 27, 2007), p. A22.

62. Naomi Klein, *Fences and Windows* (New York: Picador, 2002), p. 21.

63. Bauman, *Wasted Lives,* p. 6.

64. Wendy Brown, *Edgework: Critical Essays on Knowledge and Politics* (Princeton: Princeton University Press, 2005), p. 39.

65. See Michel Foucault, *Society Must Be Defended: Lectures at the College De France 1975–1976,* translated by David Macey (New York: Picador, 2003) and Nikolas Rose, *The Politics of Life Itself: Biomedicine, Power, and Subjectivity in the Twenty-First Century* (Princeton: Princeton University Press, 2007). See also, Thomas Lemke, "'The Birth of Bio-Politics': Michael Foucault's Lecture at the College de France on Neo-Liberal Governmentality," *Economy and Society* 30:2 (May 2001), pp. 190–207.

66. These ideas come from Kathy E. Ferguson and Phyllis Turnbull, *O, Say, Can You See? The Semiotics of the Military in Hawai'i* (Minneapolis: University of Minnesota Press, 1999), pp. 197–198.

67. Leerom Medovoi, "Peace and War: Governmentality as a Military Project," *Social Text* 25:2 (Summer, 2007), p. 69.

68. Ibid., p. 42.

69. Lynda Cheshire and Geoffrey Lawrence, "Neoliberalism, Individualisation and Community: Regional Restructuring in Australia," *Social Identities* 11:5 (September 2005), p. 438.

70. Zygmunt Bauman, *The Individualized Society* (London: Polity Press, 2001), p. 9.

71. Catherine Needham, "Customer-Focused Government," *Soundings* 26 (Spring 2004), p. 80.

72. Ruth Rosen, "Note to Nancy Pelosi: Challenge Market Fundamentalism," *CommonDreams.org* (January 30, 2007). Available online at www.commondreams.org/views07/0130-22.htm.

73. For an insightful analysis of the diverse forms that governmentality assumes under neoliberalism in different countries and contexts, see Aihwa Ong, *Neoliberalism as Exception: Mutations in Citizenship and Sovereignty* (Durham: Duke University Press, 2006). On the issue of governmentality in general, see Michel Foucault, "Governmentality," translated by Rosi Braidotti and revised by Colin Gordon, in Graham Burchell, Colin Gordon, and Peter Miller, eds., *The Foucault Effect: Studies in Governmentality* (Chicago: University of Chicago Press, 1991), pp. 87–104. For a brilliant analysis of Foucault's notion of governmentality, see Thomas Lemke, "Foucault, Governmentality, and Critique," paper presented at Rethinking Marxism Conference, University of Amherst, MA (September 21–24, 2000), available online at http://www.thomaslemkeweb.de/publikationen/Foucault,%20Governmentality,%20and%20Critique%20IV-2.pdf.

74. Tony Kashani, *Deconstructing the Mystique* (Dubuque, IA: Kendall Hunt, 2005).

75. Bauman, *Wasted Lives,* p. 27.

76. Juan Williams, "Getting Past Katrina," *New York Times* (September 1, 2006). Available online at www.iht.com/articles/2006/09/01/opinion/edjuan.php.

77. Sally Kohn, "'The Condemned' Reflects Real Life: People Are Disposable," *Common Dreams News Center* (April 11, 2007). Available online at www.commondreams.org/archive/2007/04/11/455/print/.

78. Associated Press, "Life, Death, and Ratings," *Globe and Mail* (May 30, 2007), p. A2.

79. Tamar Lewin, "A Television Audition for a Part in and of Life," *New York Times* (June 3, 2007), p. 5.

80. There is a long history of work that refuses this totalitarian coupling, one that extends from Socrates to the Frankfurt School to Hannah Arendt. The voices of three consistent defenders of democracy and dissent can be found in Howard Zinn, *A Power Governments Cannot Suppress* (San Francisco: City Lights, 2007); Noam Chomsky, *Failed States: The Abuse of Power and the Assault on Democracy* (New York: Metropolitan Books, 2006); and Gore Vidal, *Imperial America* (New York: Nation Books, 2004).

81. See Bruce Western, *Punishment and Inequality in America* (New York: Russell Sage Foundation, 2007); Jeff Manza and Christopher Uggen, *Locked Out: Felon Disenfranchisement and American Democracy* (New York: Oxford University Press, 2007); and Angela Y. Davis, *Abolition Democracy: Beyond Empire, Prisons, and Torture* (New York: Seven Stories Press, 2005).

82. Dirk Johnson, "Look at This Ad, But Don't Get Any Ideas," *New York Times* (May 13, 2007). Available online at www.nytimes.com/2007/05/13/weekinreview/13johnson.html.

83. Raina Seitel Gitlin, "The Glamorous Life: Kiddie Birthday Parties," *ABC NEWS* (June 2, 2007). Available online at http://abcnews.go.com/print?id=323811.

84. Alan Riding, "Alas, Poor Art Market: A Multimillion-Dollar Head Case," *New York Times* (June 13, 2007), pp. B1, B4.

85. William Shaw, "The Iceman Cometh," *New York Times Magazine* (June 3, 2007), p. 58.

86. Mbembe, "Necropolitics," p. 17.

87. Many books and articles have been produced on this issue. One of the most insightful commentators is David Cole. See Cole, *Enemy Aliens* (New York: The Free Press, 2003) and "Undoing Bush—1. The Constitution," *Harper's Magazine* (June 2007), pp. 43–45. See also David Rose, *Guantanamo: The War on Human Rights* (New York: The Free Press, 2006).

88. Medovoi, ibid.

89. Jeremy Rifkin, "Capitalism's Future on Trial," *Guardian* (June 22, 2005). Available online at www.guardian.co.uk/comment/story/0,3604,1511718,00.html.

90. David Kotz, "Neoliberalism and the U.S. Economic Expansion of the '90s," *Monthly Review* 54:11 (April 2003), p. 15.

91. Bauman, *The Individualized Society,* p. 79.

92. Monica Davey, "Former Bush Aide Fights Nickname: Gov. Privatize," *New York Times* (June 16, 2007), p. A8.

93. I take this issue up in great detail in Giroux, *Stormy Weather: Katrina and the Politics of Disposability.*

94. Comaroff, "Beyond Bare Life," p. 213.

95. Ferguson and Turnbull, *O, Say, Can You See?,* especially ch. 6, "The Pedagogy of Citizenship," p. 173.

96. Harvey, *A Brief History of Neoliberalism,* pp. 6–7.

97. Ibid., p. 19. For a much more capacious and theoretically developed discussion of class and power, see Stanley Aronowitz, *How Class Works: Power and Social Movements* (New Haven: Yale University Press, 2003). For an important journalistic account of neoliberalism as a kind of disaster politics, see Naomi Klein, *The Shock Doctrine: The Rise of Disaster Capitalism* (New York: Metropolitan Books: 2007).

98. Harvey, *A Brief History of Neoliberalism,* p. 3.

99. Lemke, "Foucault, Governmentality, and Critique."

100. Ellen Willis, "Escape from Freedom: What's the Matter with Tom Frank (and the Lefties Who Love Him)?" *Situations* 1:2 (2006), p. 9.

101. Grossberg, *Caught in the Crossfire,* pp. 220–221.

102. Antonio Gramsci, *Selections from the Prison Notebooks,* edited and translated by Quintin Hoare and Geoffrey Nowell (New York: International Press, 1971), p. 350.

103. I have taken up the Left's refusal to take matters of pedagogy and the politics of youth seriously in a number of books. See, most recently, Henry A. Giroux, *The Abandoned Generation: Democracy Beyond the Culture of Fear* (New York: Palgrave, 2003).

104. Brown, *Edgework: Critical Essays on Knowledge and Politics,* p. 38.

105. Ibid., pp. 39–40. Brown appropriates much of her analysis of neoliberalism from Thomas Lemke. See Lemke, "Foucault, Governmentality, and Critique."

106. Michel Foucault takes these issues up in great detail in Michel Foucault, *Society Must Be Defended: Lectures at the College de France, 1975-1976,* translated by David Macey (New York: Picador, 2003).

107. Ibid., pp. 41–45.

108. Ibid., pp. 56–57.

109. Ferguson and Turnbull, *O, Say, Can you See?*, p. 175.

110. Jean Baudrillard, *Simulacra and Simulation,* translated by Sheila Faria Glaser (Ann Arbor: University of Michigan Press, 1994), p. 15.

111. Robin Kelley, *Yo' Mama's Disfunktional!* (Boston: Beacon Press, 1997), pp. 108–109.

112. Ibid., p. 59.

113. Michael Dillon, "Sovereignty and Governmentality: From the Problematics of the 'New World Order' to the Ethical Problematic of the World Order," *Alternatives* 20 (1995), p. 330.

114. Of course, anti-intellectualism in American life has been addressed by numerous authors. See, for example, Richard Hoftstadter, *Anti-Intellectualism in American Life* (New York: Vintage, 1966); Russell Jacoby, *The Last Intellectuals* (New York: HarperCollins, 1989); and Henry A. Giroux, *Teachers as Intellectuals* (Granby, MA: Bergin and Garvey, 1988).

115. Dillon, "Sovereignty and Governmentality, p. 330.

116. Hardt and Negri, *Multitude,* p. 305.

117. Ibid.

118. Cornelius Castoriadis, "Imagining Society: Cornelius Castoriadis," Interview in *Variant* 15:3 (Autumn 1993), p. 41.

119. Antonio Gramsci, *Selections from the Prison Notebooks,* edited and translated by Quintin Hoare and Geoffrey Nowell-Smith (New York: International Press, 1971), p. 350.

120. Ellen Willis, *Don't Think, Smile* (Boston: Beacon Press, 1999), p. xiv.

121. Zygmunt Bauman, "Critical Theory," in Peter Beilharz, ed., *The Bauman Reader* (Malden, MA: Blackwell, 2001), p. 162.

122. Nick Couldry, "Dialogue in an Age of Enclosure: Exploring the Values of Cultural Studies," *Review of Education/Pedagogy/Cultural Studies* 23:1 (2001), p. 49.

123. Imre Szeman, "Introduction: Learning to Learn from Seattle," *Review of Education/Pedagogy/Cultural Studies* 24:1–2 (2002), pp. 3–4.

124. Zygmunt Bauman, *Society Under Siege* (Malden, MA: Blackwell, 2002), p. 54.

125. Lisa Duggan, *The Twilight of Equality: Neoliberalism, Cultural Politics, and the Attack on Democracy* (Boston: Beacon, Press, 2003), p. xx.

126. A conversation between Lani Guinier and Anna Deavere Smith, "Rethinking Power, Rethinking Theater," *Theater* 31:3 (Winter 2002), pp. 34–35.

127. This issue of "public connections" is taken up brilliantly in Nick Couldry, Sonia Livingstone, and Tim Markham, *Media Consumption and Public Engagement* (New York: Palgrave, 2007).

128. Couldry, "Dialogue in an Age of Enclosure," p. 68.

129. Alain Badiou, *Ethics: An Essay on the Understanding of Evil* (London: Verso, 1998), pp. 115–116.

130. Mike Davis and Daniel B. Monk, eds., *Evil Paradises: Dreamworlds of Neo-Liberalism* (New York: The New Press, 2007). For an international analysis of the anti-democratic tendencies of neoliberalism, see Leslie Holmes, *Rotten States? Corruption, Post-Communism, and Neoliberalism* (Durham: Duke University Press, 2006); Duggan, *The Twilight of Equality*; Ong, *Neoliberalism as Exception*; Neil Smith, *The*

Endgame of Globalization (New York: Routledge, 2005); and Alain Touraine, *Beyond Neoliberalism* (London: Polity Press, 2001).

131. Lewis H. Lapham, "Res Publica," *Harper's Magazine* (December 2001), p. 8.

132. Stanley Aronowitz, "The Retreat to Postmodern Politics," *Situations* 1:1 (April 2005), p. 32.

133. Zygmunt Bauman, "Has the Future a Left?" *Review of Education/Pedagogy/Cultural Studies* (in press).

134. Ibid.

135. Ibid.

136. Stanley Aronowitz, *Left Turn: Forging a New Political Future* (Boulder: Paradigm Publishers, 2006).

137. Edward Said, *The World, the Text, and the Critic* (New York: Vintage, 1983). See also, Edward Said, *Representations of the Intellectual* (New York: Vintage, 1994) and Edward Said, *Humanism and Democratic Criticism* (New York: Columbia University Press, 2004).

138. A variety of writers take up this issue in Henry A. Giroux and Kostas Myrsiades, eds., *Beyond the Corporate University* (Lanham, MD: Rowman and Littlefield, 2001). See also Giroux, *The University in Chains*; Henry A. Giroux and Susan Giroux, *Take Back Higher Education* (New York: Palgrave, 2006); Stanley Aronowitz, *The Knowledge Factory: Dismantling the Corporate University and Creating True Higher Learning* (Boston: Beacon Press, 2001); Stephen Pender, "An Interview with David Harvey," *Studies in Social Justice* 1:1 (Winter 2007), available online at http://ojs.uwindsor.ca/ojs/leddy/index.php/SSJ/article/viewFile/182/178; Stanley Aronowitz and Henry A. Giroux, *Education Still Under Siege* (New York: Bergin and Garvey, 1993); Howard Zinn, *On History* (New York: Seven Stories Press, 2001); and Edward Said, *Representations of the Intellectual* (New York: Pantheon, 1994).

139. Pender, "An Interview with David Harvey"; Aronowitz and Giroux, *Education Still Under Siege.*

140. Judith Butler, *Precarious Life: The Powers of Mourning and Violence* (London: Verso Press, 2004), p. 126.

141. Ibid., p. 104.

142. Many excellent books and articles address the various ways in which neoliberalism is being resisted. A few examples are Howard Zinn, *A Power Governments Cannot Suppress* (San Francisco: City Lights, 2007); Comaroff, "Beyond Bare Life; Stanley Aronowitz, *Left Turn: Forging a New Political Future*; Harvey, *A Brief History of Neoliberalism,* especially pp. 183–206; Grossberg, *Caught in the Crossfire*; Alfredo Saad-Filho and Deborah Johnston, eds., *Neoliberalism: A Critical Reader* (London: Pluto Press, 2005); Neil Smith, *The Endgame of Globalization* (New York: Routledge, 2005); Duggan, *The Twilight of Equality*; Touraine, *Beyond Neoliberalism*; and Ong, *Neoliberalism as Exception.*

Index

About the Author

Henry A. Giroux is the Global Television Network Chair Professor of English and Cultural Studies at McMaster University. He is the author most recently of The University in Chains (Paradigm 2007).